QUESTIONS & ANSWERS
Federal Estate
and Gift Taxation

QUESTIONS & ANSWERS
Federal Estate
and Gift Taxation

JAMES M. DELANEY
Centennial Distinguished Professor of Law, University of Wyoming College of Law

and

ELAINE HIGHTOWER GAGLIARDI
Professor of Law, University of Montana School of Law

ISBN: 978-08205-7012-9

> NOTE TO USERS
> To ensure that you are using the latest materials available in this area, please be sure to periodically check the LexisNexis Law School web site for downloadable updates and supplements at www.lexisnexis.com/lawschool.

Editorial Offices
121 Chanlon Rd., New Providence, NJ 07974 (908) 464-6800
201 Mission St., San Francisco, CA 94105-1831 (415) 908-3200
www.lexisnexis.com

MATTHEW◆BENDER

ABOUT THE AUTHORS

James M. Delaney was appointed in 2008 as the Centennial Distinguished Professor of Law at the University of Wyoming College of Law. Prior to joining the Wyoming faculty, he was a senior associate at Perkins Coie, LLP (Seattle, Washington). At Perkins Coie he advised international and domestic clients in the areas of corporate, partnership, and individual U.S. federal tax law.

Prior to his tenure with Perkins Coie, LLP, Professor Delaney served as an Attorney Advisor to the Honorable Robert P. Ruwe, Judge, United States Tax Court. He also obtained his LL.M. in taxation at the University of Florida College of Law. He served as a student editor of the Florida Tax Review and as notes and comments editor of the Gonzaga Law Review. Professor Delaney teaches courses on Federal Income Taxation, Corporate Taxation, Partnership Taxation, Estate and Gift Taxation, Estate Planning, and Trusts and Estates.

Elaine Hightower Gagliardi is the Associate Dean and a Professor of Law at The University of Montana School of Law, where she teaches Estate Planning, Taxation of Estates and Gifts, and Nonprofit Organizations. Prior to teaching, Professor Gagliardi practiced in those areas with the law firms of Perkins Coie, LLP (Seattle, Washington), and Day, Berry & Howard (Harford, Connecticut). She is an Academic Fellow of the American College of Trusts and Estates Counsel.

Professor Gagliardi earned her J.D. degree from The University of Montana School of Law. She also earned an LL.M. in taxation from New York University School of Law, where she received the Harry J. Ruddick award for distinction in the graduate tax program and served on the New York Tax Law Review as a graduate editor. She clerked for the Honorable William J. Jameson, United Stated District Court for Montana, and for the Honorable James R. Browning, Ninth Circuit Court of Appeals.

Table of Contents

QUESTIONS

Unless otherwise indicated, for all questions assume that the donor or decedent is a U.S. citizen or resident and that the beneficiaries are U.S. citizens.

Unless otherwise indicated, all references to "IRC" or to "the Code" refer to the Internal Revenue Code, all references to "Section" refer to sections of the Internal Revenue Code, and all references to "Service" refer to the Internal Revenue Service.

1. In the popular press the federal estate tax has been characterized by many labels. Which of the following labels most accurately describes the federal estate tax?

    (A) Death tax.

    (B) Inheritance tax.

    (C) Succession tax.

    (D) Wealth transfer tax.

2. In 1976, it is said that Congress "unified" the federal estate and gift tax. Then in 2001, Congress tinkered with these "unifying" features. As of 2008, which of the following enumerated features do the federal estate and gift tax still share?

    (A) The same applicable exclusion amount, the same applicable credit amount, and the same progressive rate schedule based on aggregate lifetime and deathtime transfers.

    (B) The same applicable exclusion amount, the same applicable credit amount, and the same progressive rate schedule, but the rate schedule is applied separately to lifetime and deathtime transfers.

    (C) Different applicable exclusion amounts, different applicable credits, but the same progressive rate schedule based on aggregate lifetime and deathtime transfers.

    (D) Different applicable exclusion amounts, the same applicable credit, and different progressive rate schedules based separately on aggregate lifetime transfers and aggregate deathtime transfers.

FACTS FOR QUESTIONS 3 THROUGH 5

Allan, a United States citizen and resident, made a taxable gift on January 1, 2002, of $1,000,000, and a taxable gift on January 1, 2003, of $500,000. Allan died on December 31, 2006, with a taxable estate of $2,000,000.

3. Based on the above facts, calculate the amount of federal gift tax owed by Allan on the 2002 taxable gift.

ANSWER:

4. Based on the above facts, calculate the amount of federal gift tax owed by Allan on the 2003 taxable gift.

ANSWER:

5. Based on the above facts, calculate the amount of federal estate tax owed, if any, by Allan's estate.

ANSWER:

6. Debra, who is not married, has one adult child and one grandchild. The grandchild attends an accredited college, and pays tuition of $50,000 per year. In 2008, Debra would like to transfer the maximum amount possible to child and grandchild without using any of Debra's applicable credit. What is the maximum amount of cash that Debra may transfer to her child and grandchild?

   (A) $20,000

   (B) $24,000

   (C) $62,000

   (D) $74,000

7. Barbara, who is not married and who owns assets in excess of $10 million, has decided to make gifts to her only child to minimize federal estate and gift tax. Indicate which of the following assets you would recommend that Barbara give to her child:

   (A) Apartment building, which produces income that Barbara uses to pay personal expenses.

   (B) Company X stock, which has recently been declining in value.

(C) Lake home, which has recently begun to appreciate rapidly.

(D) Residence, which Barbara intends to live in long-term.

8. Charles, who owns property in excess of $10,000,000, would like to transfer the greatest amount of property possible to Charles' five grandchildren without incurring generation-skipping transfer tax. Charles would like to place the entire amount to be transferred in trust for the benefit of the grandchildren. What is the maximum amount of property Charles may transfer to grandchildren free of generation-skipping transfer tax?

   (A) $0

   (B) Aggregate assets equal to the applicable exclusion amount.

   (C) All Charles' assets.

   (D) Assets equal to the applicable exclusion amount to each of his five grandchildren.

9. Explain why the federal gift tax and generation-skipping transfer tax are said to work as a "back-stop" to the federal estate and income taxes.

ANSWER:

10. What will the estate tax applicable exclusion amount be in the year 2010?

   (A) $1 million

   (B) $3.5 million

   (C) uncertain

   (D) zero

11. Indicate which of the following interests owned by Ellen will not be included in Ellen's gross estate pursuant to Section 2033.

   (A) Community property interest in land.

   (B) General power of appointment.

   (C) Tax-exempt municipal bonds.

   (D) Tenant-in-common interest in land.

12. Fred holds the following interests in trust. Each of the trusts were created and funded by someone other than Fred. Fred holds only the interests indicated, and no other interest in the trust. Indicate which of the following interests will be included in Fred's gross estate pursuant to Section 2033.

   (A) Fred's life estate in trust 1, with Fred's interest being terminated at death and trust property passing to the named remainder person on Fred's death.

   (B) Fred's contingent remainder interest in trust 2, with Fred's interest being terminated at death and trust property passing to the other named remainder person.

   (C) Fred's vested remainder interest in trust 3, with Fred's interest surviving death, and passing to Fred's estate.

   (D) Fred's legal title to trust property as trustee of trust 4, with Fred's interest as trustee terminating at death, and legal title passing to the named successor trustee.

13. Geri was involved in a car accident. Recovery for losses due to the accident depends on state law. Indicate which of the following recoveries that, if provided for by state law, would result in estate tax inclusion pursuant to IRC § 2033.

   (A) Geri's personal representative is entitled to bring an action for Geri's wrongful death, and does so successfully.

   (B) Harold, a surviving spouse of Geri, is entitled to bring an action for Geri's wrongful death, and does so successfully.

(C) Geri's personal representative is entitled to bring an action for Geri's pain and suffering, and does so successfully.

(D) Geri's no-fault insurance policy pays a state required survivor's benefit to Harold.

14. John was employed by Company X, a publicly traded company. On the death of an employee, Company X's employee manual provided that the company would "at its option" pay a death benefit amount equal to the bonus the decedent would have earned had decedent lived. The manual indicated the amount would be paid to a decedent's estate or a beneficiary, as determined by the company's officers. On the death of an employee, the company's board of directors typically investigated whether circumstances justified payment of the amount. Company X paid a death benefit to John's estate, which was distributed pursuant to John's will. Does John's gross estate include the death benefit paid by Company X to John's estate pursuant to Section 2033, and why?

(A) Yes, because John's estate in fact received the death benefit, and as a result, it is property subject to probate.

(B) Yes, because John was deemed to transfer the death benefit to John's estate by the act of consenting to employment.

(C) No, because John held no more than a mere expectancy at death and as such did not hold an interest in property.

(D) No, because only Section 2039 applies to determine whether the gross estate includes death benefits.

15. Kathy makes a loan to her sibling, and takes back a promissory note. Kathy dies holding the promissory note. Kathy's will forgives all remaining payments due on the note. Will Kathy's gross estate include the value of the remaining payments due pursuant to Section 2033, and why?

(A) Yes, because Kathy made a transfer of an interest in property held at death by forgiving the promissory note.

(B) Yes, because Kathy retained an interest in property transferred during life by taking back the promissory note.

(C) No, because Kathy terminated the property interest by forgiving the promissory note, and no transfer occurred.

(D) No, because Kathy received adequate consideration for the note so that the forgiveness did not amount to a transfer.

16. Lance died owning a sport utility vehicle. Briefly explain how the vehicle should be valued for inclusion in the decedent's gross estate.

ANSWER:

17. Melanie died owning stock in a publicly traded corporation. The highest reported trading price per share of stock on the date of decedent's death was $100. The lowest reported trading price was $50. Most shares traded for $80 that day. Choose the value at which the stock should be reported on Melanie's federal estate tax return.

    (A) $50

    (B) $75

    (C) $80

    (D) $100

18. Norman died holding a vested remainder interest in a trust following a life income interest payable annually to the life tenant. Trust property as of Norman's date of death totaled $100,000. The applicable federal rate at that time was 10 percent, and the age of the life tenant was 60. The remainder factor provided by actuarial tables for the remainder interest is ".21196." Determine the value of the Norman's remainder interest for purposes of determining the gross estate.

ANSWER:

19. Laura transferred property to a trust, with Mary as trustee. Laura retained certain rights and interests in the trust. Indicate the code section that will most likely apply to include the entire value of the trust property on Laura's date of death in the gross estate of Laura.

    (A) IRC Section 2033.

    (B) IRC Section 2036.

    (C) IRC Section 2040.

    (D) IRC Section 2041.

20. Lance transferred property to a trust with Martin as trustee. Pursuant to the trust, Lance gave Oscar, who is a life income beneficiary of the trust, the power to determine who receives the trust principal on termination of the trust, including payment to Oscar. Indicate the code section that will most likely apply to include the trust property in the gross estate of Oscar as beneficiary of the trust.

    (A) IRC Section 2033.

    (B) IRC Section 2036.

    (C) IRC Section 2038.

    (D) IRC Section 2041.

21. Livvy transferred property to a trust, with Max as trustee. Max is also a beneficiary. Pursuant to the trust, Max possesses the power as trustee to distribute trust income and principal among beneficiaries. Indicate the code section that will most likely apply to include the trust property in the gross estate of Max, as trustee.

    (A) IRC Section 2033.

    (B) IRC Section 2036.

    (C) IRC Section 2037.

(D) IRC Section 2041.

22. Lanna and Lanna's spouse, Paul, own Greenacre as joint tenants with right of survivorship. Indicate the code section that will most likely apply to include a portion of Greenacre in the gross estate of Lanna.

(A) IRC Section 2033.

(B) IRC Section 2034.

(C) IRC Section 2040.

(D) IRC Section 2044.

23. Lucy owns a life insurance policy on the life of her spouse. Indicate the code section that will most likely apply to include the life insurance policy in the gross estate of Lucy.

(A) IRC Section 2033.

(B) IRC Section 2036.

(C) IRC Section 2042.

(D) IRC Section 2044.

FACTS FOR QUESTIONS 24 AND 25

Any State, USA, has abolished dower and curtesy. Instead, Any State allows a surviving spouse to take an elective share amount in the event decedent fails on death to make sufficient provision for the surviving spouse. The surviving spouse is not entitled to an elective share amount unless the surviving spouse makes a timely election. In Any State the surviving spouse must make any election within nine months of the death of the first spouse to die. The law of Any State also prohibits an election after the death of the surviving spouse. This right to take an elective share amount is often referred to as a "right of election."

Anna and Barry are married and domiciled in Any State. Anna dies when Anna is married to Barry. Barry dies six months following Anna's death without having exercised his right of election.

24. Based on the above facts, will Anna's gross estate include the property owned by Anna that is subject to Barry's right of election?

   (A) Yes, because Barry's right of election is a statutory interest created in Anna's surviving spouse as a result of her death.

   (B) Yes, because Barry's right of election is a contingent interest that may never vest in Barry.

   (C) No, because Barry's right of election is a general power of appointment in Barry, not Anna.

   (D) No, because Barry's right of election amounts to a valid claim against Anna's property.

25. Based on the above facts, discuss whether Barry's gross estate includes the value of the elective share amount.

ANSWER:

26. Celeste and Eric enter into a prenuptial agreement. Pursuant to the agreement, Celeste gives Eric a life interest in Celeste's apartment in consideration for Eric's agreement to waive any marital or other rights upon Celeste's death. Celeste dies at a time when Celeste and Eric are happily married, and Eric enforces the

agreement. The prenuptial agreement is based on adequate consideration and is enforceable under state law. Section 2053 of the Code allows a deduction for bona fide claims against the estate supported by full and adequate consideration. Indicate whether Celeste's estate may deduct the value of Eric's life interest in Celeste's apartment pursuant to Section 2053.

(A) Yes, because the prenuptial agreement is supported by adequate consideration and enforceable under state law.

(B) Yes, because Eric has enforced Eric's claim under the prenuptial agreement, and caused a life estate in the apartment to vest in Eric.

(C) No, because a waiver of marital rights does not amount to full and adequate consideration for federal estate tax purposes.

(D) No, because Eric did not enter into the agreement within the three-year period beginning one year prior to Celeste's date of death.

ADJUSTMENTS FOR CERTAIN GIFTS MADE WITHIN THREE YEARS OF DECEDENT'S DEATH, IRC § 2035

IRC § 2035 generally serves two purposes. First, it acts as a stop-gap to IRC §§ 2036, 2037, 2038, and 2042. For this reason, you may wish to come back to this Topic 5 after reviewing the topics addressing these sections. Second, IRC § 2035 acts to prevent the gift tax exclusive impact of gifts made within three years of decedent's death.

The following questions assume the transfer at issue occurred after 1981. Prior to 1982 the reach of IRC § 2035 was much broader than it is today. (Note that, while the substance of IRC § 2035 did not materially change, the numbering of the subsections changed in 1997.)

27. Alice transfers cash to herself as trustee of an irrevocable trust for the benefit of her adult child and grandchild. As trustee, Alice may distribute income in her discretion to her child and grandchild. On the death of Alice's child, the remainder of trust property passes to Alice's grandchild or the grandchild's estate. Alice consults with her attorney, and irrevocably resigns as trustee of the trust on March 6, 2005, in order to avoid any concern that IRC §§ 2036 and 2038 would apply to include the trust property in her gross estate. Alice dies on March 6, 2008. Indicate whether Alice successfully avoided inclusion of the trust property in her gross estate, and why.

    (A) Yes, Alice avoided inclusion in her gross estate because Alice never held any interest in or power that would have caused inclusion under IRC §§ 2036 through 2038, thereby making IRC § 2035 irrelevant.

    (B) Yes, Alice avoided inclusion in her gross estate because Alice irrevocably relinquished her power over the trust more than three years prior to her date of death, thereby avoiding application of IRC § 2035.

    (C) No, Alice's gross estate includes a portion of the trust property because Alice relinquished her power over the trust assets within three years of her date of death thereby triggering application of IRC § 2035.

    (D) No, Alice's gross estate includes a portion of the trust property because Alice originally retained a power over trust income, and relinquishment of the power, regardless of when, causes IRC § 2035 to apply.

28. Indicate whether your answer to question 27 would change if Alice made the transfer one week prior to her death.

ANSWER:

29. Barney transfers $1 million in trust and retains the power to revoke the trust during his lifetime. The trust requires trustee to pay income and principal as directed by Barney. One month prior to his death, Barney directs trustee to transfer $100,000 cash from the trust to Barney's niece. On Barney's date of death, the trust assets total $900,000. Will Barney's gross estate include any portion of the $1 million, and, if so, why and how much?

    (A) No, Barney's gross estate will not include any portion of the amount transferred.

    (B) Yes, Barney's gross estate will include $900,000 per IRC § 2038, and $100,000 per IRC § 2035.

    (C) Yes, Barney's gross estate will include only $100,000 pursuant to IRC § 2035.

    (D) Yes, Barney's gross estate will include only $900,000 pursuant to IRC § 2038.

30. Collin purchased a life insurance policy on his own life two years prior to his death. Collin paid the initial premium payment of $20,000, then immediately transferred ownership of the policy to his child. On Collin's death, the insurance proceeds of $1 million were paid to Collin's child as beneficiary. Will Collin's gross estate include the policy proceeds, and, if so, how much?

    (A) No, Collin's gross estate will not include the policy proceeds because Collin did not retain any incidents of ownership over the policy as of the date of his death, nor did Collin's estate receive policy proceeds.

    (B) Yes, Collin's gross estate will include the value of the initial premium payment of $20,000 because Collin transferred the policy during the three-year period ending on decedent's death.

    (C) Yes, Collin's gross estate will include the $1 million of policy proceeds because Collin transferred the policy during the three-year period ending on decedent's death.

    (D) Yes, Collin's gross estate will include both the $1 million of policy proceeds and the $20,000 premium payment because Collin transferred the policy during the three-year period ending on decedent's death.

31. Dorthea transfers $12,000 outright to her child on January 1, 2007. Child invests the cash in Public Corporation stock, and as of Dorthea's death on August 1, 2008, the Public Corporation stock has appreciated to $20,000. Indicate whether Dorthea's gross estate includes the value of the gift made by Dorthea, and, if so, why and how much.

(A) Dorthea's gross estate does not include any portion of the value of the gift because the gift was an outright transfer to Dorthea's child.

(B) Dorthea's gross estate includes the $12,000 date-of-gift value because the gift occurred within three years of Dorthea's death.

(C) Dorthea's gross estate includes the $20,000 date-of-death value because the gift occurred within three years of Dorthea's death.

(D) Dorthea's gross estate includes the stock value as of the filing of Dorthea's gift tax return because the gift occurred within three years of Dorthea's death.

32. Elise makes a cash gift to her child three years and one month prior to Elise's death. Elise and Elise's spouse choose to split the gift. Two years prior to her death, Elise pays $50,000 of gift tax with respect to the gift, and Elise's spouse also pays $50,000 of gift tax with respect to the split gift. Indicate the amount, if any, included in Elise's gross estate.

(A) Elise's gross estate will not include any portion of the transfer to Elise's child or any gift tax paid on that amount.

(B) Elise's gross estate will include only the $50,000 of gift tax paid by Elise during the three-year period ending on her date of death.

(C) Elise's gross estate will include only the $100,000 of gift tax paid by Elise and Elise's spouse during the three-year period ending on Elise's date of death.

(D) Elise's gross estate will include the value of the cash gift, and the $100,000 of gift tax paid.

33. One year before his death Fred makes a taxable gift to Fred's child. The transfer is not included in Fred's gross estate under IRC § 2035. Discuss whether the transfer would be taken into account for purposes of determining whether the estate qualifies for special use valuation under IRC § 2032A.

ANSWER:

Unless otherwise indicated in the problems below, assume (1) any trust is irrevocable, (2) trustor and trustee are not related or subordinate to each other, and (3) all transfers of property occurred on or after June 7, 1931.

34. Alyssa transferred her home to a trust and retained the right to use the home for a period of 10 years. At the end of the 10-year period the property passed to Bobby, Alyssa's friend. At the end of the 10-year period, Alyssa moved to an apartment. Alyssa died in year 14. Indicate whether Alyssa's gross estate will include the trust property, and the reason for your answer.

    (A) Yes, IRC § 2036 includes the trust property because Alyssa retained the right to possess the home for a period beginning upon its transfer.

    (B) Yes, IRC § 2038 includes the trust property because Alyssa retained the right to possess the home for a period beginning upon its transfer.

    (C) No, IRC § 2036 does not include the trust property because Alyssa retained the right to possess the home for a period that ended prior to her death.

    (D) No, IRC § 2038 does not include the trust property because Alyssa retained the right to possess the home for a period not ascertainable with reference to her death.

35. Assume the same facts as in Question 34, above, except that Alyssa now dies within the 10-year period during which she had the right to use the home. Indicate how your answer will change based on this new fact.

ANSWER:

36. Barry transferred stock to a corporate trustee, and retained the right to all income and dividends earned by the trust during his life. On Barry's death, the trust property passes to Barry's child Cassie or, if Cassie is not then living, to Cassie's estate. Indicate whether Barry's gross estate will include the trust property, and the reason for your answer.

    (A) IRC § 2036 includes the trust property in Barry's gross estate because Barry retained the right to income from the trust for life.

(B) IRC § 2038 includes the trust property in Barry's gross estate because Barry retained the right to income from the trust for life.

(C) IRC § 2037 includes the trust property in Barry's gross estate because Barry retained the right to income from the trust for life.

(D) The trust property is not included in Barry's gross estate under IRC §§ 2036, 2037, or 2038 because a corporate trustee, and not Barry, possesses the right to manage the trust property.

37. Assume the same facts as in Question 36, above, except assume instead that Barry retained only the right to distribute income among Barry's children in Barry's sole discretion. Indicate how your answer will change based on this new fact.

ANSWER:

38. Cory transfers income-producing property to a trust, and retains the right to an annuity interest for a period of 10 years. The remainder interest in trust passes to Cory's adult child or, if Cory's child does not survive, to the estate of Cory's child. Cory dies 12 years after creation of the trust. Will Cory's gross estate include a portion of the trust assets pursuant to IRC § 2036?

(A) Yes, IRC § 2036 includes a portion of the trust in Cory's gross estate because Cory retained an income interest in the trust.

(B) Yes, IRC § 2036 includes a portion of the trust in Cory's gross estate because Cory retained an income interest in the trust and died within three years of its termination.

(C) No, IRC § 2036 does not apply to include a portion of the trust in Cory's gross estate because at death Cory has no interest in the trust.

(D) No, IRC § 2036 does not apply to include a portion of the trust in Cory's gross estate because Cory retained only an annuity interest in the trust.

39. Daisy transfers her home and income-producing property in trust. Daisy directs trustee to hold the trust property for the benefit of Daisy's adult child, and to use the trust property for the support of her child. Even though the trust terms do not allow trustee to use trust property for the benefit of anyone other than Daisy's child, trustee (with the child's consent) allows Daisy to live rent-free in the home, and uses a portion of the income to pay Daisy's living expenses up to the time of Daisy's death. Will IRC § 2036 include any portion of the trust property Daisy's gross estate?

(A) Yes, IRC § 2036 includes the trust property in Daisy's gross estate based on evidence of an implied agreement that Daisy would retain use of the property.

(B) Yes, IRC § 2036 includes the trust property in Daisy's gross estate because Daisy owed a duty of support to her adult child.

(C) No, IRC § 2036 does not apply to include the trust property in Daisy's gross estate because Daisy did not retain a legally enforceable interest in the trust.

(D) No, IRC § 2036 does not apply to include the trust property in Daisy's gross estate because Daisy did not retain any rights as trustee.

40. Eva transfers property to a corporate trustee for the benefit of Eva's child, to whom Eva owes a duty of support under state law. The trust terms direct the trustee to distribute trust income and principal for the support of Eva's child until such child attains age 18, and thereafter to terminate the trust and pay over remaining trust property to Eva's child, or the child's estate. Will Eva's gross estate include any portion of the trust property pursuant to IRC § 2036 if Eva dies during the term of the trust?

(A) Yes, because under the trust terms Eva, as child's parent, legally has the right to control child's income and property for a period that does not end before Eva's death.

(B) Yes, because Eva receives the benefit of the trust income used to satisfy her obligation of support for a period that does not end before Eva's death.

(C) No, because Eva is not entitled to any distribution of income or right to enjoy the trust property prior to Eva's death.

(D) No, because Eva has transferred all power over the trust property to a corporate trustee.

41. Client Frank asks whether the following scenarios will cause inclusion in Frank's gross estate, if Frank transfers property to himself as trustee for the benefit of his descendants. Indicate which of the scenarios (there may be more than one) will cause inclusion in Frank's gross estate pursuant to IRC § 2036(a)(2), and why.

(A) In scenario A, trustee pays all income to Frank's daughter for life. Trustee may, in his discretion, distribute principal to Frank's grandchild. Remainder passes to grandchild or grandchild's estate.

(B) In scenario B, trustee pays all income to Frank's daughter for life. Trustee may, in his discretion, also distribute trust principal to Frank's daughter. Remainder passes to daughter or daughter's estate.

(C) In scenario C, trustee may distribute income to Frank's daughter and grandchild in trustee's discretion. Remainder passes to daughter or daughter's estate.

(D) In scenario D, trustee may pay trust income to Frank's daughter, or trustee may accumulate trust income, and add it to principal. Remainder passes to Frank's grandchild or grandchild's estate.

42. Greg transfers property to an unrelated trustee, who is not subordinate to Greg. Greg retains the right to remove trustee, and name a new trustee. There are no restrictions on who may be appointed as successor trustee. The trust terms allow trustee, in trustee's discretion, to distribute trust income to Helia or Ignacio. On Helia's death all remaining trust assets pass to Ignacio or Ignacio's estate. Discuss whether IRC § 2036(a)(2) will cause inclusion of trust property in Greg's gross estate if Greg survives Helia and Ignacio.

ANSWER:

43. Julius owns 25 percent of Yak Corporation stock. Yak Corporation has only one class of stock. Julius gives 20 percent of his stock in Yak Corporation to his son, but Julius makes the gift of stock subject to an agreement that Julius votes the gifted stock until he dies. Will the 20 percent of Yak stock Julius transferred to his son be included in Julius' gross estate under IRC § 2036 and, if so, why?

   (A) Yes, because Julius gave at least 20 percent of the Yak Corporation stock to his son.

   (B) Yes, because after the transfer Julius had the right to vote at least 20 percent of the Yak Corporation stock.

   (C) No, because after the transfer Julius owned less than 20 percent of the Yak corporation stock.

   (D) No, because Julius gave 20 percent of the stock outright to his son, and not in trust.

44. Zany Corporation has two classes of stock, voting and non-voting. Kristina owns 25 percent of each class of stock. Kristina transfers 25 percent of the non-voting stock to her grandchild. Will Kristina's gross estate include any portion of the non-voting stock transferred to grandchild?

ANSWER:

45. Lacey and Marik are siblings. Lacey transfers $1 million in assets to a trust for the benefit of Marik and Marik's family. The trust distributes all income to Marik for life, with remainder to Marik's child or the child's estate. One week later Marik transfers $1 million in assets to a trust for the benefit of Lacey and Lacey's family. The trust created by Marik for Lacey mirrors the terms of the earlier trust created by Lacey for Marik. Will IRC § 2036 cause inclusion of any of the trust assets in Lacey's gross estate?

(A) Yes, because the trusts are interrelated and leave Lacey and Marik in substantially the same economic position, Lacey's gross estate will include the value of the assets held in trust created by Marik for Lacey's benefit.

(B) Yes, because Lacey is the income beneficiary of the trust created by Marik and is entitled to income for life, Lacey's gross estate will include the value of the assets held in the trust created by Marik for Lacey's benefit.

(C) No, because Lacey did not retain any possession or enjoyment of, or the right to income from, the trust property transferred by Lacey, Lacey's gross estate avoids inclusion of the value of any trust assets.

(D) No, because Lacey's interest in the trust for her benefit ceases as of her death and she is unable to direct its transfer, Lacey's gross estate avoids inclusion of the value of any trust assets.

46. Nels transferred property to trustee for the benefit of Nels and Nels' child. The trust directed trustee to distribute one-half the income to Nels and one-half the income to Nels' child. On Nels' death, the remainder passes to Nels' child. What amount of the trust property is includible in Nels' gross estate under IRC § 2036?

(A) All of the trust property.

(B) One-half the trust property.

(C) The value of Nels' life interest.

(D) None of the trust property.

47. Olivia sells her home to her son for cash and receives fair market value. Following the sale Olivia continues to live in the home and pays fair rental value until her death. Will IRC § 2036 cause the value of the home to be included in Olivia's gross estate?

(A) Yes, because Olivia transferred her home, and impliedly retained possession of the home for a period not ending before her death.

(B) Yes, because Olivia transferred her home solely to avoid estate tax, and did not transfer the home for a bona fide non-tax reason.

(C) No, because Olivia paid rent for the home to her son following the transfer.

(D) No, because Olivia received fair market value for the home when she sold it to her son.

48. Assume the same facts as in Question 47, except that Olivia sells her home for less than adequate consideration to her son and does not pay rent. The bona fide sale for adequate consideration exception does not apply. What amount, if any, will be included in Olivia's gross estate under IRC § 2036?

(A) The fair market value of the home as of Olivia's date of death.

(B) The fair market value of the home as of Olivia's date of death less an amount proportionate to the value of the consideration paid by son divided by the fair market value as of date of death.

(C) The fair market value of the home less the actual amount of consideration paid by son.

(D) Nothing.

49.   Paul sells a remainder interest in his home to his friend Quixote, and retains a life estate. Quixote pays consideration to Paul equal to the fair market value of the remainder interest. Analyze the amount of the home includible in Paul's gross estate, if any.

ANSWER:

There is a great deal of overlap between IRC § 2036(a)(2) and § 2038. In addition to focusing on the broad application of IRC § 2038, this topic explores the similarities and differences between the two sections. Unless otherwise indicated in the problems below, assume (1) the trust is irrevocable, (2) trustor and trustee are not related or subordinate to each other, and (3) all transfers of property occurred on or after June 23, 1936.

50. Andy transfers property to trustee, and retains the right to revoke the trust at any time upon giving trustee 60 days written notice of the intent to revoke. During Andy's life, trustee, in its discretion, may pay income to Andy or Andy's child. On Andy's death, the trust property passes to Andy's child or the child's estate. Andy does not exercise the power to revoke. Will IRC § 2038 include trust property in Andy's gross estate, and on what basis?

    (A) Andy's gross estate includes all property because all property is subject to the power to revoke as of Andy's date of death.

    (B) Andy's gross estate includes only the value of the remainder interest payable to Andy's child because that is the interest returned to Andy in the event of revocation.

    (C) Andy's gross estate avoids inclusion of the property subject to the power to revoke because Andy did not in fact exercise the power.

    (D) Andy's gross estate avoids inclusion of the property subject to the power to revoke because revocation does not occur until 60 days after notice to trustee.

51. Becca transfers property to herself and her spouse as trustees. The trust terms allow trustees to accumulate trust income until Becca's child attains age 25, at which time accumulated income and principal pass outright to Becca's child or the child's estate. Trustees, in their discretion, also may pay trust principal to Becca's child prior to the time the child reaches age 25. Will IRC § 2038 include trust property in Becca's gross estate, and on what basis?

    (A) Becca's gross estate includes the value of all trust property under IRC § 2038 because Becca, with her spouse, has the power to determine when Becca's child receives trust property.

(B) Becca's gross estate includes the value of all trust property under IRC § 2038 because the power extends beyond the minority of Becca's child.

(C) Becca's gross estate avoids inclusion of the trust property under IRC § 2038 because Becca does not retain the power to alter who in fact receives the trust property.

(D) Becca's gross estate avoids inclusion of the trust property under IRC § 2038 because Becca cannot exercise the power alone and in all events.

52. Cindy transfers property to trustee for the benefit of Cindy's adult child. Trustee, in its discretion, may pay income to Cindy's adult child for the child's support. On Cindy's death, her child or her child's estate receives all remaining trust property outright. Cindy has the power to remove and replace trustee with another trustee, including herself. Will IRC § 2038 include the value of the trust in Cindy's gross estate, and on what basis?

(A) IRC § 2038 includes the value of all trust property in the gross estate because trustee may determine when child receives income and Cindy may remove and replace the trustee with herself.

(B) IRC § 2038 includes the value of all trust property in the gross estate because trustee may satisfy a duty of support to child and Cindy may remove and replace trustee with herself.

(C) Cindy's gross estate avoids inclusion under IRC § 2038 even though Cindy may remove and replace trustee because the trustee's power to alter Cindy's interest is only with respect to trust income, and not principal.

(D) Cindy's gross estate avoids inclusion under IRC § 2038 even though Cindy may remove and replace trustee because the trustee's power is subject to an ascertainable standard.

53. Assume the same facts as in Question 52, above. Discuss how your answer would change if the question was whether IRC § 2036 applies to include the trust property in the gross estate.

ANSWER:

54. Demetra transfers property to herself as trustee. As trustee, Demetra may distribute trust income among her nieces, Effie, Faye, and Gabriela, in her sole discretion. On Demetra's death the property passes to Mensa University. Indicate whether Demetra's estate will include the full value of all trust property under either IRC § 2036 or § 2038.

(A) Only IRC § 2036 includes the full value of trust property in Demetra's gross estate.

(B) Only IRC § 2038 includes the full value of trust property in Demetra's gross estate.

(C) Both IRC § 2036 and § 2038 include the full value of the trust property in Demetra's gross estate.

(D) Neither IRC § 2036 nor § 2038 include the full value of the trust property in Demetra's gross estate.

55. Hanson transfers property to trustee. Hanson does not retain any power over the trust. Trustee may, in its discretion, pay income and principal from the trust property to and among Hanson's descendants. At such time as there is no descendant of Hanson then living, the trust property passes to charity. Indicate whether Hanson's gross estate will include any portion of the trust property under either IRC § 2036 or § 2038.

(A) Only IRC § 2036 will include trust property in Hanson's gross estate.

(B) Only IRC § 2038 will include trust property in Hanson's gross estate.

(C) Both IRC § 2036 and § 2038 will include trust property in Hanson's gross estate.

(D) Neither IRC § 2036 nor § 2038 will include trust property in Hanson's gross estate.

56. Jaime transfers property to co-trustees. The trust directs Jaime to appoint a successor trustee if a trustee vacancy occurs because of death, resignation, or removal of trustee by a proper court for cause. During Jaime's life, a vacancy in the trusteeship occurred, and Jaime appointed a successor trustee. At Jaime's death, however, no vacancy existed. Trustee possesses discretion to pay income and principal among Kalla, Larimie, and Megan, or to the survivor of them. Indicate whether Jaime's gross estate will include any portion of the trust property under either IRC § 2036 or § 2038.

(A) Only IRC § 2036 will include trust property in Jaime's gross estate.

(B) Only IRC § 2038 will include trust property in Jaime's gross estate.

(C) Both IRC § 2036 and § 2038 will include trust property in Jaime's gross estate.

(D) Neither IRC § 2036 nor § 2038 will include trust property in Jaime's gross estate.

Although formally titled "Transfers Taking Effect at Death," IRC § 2037 more aptly applies to reversionary interests, whether arising under the terms of the governing instrument or by operation of law. Only on rare occasion does IRC § 2037 apply to cause inclusion in the gross estate. The infrequency of its application is due to the fact that transferors of interests rarely reserve a reversion under the narrow circumstances of IRC § 2037 application.

Unless otherwise indicated in the problems below, assume (1) the trust is irrevocable, (2) trustor and trustee are not related or subordinate to each other, and (3) all transfers of property occurred on or after October 8, 1949. Also, unless otherwise indicated, assume the value of any reversionary interest immediately before decedent's death exceeds 5 percent of the value of the property transferred.

57. Anderson transferred property to trustee. The trust directs trustee to pay income to Anderson's spouse for her life, with remainder to Anderson or, if he is not living at his spouse's death, to Anderson's child or to the child's estate. Anderson predeceases his spouse and his child. Indicate whether Anderson's gross estate will include any portion of the trust property under either IRC § 2033 or § 2037.

   (A) Only IRC § 2033 will include trust property in Anderson's gross estate.

   (B) Only IRC § 2037 will include trust property in Anderson's gross estate.

   (C) Both IRC § 2033 and § 2037 will include trust property in Anderson's gross estate.

   (D) Neither IRC § 2033 nor § 2037 will include trust property in Anderson's gross estate.

58. Based on your answer in Question 50, indicate what amount of trust assets, if any, will be included in Anderson's gross estate.

ANSWER:

59. Bob transfers property in trust, and directs trustee to pay income to his sister for her life, with remainder to his sister's surviving children, or if none, to Bob or Bob's estate. Bob dies survived by his sister and her children. Indicate whether Bob's gross estate will include any portion of the trust property under either IRC § 2033 or § 2037.

(A) Only IRC § 2033 will include trust property in Bob's gross estate.

(B) Only IRC § 2037 will include trust property in Bob's gross estate.

(C) Both IRC § 2033 and § 2037 will include trust property in Bob's gross estate.

(D) Neither IRC § 2033 nor § 2037 will include trust property in Bob's gross estate.

60. Cynthia transfers property in trust, and directs income to be accumulated for Cynthia's life. At Cynthia's death accumulated income and principal pass to Cynthia's surviving descendants, or, if none, to David or David's estate. Indicate whether Cynthia's gross estate will include any portion of the trust property under either IRC § 2033 or § 2037.

(A) Only IRC § 2033 will include trust property in Cynthia's gross estate.

(B) Only IRC § 2037 will include trust property in Cynthia's gross estate.

(C) Both IRC § 2033 and § 2037 will include trust property in Cynthia's gross estate.

(D) Neither IRC § 2033 nor § 2037 will include trust property in Cynthia's gross estate.

61. Ellen transfers property in trust, and directs trustee to pay income and principal to Ellen's friend for friend's life. Ellen retained the power to designate who will receive the trust property on the death of Ellen's friend, if Ellen is then living. If Ellen is not then living, the trust property passes to Ellen's niece, or if she is not then living, to her estate. Indicate whether Ellen's gross estate will include any of the trust property under IRC § 2037 and why.

(A) Ellen's gross estate will include trust property under IRC § 2037 because Ellen retained the possibility of exercising power over the trust property, and her niece could only possess the trust property by surviving Ellen.

(B) Ellen's gross estate will include trust property under IRC § 2037 because Ellen retained the right to determine who will possess and enjoy the trust property, and did so for a period not in fact ending before Ellen's death.

(C) Ellen's gross estate avoids inclusion of trust property under IRC § 2037 because Ellen did not retain the required reversionary interest in trust property even though Ellen's niece would benefit only upon surviving Ellen.

(D) Ellen's gross estate avoids inclusion of trust property under IRC § 2037 because Ellen transferred trust property for the benefit of an unrelated person, and Ellen retained no power over the property during Ellen's friend's life.

62. Frances transfers property in trust, and directs that income be accumulated for her life. At her death, principal and accumulated income pass to Frances' surviving children. Frances gives her spouse an unrestricted general power of appointment. Frances' spouse survives Frances but does not exercise the power given him under the trust instrument. Will Frances' gross estate include any portion of the trust under IRC § 2037?

(A) Yes, because if Frances had survived Frances' spouse, the trust property could have reverted to Frances, and Frances' children would take only by surviving Frances.

(B) Yes, because the power granted to Frances' spouse is attributed to Frances, Frances retains a reversionary interest, and Frances' children must survive Frances to take.

(C) No, because Frances' spouse could have possessed trust property immediately before Frances' death by exercising his general power of appointment.

(D) No, because Frances' spouse did not in fact exercise the general power of appointment prior to Frances' death to prevent any reversion to Frances.

63. Greg transfers property in trust with income to Greg's niece for life, remainder to niece's child if Greg predeceases niece, but if Greg survives niece, the property reverts to Greg. Discuss the method for determining whether Greg's reversionary interest immediately before death exceeds 5 percent of the trust property.

ANSWER:

An annuity is a financial arrangement where in exchange for consideration a person receives periodic payments for a specified period of time or until a specified event occurs. Both commercial annuities and private annuities fall within this definition. Many banks, brokerage houses, and life insurance companies provide commercial annuities. Retirement benefits are often paid in the form of an annuity. Private annuity arrangements exist between private individuals, although income tax regulations issued in 2006 have significantly diminished the income tax advantages of a private annuity.

The following problems assume the decedent entered into the annuity arrangement after 1986. In 1984 Congress eliminated certain exclusions that had previously applied to qualified employee retirement plans, and in 1986 it significantly amended the statute again.

64. Indicate under which of the following scenarios the Service will likely argue that IRC § 2039 applies to include an amount in the decedent's gross estate.

    (A) Annuity payment paid to a beneficiary for life pursuant to a life insurance policy on decedent's life.

    (B) Annuity payment to a beneficiary of a grantor retained annuity trust following decedent's death.

    (C) Annuity payment made to a beneficiary under a qualified retirement plan with a joint and survivor payout.

    (D) Annuity payments made to the beneficiary pursuant to a benefit provided under the Railroad Retirement Act.

65. Alice bought a lottery ticket for $1. When Alice won the lottery, she chose to receive the proceeds in the form of an annuity payable over 20 years. On Alice's death, any annuity payments still owing continue to be paid to Alice's surviving descendants pursuant to the terms of the lottery rules. Will IRC § 2039 include the value of the annuity payments remaining to be paid as of Alice's death?

    (A) Yes, the value of the annuity payments as of Alice's death will be included in Alice's gross estate.

    (B) Yes, but only a portion of the value of the annuity as of Alice's death equal to $1 over all tickets purchased will be included in Alice's gross estate.

(C) No, Alice was unable to direct transfer of the annuity to anyone other than Alice's descendants pursuant to the lottery rules.

(D) No, the annuity was for a term of years and was not dependent on Alice's death.

66. Public company employed Bill, and made contributions to a retirement fund. Upon retirement at age 65, Bill would receive an annuity for Bill's life, and the annuity would continue for Bill's designated beneficiary upon Bill's death. However, if Bill died before attaining age 65, no benefits would be payable. On Bill's death at age 59, however, Public Company in an unusual move voluntarily paid a lump sum to Bill's designated beneficiary. Indicate whether IRC § 2039 would include the lump sum paid to Bill's designated beneficiary in Bill's gross estate, and why.

(A) Yes, Bill's gross estate includes the lump-sum amount to the beneficiary because an annuity was payable to decedent had he lived to age 65.

(B) No, Bill's gross estate does not include the lump-sum amount because the designated beneficiary did not receive a series of annuity payments.

(C) No, Bill's gross estate does not include the lump-sum amount because Bill was not in pay status as of his death.

(D) No, Bill's gross estate does not include the lump-sum amount because it was not paid pursuant to a contract or agreement.

67. Pursuant to employer's retirement fund, employer made contributions to two different funds under the terms of two different agreements. Plan 1 provided employee Clarice with an annuity for Clarice's life upon retirement at age 65. Plan 2 provided Clarice's spouse a similar annuity amount for life upon Clarice's death. Under both Plans 1 and 2, if Clarice was not employed or died prior to age 65, Clarice forfeited the benefits under the plan. Under Plan 2, if Clarice's spouse remarries after Clarice's death, payments under the plan cease. Clarice died at age 66, after receiving payments under Plan 1. Indicate whether any portion of the annuity under Plan 2 will be included in Clarice's gross estate, and why.

(A) Yes, the annuity payable under Plan 2 will be included in Clarice's gross estate because pursuant to the arrangement Clarice received an annuity under Plan 1, and Clarice's spouse received the annuity on Clarice's death under Plan 2.

(B) No, the annuity payable under Plan 2 will not be included in Clarice's gross estate because the payments could be forfeited by Clarice's spouse upon remarriage leaving the amount receivable by Clarice's spouse uncertain.

(C) No, the annuity payable under Plan 2 will not be included in Clarice's gross estate because the payments could have been forfeited under either Plan if Clarice had not lived or been employed at age 65.

(D) No, the annuity payable under Plan 2 involved a separate contract than that under Plan 1, and under Plan 2 Clarice did not have any right to receive any annuity payments.

68. Under her retirement plan, Dani elected to receive a joint and survivor annuity for the benefit of herself and her spouse for the period of their joint lives. Dani died prior to receiving any payments. Payments were made to Dani's spouse under the terms of the plan. Dani paid one-half of the value of the contributions to the retirement plan. The other one-half of the contributions were made by her employer. Indicate whether any amount will be included in Dani's gross estate, and, if so, how much.

(A) The entire value of the annuity will be included in Dani's gross estate because Dani had a right to receive the benefits under the plan, and Dani and Dani's employer made all contributions to the plan.

(B) One-half the value of the annuity will be included in Dani's gross estate because, although Dani had a right to receive benefits under the plan, Dani only contributed one-half of the consideration for the plan.

(C) None of the value of the annuity is includible in Dani's gross estate because Dani never in fact received benefits under the plan, and all payments were made only to Dani's spouse.

(D) None of the value of the annuity is includible in Dani's gross estate because Dani did not survive for a sufficient amount of time and Dani's spouse was to receive benefits regardless of whether he survived Dani.

Because of the unique characteristics of joint with right of survivorship property, Congress enacted IRC § 2040 to specifically deal with its inclusion in the gross estate. Congress enacted simplified rules in 1981 to deal with joint tenancies held between spouses. Unless otherwise indicated, the problems below address joint tenancy with right of survivorship property after 1981.

69. Individuals may hold property either as a tenancy in common, joint tenancy with right of survivorship, tenancy by the entirety, or community property. For purposes of determining inclusion in a decedent's gross estate, indicate the tenancies governed by IRC § 2040.

    (A) Community property.

    (B) Joint tenancy with right of survivorship.

    (C) Tenancy in common *and* joint with right of survivorship property.

    (D) Tenancy by the entirety *and* joint with right of survivorship property.

70. Abbey and Bob are married. Abbey contributed 70 percent of the funds to purchase an apartment building, and Bob contributed 30 percent of the funds to purchase the building. Abbey and Bob took title to the apartment building as joint tenants with right of survivorship. Indicate the portion of the apartment building includible in Abbey's gross estate on her death.

    (A) The entire value of the apartment building will be included in her gross estate because a joint tenant may enjoy the entire property subject to use of the other tenant.

    (B) Seventy percent of the value of the property will be included in her gross estate because that is the portion of the purchase price contributed by Abbey.

    (C) Fifty percent of the value of the property will be included in her gross estate because Abbey and Bob are married, and are the sole joint tenants.

    (D) None of the property will be included in Abbey's gross estate because the entire value of the property will be included in Bob's gross estate.

71. Carl, David, and Ellie received a gift of land from their mother as joint tenants with right of survivorship. Mom provided the entire consideration for the land. When Ellie dies survived by Carl and David, what portion of the land, if any, will be included in her gross estate?

(A) The entire value of the land will be included in her gross estate because none of the tracing rules regarding contributions apply to property received by gift.

(B) One-third the value of the land will be included in her gross estate because a fractional portion of joint tenancy with right of survivorship interests received by gift is included.

(C) One-half the value of the land will be included in her gross estate because Carl and David each receive a one-half interest in the joint with right of survivorship property on Ellie's death.

(D) None of the value of the land will be included in her gross estate because Ellie did not provide any consideration toward the purchase of the land received by gift.

72. Fred opened a brokerage account, and provided the entire contribution to the account. Fred then named Gavin as joint tenant with right of survivorship on the account. With Fred's consent, Gavin withdrew two-thirds of the dividends from the account each year. Gavin dies survived by Fred. On Gavin's death, indicate the proportionate amount of the brokerage account, if any, included in Gavin's gross estate.

(A) The entire value of the brokerage account is included in Gavin's gross estate because Gavin had access to the entire amount held in the account during his life.

(B) One-half of the value of the brokerage account is included in Gavin's gross estate because he received his interest in the brokerage account by gift from Fred.

(C) Two-thirds of the value of the brokerage account is included in Gavin's gross estate because he annually received from Fred two-thirds of the dividend income earned on the brokerage account.

(D) None of the value of the brokerage account is included in Gavin's gross estate because the estate can show he did not contribute any of the funds held in the brokerage account.

73. Heidi made a gift to her daughter of land valued at $50,000 on the date of gift. At a time when the land was worth $100,000, Heidi's daughter and Heidi decided to build a home on the land. The home was built with $100,000 contributed by Heidi. At the time the home was built, Heidi and her daughter decided to hold title to the

land and home worth $200,000 as joint tenants with right of survivorship. Heidi dies survived by her daughter. Indicate what portion of the home, if any, is included in Heidi's gross estate.

(A) The entire value of the land and home is included in Heidi's gross estate because all consideration can be traced to Heidi.

(B) One-half the value of the land and home is included in Heidi's gross estate because each contributed one-half the value of the land and home.

(C) Three-fourths the value of the land and home is included in Heidi's gross estate because only the $50,000 appreciation is traceable to daughter.

(D) None of the value of the land and home is included in Heidi's gross estate because title automatically passes to Heidi's daughter under state law.

74. Assume instead that Heidi transferred land to her daughter worth $50,000. When the land had appreciated to $100,000, Heidi's daughter sold the land and realized a capital gain of $50,000. Heidi's daughter invested the proceeds in a brokerage account. Heidi's daughter then used $100,000 of the brokerage account to invest in a $200,000 condominium as joint tenants with right of survivorship with Heidi, who contributes the other $100,000. Heidi dies survived by her daughter at a time when the condominium is worth $200,000. Indicate the portion of the condominium included in Heidi's gross estate.

ANSWER:

75. Ingrid and her sister Joan own an apartment building as joint tenants with right of survivorship. Ingrid contributed the funds for the entire purchase price of the apartment building. Ingrid and Joan die simultaneously in a car accident. Pursuant to state law, one-half the apartment building passes through each of their estates. Indicate the portion of the apartment building included in each of their gross estates.

(A) The entire date-of-death value is included in Ingrid's gross estate, and none of the value is included in Joan's gross estate.

(B) The entire date-of-death value is included in Ingrid's gross estate, and one-half the value is included in Joan's gross estate.

(C) One-half the date-of-death value is included in each of Ingrid's and Joan's gross estates.

(D) One-half of the date-of-death value is included in Ingrid's gross estate, and the entire date of death value is included in Joan's gross estate.

A third party may grant decedent powers over property owned or transferred by the third party, including powers to determine who will receive income and principal of a trust, and powers to determine who will receive ultimate ownership of property held in trust or otherwise. IRC Section 2041 may apply when decedent holds a power over property that is equivalent to ownership, and when decedent was not the transferor of the property subject to the power. In other words, IRC Sections 2036 through 2038 apply when decedent transfers property and retains powers over or interests in the property transferred by decedent. IRC Section 2041 applies when decedent holds a power over property that was owned or transferred by another.

Congress enacted IRC Section 2041 to include in the gross estate powers held by a decedent that are the equivalent of ownership of property. Because powers held by a decedent do not amount to ownership of the underlying property, IRC Section 2033 fails to include in the gross estate property transferred by another over which decedent held a power.

Different rules apply to powers of appointment created prior to October 22, 1942. For purposes of the following questions, assume the powers at issue were created after October 21, 1942.

For Questions 76 through 82 indicate whether, under IRC § 2041, the power is a general power of appointment or a special power of appointment (sometimes also referred to as a limited power of appointment).

76. Alison's mother created a trust for the benefit of Alison. The trust grants Alison, as beneficiary of the trust, the power to appoint by will all remaining trust property to any person she chooses, including her estate or the creditors of her estate. In absence of an exercise of the power of appointment, the trust property passes to Alison's descendants by representation.

    (A) General power of appointment.

    (B) Special power of appointment.

77. Bob's father created a trust for Bob's benefit. The trust grants Bob the power to appoint trust property during life or by will to pay his taxes or the taxes of his estate. In the absence of an exercise of the power of appointment, the trust property passes to Bob's descendants by representation.

    (A) General power of appointment.

(B) Special power of appointment.

78. Carl's mom created a trust for the benefit of her children and appointed Carl to act as trustee of the trust. As trustee, Carl could distribute trust property to himself or to his siblings in any proportion he chose.

    (A) General power of appointment.

    (B) Special power of appointment.

79. Diane's mom created a trust for the benefit of her children and appointed Diane to act as trustee of the trust. As trustee, Diane could distribute trust property to herself or to her siblings as needed for their support, health, maintenance, and education.

    (A) General power of appointment.

    (B) Special power of appointment.

80. Elise's dad created a trust for the benefit of Elise's descendants and appointed Elise to act as trustee of the trust. As trustee, Elise could distribute property to her minor children for their support.

    (A) General power of appointment.

    (B) Special power of appointment.

81. Frank's grandfather created a trust for the benefit of his descendants, and Frank became successor trustee of the trust. The trustee of the trust could distribute income and principal of the trust as needed for the descendants' support in their accustomed manner of living. Frank, who is one of the descendant's, may now exercise this power as trustee.

    (A) General power of appointment.

    (B) Special power of appointment.

82. As beneficiary of a trust created by his relative, Gary could appoint the trust property to anyone other than himself, his creditors, his estate, or the creditors of his estate. In the absence of an exercise of the power of appointment, trust property passes to Gary's descendants by representation.

    (A) General power of appointment.

    (B) Special power of appointment.

83. Hans served as trustee of a trust created for his benefit by Izzy. All trust income was payable to Hans. In addition, as trustee, Hans could appoint trust principal to himself in the event of an emergency or illness. Discuss whether Hans' ability to

appoint principal to himself in the event of emergency or illness amounts to a general power of appointment.

ANSWER:

84. Jacob was the beneficiary of a trust created by his father. Trustee could distribute property to Jacob during his life for his support. On Jacob's death, the trust directed trustee to distribute property as appointed by Jacob in his will, including appointment to Jacob's estate. In the absence of appointment, trust property passed by representation to Jacob's descendants. Jacob died intestate, and never attempted to exercise the power of appointment. Indicate whether the property held in trust will be included in Jacob's gross estate.

(A) Yes, the property will be included in Jacob's gross estate because Jacob held a general power of appointment over the trust property at the time of his death.

(B) Yes, the property will be included in Jacob's gross estate because Jacob retained an interest in the trust property during his life, and the property passed to his descendants.

(C) No, the property will avoid gross estate inclusion because, although Jacob held a general power of appointment, he did not exercise the power as of his death.

(D) No, the property will avoid gross estate inclusion because the life interest for the benefit of Jacob is subject to an ascertainable standard, and Jacob did not exercise the power.

85. Assume the same facts as in the preceding Question 84 except that prior to his death a court had declared Jacob incompetent and placed him under a guardianship. Pursuant to state law, persons placed under a guardianship cannot exercise any power of appointment. Based on these changed facts, indicate whether the property held in trust will be included in Jacob's gross estate.

(A) Yes, the property will be included in Jacob's gross estate because Jacob held a general power of appointment over the trust property at the time of his death.

(B) Yes, the property will be included in Jacob's gross estate because, at the time the court declared Jacob incompetent, Jacob's power lapsed and Jacob continued to retain an interest in trust.

(C) No, the property will not be included in Jacob's gross estate because even though the trust granted Jacob a general power of appointment, Jacob could not exercise the power as of his death.

(D) No, the property will not be included in Jacob's gross estate because Jacob had not executed a will exercising the power as of the date that he was placed under the guardianship.

86. Kathy was the trustee and beneficiary of a trust created by her partner Lois. The trust terms granted Kathy, as trustee, a lifetime power to appoint the trust property to herself as she desired. The power terminated as of her death. As of Kathy's death the trust property passed to the descendants of Lois' siblings. Indicate whether any portion of the trust property will be included in Kathy's gross estate under IRC § 2041.

   (A) The entire value of the trust property will be included in Kathy's gross estate because she was both the trustee and the beneficiary of the trust during her life.

   (B) The entire value of the trust property will be included in Kathy's gross estate because up to the moment of her death Kathy held a general power of appointment over trust property.

   (C) None of the trust property will be included in Kathy's gross estate because the general power of appointment terminated the moment before her death.

   (D) Only that portion of the trust property distributed by Kathy as trustee to herself will be included in her gross estate because Kathy held the power only until her death.

87. Monty, who worked as a barista at a popular coffee house, was a discretionary beneficiary of a credit shelter trust and an income beneficiary of a general power of appointment marital deduction trust created by the will of his spouse. A bank trustee could in its discretion distribute income from the credit shelter trust to Monty. In addition, Monty held a power to annually appoint 5 percent of the property held in a credit shelter trust to himself. The 5 percent annual general power of appointment lapsed at the end of each year. The exercise of the 5 percent general power, however, was conditioned on exhaustion of the assets of the marital deduction trust over which Monty also held a general power of appointment. At the time of Monty's death, the marital deduction trust held substantial assets. Indicate what portion of the property held in the credit shelter trust, if any, will be includible in Monty's gross estate under IRC § 2041.

   (A) Monty's gross estate will not include any assets held in the credit shelter trust because the condition placed on exercise of the 5 percent general power of appointment precluded Monty from holding the power at death.

   (B) Monty's gross estate will not include any assets held in the credit shelter trust because the Code excepts from the definition of general powers of appointment those powers limited to 5 percent of the trust assets.

(C) Monty's gross estate will include only 5 percent of the assets held in the credit shelter trust because conditions on exercise of a power within the control of the beneficiary are disregarded.

(D) Monty's gross estate will include all assets held in the credit shelter trust because the 5 percent general power of appointment lapsed each year, and he was also a discretionary beneficiary of the credit shelter trust.

88. Nancy was the beneficiary of a trust created by her father in year 1. Pursuant to the trust agreement, Nancy received all income and so much of the principal as necessary for her support. In addition, Nancy had the right to withdraw up to $5,000 of the trust property each year. The $5,000 withdrawal power lapsed on December 31 of each year. The power terminated on her death. Nancy never exercised the $5,000 withdrawal power. Nancy died in year 3. At her death the trust assets were worth $50,000. Indicate the amount of trust assets, if any, includible in Nancy's gross estate under IRC § 2041.

(A) None of the assets.

(B) $5,000.

(C) $10,000.

(D) $15,000.

89. Oscar was the beneficiary of a trust created by his mother in year 1. Pursuant to the trust agreement, Oscar was entitled to all income from the trust. In addition, Oscar had the right to withdraw $10,000 per year. The annual $10,000 withdrawal right lapsed on December 31 each year. Oscar dies in year 4. On Oscar's death, remaining trust assets pass to Penelope. Trust assets remained at $60,000 from inception to termination of the trust on Oscar's death. Indicate the amount of trust assets, if any, includible in Oscar's gross estate under IRC § 2041.

(A) None of the assets.

(B) $10,000.

(C) $25,000.

(D) $31,000.

90. Assume the same facts as in Question 89, except that Oscar was not entitled to receive any income from the trust. In fact, Oscar held no beneficial interest in the trust. The only access held by Oscar to trust assets was the $10,000 annual withdrawal right. Indicate to what extent your answer to Question 89 will change based on this changed fact.

ANSWER:

91. Assume the same facts as in Question 90, except that the $10,000 annual withdrawal right can be exercised only in the month of November. Also assume for purposes of this question that Oscar dies in October of year 4. Indicate to what extent your answer to Question 90 will change based on these additional changed facts.

ANSWER:

92. Quincy transferred property to a trust, and named Peter as trustee. The trust agreement directed trustee to pay income to Peter. The trust agreement also provided that Peter, as trustee, after obtaining Quincy's consent, could pay so much of the principal to himself or to his two brothers as Peter desires. On Peter's death all remaining trust assets pass to Peter's descendants. Indicate the portion of the trust assets, if any, includible in Peter's gross estate under IRC § 2041.

(A) None.

(B) One-third.

(C) One-half.

(D) All.

93. Rylan and Sonja were co-trustees of a trust created by their uncle. The trust provided that all income be paid to Rylan for life, and on Rylan's death, the remainder passes to Sonja. Rylan and Sonja, as trustees, jointly had discretion to pay principal to Rylan during his life. The value of Sonja's interest in the trust is substantial. Indicate the portion of the trust, if any, includible in Rylan's gross estate if he is survived by Sonja.

(A) None.

(B) One-half.

(C) The value of the trust less the actuarial value of Sonja's remainder interest just before death.

(D) All.

94. Tina, Vicky, and Wendy are beneficiaries of a trust created by their aunt. The trust agreement allows Tina, Vicky, and Wendy to jointly agree to distribute trust property to themselves and other descendants of their common grandparent. The trust agreement provides that on the death of Tina, Tina's daughter steps into Tina's shoes for purposes of exercising the power. Indicate the portion of the trust, if any, includible in Tina's gross estate if she is survived by Vicky and Wendy.

(A) None.

(B) One-fourth.

(C) One-third.

(D) All.

95. Alena owned a life insurance policy on her own life, and named her estate as beneficiary. In the aggregate she paid premiums on the policy of $35,000. On her death Alena's estate received proceeds of $500,000 on the life insurance policy. Indicate the amount, if any, of life insurance proceeds includible in Alena's gross estate under IRC § 2042.

(A) None.

(B) $35,000.

(C) $465,000.

(D) $500,000.

96. Indicate how your answer to Question 95 would change if instead Alena named her daughter as beneficiary of the policy.

ANSWER:

97. Assume instead that Hometown Bank, as trustee of an irrevocable life insurance trust, purchased a $500,000 life insurance policy under which Alena was the insured. Alena was not entitled to any benefits from the life insurance policy; however, the trust provided that trustee, in its discretion, may use trust assets to pay any estate tax owed by Alena's estate. Prior to Alena's death, trustee paid policy premiums in the aggregate of $35,000. What amount, if any, of the $500,000 life insurance proceeds would be includible in Alena's gross estate under IRC § 2042?

(A) None.

(B) $35,000.

(C) $465,000.

(D) $500,000.

98. Bob owned a life insurance policy on the life of his sister. The face amount of the policy is $200,000. The value assigned to the policy by the insurance company on Bob's death was $55,000. Bob paid aggregate insurance premiums of $70,000.

Indicate the amount, if any, included in Bob's gross estate under IRC § 2042.

(A) None.

(B) $55,000.

(C) $70,000.

(D) $200,000.

99. Clara owned 49 percent of the stock of Family Corporation, and her daughter held 51 percent of the stock. Family Corporation purchased a life insurance policy on Clara's life, and named Clara's descendants as beneficiaries. Indicate the extent to which the policy proceeds will be included in Clara's gross estate, if at all, and why.

(A) Yes, Clara's gross estate includes 49 percent of the policy proceeds because Clara owned 49 percent of the corporation stock and the proceeds were payable to her descendants.

(B) Yes, Clara's gross estate includes the entire value of the policy proceeds because Clara is deemed to own more than 50 percent of the stock after attribution of her daughter's shares.

(C) No, Clara's gross estate does not include any part of the value of the policy proceeds because the Corporation's board of directors, and not Clara, holds all incidents of ownership to the policy as owner.

(D) No, Clara's gross estate does not include any part of the value of the policy proceeds because the value of the proceeds is reflected in the value of the corporation included in Clara's gross estate, and the regulations avoid double inclusion.

100. Dad takes out and pays for a policy on his son David's life, and names David as owner of the policy and Dad as beneficiary of the policy. Dad never tells David about the policy, Dad keeps the policy in a place hidden from David, and Dad is the only person to makes changes to the policy as if he were in fact the owner. When David dies, indicate whether any portion of the policy proceeds are included in David's gross estate, and why.

(A) Yes, David's gross estate includes the proceeds because under the policy terms David is the owner of the policy, and, thus, holds incidents of ownership under the policy.

(B) No, the policy proceeds avoid inclusion in David's gross estate because David could not practically exercise any of the incidents of ownership under the policy.

(C) No, the policy proceeds avoid inclusion in David's gross estate because David in fact did not exercise any incidents of ownership under the policy.

(D) No, the policy proceeds avoid inclusion in David's gross estate because Dad, and not David's estate, is the named beneficiary of the policy proceeds.

101. Eleni purchased an insurance policy on the life of her husband, Hayden, and she transferred the policy to her irrevocable trust. On Eleni's death, Hayden became trustee of the trust that held the policy on his life. The trust agreement made no provision for Hayden. It directed Hayden as trustee to use trust assets for the benefit of his grandchildren. As trustee of Eleni's trust, Hayden held all incidents of ownership over the policy. Indicate whether Hayden's gross estate will include any portion of the life insurance proceeds under IRC § 2042, and why.

(A) Yes, Hayden's gross estate will include all trust proceeds because as trustee he held the legal right to exercise incidents of ownership over the policy, and it does not matter that Hayden held those incidents only as a fiduciary.

(B) Yes, Hayden's gross estate will include all trust proceeds because it was within Hayden's control to resign as trustee of the trust, and he chose to continue to serve as trustee and to exercise incidents of ownership over the policy.

(C) No, the insurance proceeds avoid inclusion in Hayden's gross estate because he did not transfer the policy to the trust and he held incidents of ownership only as a fiduciary with no ability to benefit himself under the trust.

(D) No, the insurance proceeds avoid inclusion in Hayden's gross estate because the transfer to the trust was by Hayden's wife and the transfer qualifies for the marital deduction.

102. Ingrid purchases a life insurance policy on her life, and transfers ownership of the policy to her child. Ingrid reserves only the right to cancel the policy at any time. She reserves no other rights over the policy. As owner of the policy, Ingrid's child has the right to borrow against the policy and to name the beneficiary. Six years following the transfer to her child, Ingrid dies. Discuss whether Ingrid's gross estate includes any portion of the policy proceeds.

ANSWER:

103. Indicate how your answer to Question 101 would change if instead Ingrid could exercise the right to cancel the policy only with the consent of her child.

ANSWER:

104. Jamie purchased a life insurance policy on her life and transferred ownership of the policy to an irrevocable life insurance trust. As trustee, National Bank holds all incidents of ownership. Jamie does not retain any right, power, or interest in the life insurance trust. Jamie paid one $10,000 annual premium before the transfer to the trust, and Jamie continued to pay two more $10,000 annual premiums after the transfer to the trust. Jamie dies two years after the transfer of the policy to the life insurance trust. The policy proceeds are paid to the irrevocable life insurance trust as named beneficiary of the policy. Indicate the portion of the life insurance proceeds, if any, includible in Jamie's gross estate.

(A) None, because Jamie held no incidents of ownership as of the date of her death.

(B) One-third, because Jamie died within three years of the transfer and paid one-third of total premiums prior to transferring the policy to the trust.

(C) Two-thirds, because Jamie died within three years of the transfer and paid two-thirds of total premiums following the transfer to the trust.

(D) All proceeds because Jamie transferred the policy within three years of death.

105. Mary creates and transfers $10,000 cash to an irrevocable trust of which State Bank is trustee. Mary does not retain any interest in or power over the irrevocable trust. State Bank, as trustee, purchases a life insurance policy on Mary's life with a $1 million face value, and uses the $10,000 to pay the initial annual premium. Mary pays the second annual $10,000 premium directly to the insurance company on behalf of the trust. Mary dies two years after State Bank purchased the life insurance policy. The irrevocable trust receives the policy proceeds on Mary's death as the named beneficiary. Indicate the portion of the life insurance proceeds, if any, includible in Mary's gross estate.

(A) None, because Mary held no incidents of ownership in the life insurance policy as of the date of her death.

(B) One-half the policy proceeds, because Mary paid one-half of the policy premiums directly to the insurance company within three years of her death.

(C) The policy proceeds less the $10,000 policy premium paid by the bank trustee when it purchased the policy within three years of Mary's death.

(D) All policy proceeds because trustee purchased the policy within three years of Mary's death.

106. Karen and Luke were married and lived in a community property state. Luke purchased a life insurance policy on his life with community funds. Under the policy terms, Luke had the sole power to exercise incidents of ownership. Luke named his children from a prior marriage as beneficiaries. Luke dies survived by Karen. Indicate the portion of the life insurance policy, if any, includible in Luke's gross estate under IRC § 2042.

(A) The entire date-of-death value of the policy.

(B) One-half the date-of-death value of the policy.

(C) The portion equal to Luke's support obligation to his children.

(D) None of the date-of-death value of the policy.

107. Wilma was survived by her husband Henry. On Wilma's death, her executor elected Qualified Terminable Interest Property ("QTIP") treatment pursuant to IRC § 2056(b)(7) for that property passing from Wilma to a trust for Henry's benefit. The trust provided a life income interest to Henry that met the requirements of a "qualifying income interest." On Henry's death, the trust assets pass to Wilma's daughter. As of Wilma's death, QTIP trust assets were valued at $750,000. As of Henry's later death, QTIP trust assets appreciated to $1 million. Indicate the amount of QTIP trust assets includible in Henry's gross estate under IRC § 2044.

(A) None, because the trust assets were already included in Wilma's gross estate.

(B) The value of Henry's life interest in the trust, because he only received income from the trust assets.

(C) $750,000, because that was the value of QTIP trust assets for which Wilma's estate received a marital deduction.

(D) $1 million, because it is the value of QTIP trust assets as of Henry's date of death.

108. Assume that Henry's estate incurs $450,000 additional federal estate tax due to the inclusion of the QTIP trust for his benefit created under Wilma's testamentary documents. Neither Wilma's nor Henry's testamentary documents address who will bear the burden for paying the tax incurred on the QTIP trust assets. Indicate who bears the burden of the tax and how the burden is allocated pursuant to the default rules of the Code.

(A) Henry's estate bears the burden for the proportionate amount of tax attributable to the QTIP assets on Henry's death.

(B) Wilma's estate bears the burden for the incremental amount of tax caused by inclusion of the QTIP assets on Henry's death.

(C) The QTIP trust bears the burden for the proportionate amount of tax attributable to the QTIP assets on Henry's death.

(D) Wilma's daughter, who is the trust remainder beneficiary, bears the burden for the incremental amount of tax caused by inclusion of the QTIP assets on Henry's death.

109. Ellie and Tom were married. On Ellie's death, her executor made a QTIP election for assets passing to a trust for Tom's benefit, and as a consequence of the marital deduction Ellie's estate did not have to pay any estate tax. On Tom's death, Tom's executor discovered that the trust for which a QTIP election had been made did not meet the definition of a "qualifying income interest." As a result, Tom's executor decided not to include the assets for which a QTIP election had been made on Ellie's estate tax return. At the time of Tom's death the statute of limitations had run on the collection of estate tax from Ellie's estate. The decision of Tom's executor resulted in a substantial estate tax savings on the return. Indicate whether Tom's executor was correct in not including the trust assets in Tom's gross estate, and why.

   (A) Yes, Tom's executor should not have included the trust assets in his gross estate because Ellie's estate was not entitled to make the QTIP election.

   (B) Yes, Tom's executor should not have included the trust assets in his gross estate because the QTIP election was null and void due to the fact that it was unnecessary to make a QTIP election.

   (C) No, Tom's executor should have included the trust assets in Tom's gross estate because courts impose a duty of consistency requiring inclusion in the survivor's estate when the predeceased spouse's estate enjoyed the benefit of a deduction.

   (D) No, Tom's executor should have included the trust assets in Tom's gross estate because regardless of the QTIP election, he held an income interest in trust.

110. Aaron dies in 2009. Aaron has never made any gifts. Indicate the amount of unified credit under IRC § 2010 available to his estate.

(A) $1,000,000.

(B) $1,445,800.

(C) $2,000,000.

(D) $3,500,000.

111. Betty dies in 2009. Betty made a $1 million gift in 2005, and completely used her available gift tax unified credit amount under IRC § 2505. When computing estate tax on Betty's gross estate, discuss whether the executor should reduce the IRC § 2010 estate tax unified credit amount by the amount of the IRC § 2505 gift tax credit amount previously used.

ANSWER:

112. Callie dies in 2009. Callie pays $400,000 in state estate taxes to the state of her domicile. Callie's taxable estate for federal estate tax purposes is $4,100,000. Indicate how Callie's executor will take state estate taxes paid into account in determining federal estate taxes.

(A) Callie's estate will receive a state death tax credit equal to $290,800.

(B) Callie's estate will receive a state death tax credit equal to $400,000.

(C) Callie's estate will receive a state death tax deduction equal to $290,800.

(D) Callie's estate will receive a state death tax deduction equal to $400,000.

113. Dirk dies in 2005 survived by his brother Ed. Dirk's will devises stock to his brother Ed. After payment of federal estate tax, Ed receives $3 million of stock from Dirk's estate. The portion of Dirk's estate tax attributable to the stock received by Ed equals $600,000. Ed sells the stock and reinvests in an apartment complex. Ed dies three years after Dirk in 2008. The amount of Ed's estate tax

attributable to the $3 million received from Dirk's estate equals $400,000. Indicate whether and to what extent Ed's estate will receive an IRC § 2013 tax on prior transfers credit.

(A) Ed's estate is not entitled to an IRC § 2013 credit because Ed sold the stock received from Dirk.

(B) Ed's estate is limited to an IRC § 2013 credit equal to $320,000 because Ed died three years after Dirk and must calculate the credit based on the smaller $400,000 amount.

(C) Ed's estate is entitled to an IRC § 2013 credit equal to $400,000 because it is the amount of Ed's estate tax attributable to the property received from Dirk.

(D) Ed's estate is entitled to an IRC § 2013 credit equal to $600,000 because it is the amount of Dirk's estate tax attributable to the property devised to Ed.

114. Prior to his death in 2008, Fred made a taxable gift in 2007. Fred paid gift tax of $100,000 on the 2007 gift. Fred made no other taxable gifts during his life. Because Fred retained a prohibited interest in the taxable gift, the gift is included in his gross estate. Discuss whether Fred's estate will receive an IRC § 2012 credit for gift tax paid on the 2007 transfer.

ANSWER:

115. Gary, a U.S. citizen, owned property in a foreign country. Gary's estate paid tax to the foreign country on the property situated there. Gary also included the property in his gross estate, and paid tax to the United States on the foreign property. Discuss whether Gary's estate will pay a double tax on the property situated in the foreign country.

ANSWER:

Except where otherwise indicated, assume the donor is a U.S. citizen and resident, and any beneficiary also is a U.S. citizen and resident. Additionally, unless otherwise indicated, assume that the donor has no remaining gift tax credit and that all annual exclusions have been exhausted.

116. Under which of the following sets of circumstances will the transfer from Adam to Bernice NOT be subject to the gift tax pursuant to IRC § 2501?

    (A) Adam, a U.S. citizen and resident, possesses a valuable gem, which he gifts to Bernice. Bernice is neither a citizen nor resident of the United States.

    (B) Adam, an English citizen and resident who is not a citizen of the United States, gifts a parcel of land located in Jackson Hole, Wyoming, to Bernice. Bernice is neither a citizen nor a resident of the United States.

    (C) Adam, a U.S. citizen and resident, gifts a parcel of land located in Missoula, Montana, to Bernice. Bernice is a citizen and resident of the United States.

    (D) Adam, an English citizen and resident who is not a citizen of the United States, possesses a valuable gem, which he gifts to Bernice. Bernice is a U.S. citizen and resident.

117. Grant, at age 50, transferred $1,000,000 to a trust he created for the benefit of Leta, his daughter. The terms of the trust provided that Leta would receive all trust income annually and, upon Grant's death, all remaining trust assets would be distributed to Leta. Upon creation of the trust, Grant retained unrestricted power to modify, alter, or revoke the trust at any time. On January 1, 10 years after the creation of the trust, when the trust still contained $1,000,000, Grant amended the trust to provide that it was irrevocable. Indicate when, if ever, Grant made a gift to Leta for federal gift tax purposes.

    (A) Grant made a taxable gift of $1,000,000 to Leta upon his initial contribution of the funds to the trust.

    (B) Grant only made a taxable gift of $1,000,000 to Leta on January 1st, 10 years later, when he amended the trust to be irrevocable.

    (C) Grant never made a taxable gift to Leta.

(D) Grant made a taxable gift to Leta each year when the trust distributed annual income, and he also made a gift of $1,000,000 on January 1st, 10 years later, when he amended the trust to be irrevocable.

118. Anne is the income beneficiary of Trust Z for life. The terms of Trust Z provide that in the event Anne marries, all of the trust assets are to be distributed to Chad, Anne's child. Bob proposes to marry Anne, but Anne declines based upon the loss of trust income. In an effort to induce Anne to accept the marriage proposal, Bob offers to transfer a sufficient amount of cash into an interest-bearing account that pays Anne annual interest amounts equal to Trust Z annual income. Anne accepts Bob's offer, marries Bob, and loses the right to income from Trust Z. Indicate whether Bob has made a gift to Anne and the reasons for your answer.

(A) No, because Anne's relinquishment of the right to income from Trust Z in return for the cash in the bank account is a sale supported by adequate and full consideration in money's worth.

(B) No, because Anne's promise to marry Bob in exchange for Bob's transfer of the cash to the account is adequate and full consideration in money or money's worth.

(C) Yes, because Anne's promise to marry Bob in return for the cash account from Anne is not a sale supported by adequate and full consideration in money's worth.

(D) Yes, but it is a gift only to the extent of the difference between the fair market value of Anne's promise to marry Bob and the amount of cash in the account.

119. Mom owned a home valued by a qualified appraiser at a fair market value of $250,000. In an effort to give her daughter Ally a "good start in life," Mom sold the home to Ally for $200,000. Which of the following describes the correct amount of taxable gift or gifts, if any, made in relation to the two transfers?

(A) Mom made a $250,000 taxable gift of the home to Ally.

(B) Mom made a $50,000 taxable gift to Ally.

(C) Mom made a $250,000 taxable gift of the home to Ally, and Ally made a $200,000 gift in cash to Mom.

(D) No gifts were made, as the transfers constituted a purchase by Ally of the home from her mom.

120. Would your answer to Question 119, above, be different if rather than the participants in the transfer being mother and daughter, they were two unrelated persons? Assume that Seller was initially asking $250,000 for the home but

purchaser offered $200,000

ANSWER:

121. Mom owns a condominium in downtown Manhattan, New York. Mom retired "young" from her position as a securities trader on Wall Street and moved to Florida to enjoy the sunnier climate. Mom kept her condo in Manhattan, now worth $2,000,000, as she was not altogether sure she was through with her career. In past years, Mom rented the Manhattan condo out on an annual basis for $120,000 per year. Mom did not intend to increase the rent in the coming year. However, this year, Mom's 27-year-old son Junior was accepted to New York University (NYU) Law School, and Mom decided that instead of renting the Manhattan condo this coming year, she would allow her son to stay in the condo rent-free beginning on January 1. Junior lived in the condo for the full year. Mom now asks you whether with respect to the condo she has made a taxable gift to Junior this past year, and, if a gift was made, the amount of the taxable gift. Indicate the most accurate response.

(A) Mom made a $2,000,000 taxable gift to Junior.

(B) Mom made a $120,000 taxable gift for the year to Junior.

(C) Mom has made a $2,120,000 taxable gift for the year to Junior.

(D) Mom has not made a taxable gift to Junior.

122. On the first day of the year, in an effort to help his son Martin get a "good start in life," Gary loaned $100,000 to Martin in exchange for a promissory note. The terms of the promissory note required that Martin pay the full $100,000 upon Gary's demand, with stated interest equal to 9 percent. Interest was payable on the note semiannually, and Martin paid Gary $4,500 in interest on June 30 and $4,500 on December 31. Assuming the loan remained outstanding at the end of the year, calculate the amount of the taxable gift for the year and explain how you arrived at the amount. For purposes of making the calculation, assume that the applicable IRC § 7872 rate (the blended annual rate) for the year was 10.45 percent and ignore any annual exclusions or gift tax credit that may exist.

ANSWER:

TOPIC 16   **QUESTIONS**

POWERS OF APPOINTMENT, RETAINED POWERS, AND RETAINED INTERESTS

123. Under which of the following sets of circumstances does Ally have a general power of appointment over all of the trust property? Assume the power of appointment was created after October 21, 1942.

(A) Ally has the right to appoint any portion or the entire corpus of a trust created by her father Jim to anyone other than Ally's sister Betty.

(B) Ally and Cindy jointly have the right to appoint any portion or the entire corpus of a trust created by Ally's father Jim to anyone including themselves. Upon Ally's death, the power to appoint does not pass solely to Cindy.

(C) Ally has the right to appoint any portion or the entire corpus of a trust created by her father Jim except that Ally can exercise her power only with Jim's consent.

(D) Ally has the right to appoint any portion or the entire corpus of a trust created by her father Jim except that Ally's power can be exercised only with the consent of George who, upon Ally's death, will alone have the power to appoint the trust corpus to anyone including himself.

124. How, if at all, would your answer to Question 123, above, change if the power of appointment in that question had been created on or before October 21, 1942?

ANSWER:

125. On January 27, 2002, Dimitri created a trust for the benefit of his three children. Trust income was to be accumulated during Dimitri's life and, at his death, principal and accumulated income was to be distributed to Dimitri's then-surviving children. Under the terms of the trust, Dimitri's wife, Martine, was given unrestricted power to alter, amend, or revoke the trust. Under which of the following additional factual scenarios will Martine make a taxable gift of the entire interest in the trust?

(A) Martine survived Dimitri but did not, in fact, exercise her power of appointment during her lifetime.

63

(B) In July of 2007, Martine amended the trust to provide that Martine would receive trust income for life, and her sister Cindy would receive all remaining trust property upon Martine's death. Martine retained the right to alter, amend, or revoke the trust.

(C) In July of 2007, Martine amended the trust to provide that Martine would receive trust income for life, and her sister Cindy would receive all remaining trust property upon Martine's death. The amended trust was irrevocable.

(D) In July of 2007, Martine irrevocably gave up her interest in the trust.

126. After October 21, 1942, Sharon transferred property into a trust. Under the terms of the trust, the remainder of the trust property was payable to Randall upon Lisa's death. Assume that neither Lisa nor Randall has any interest in or power over the enjoyment of the property except as indicated separately in the answer choices below. Under which of the following additional factual scenarios will a taxable gift from Lisa to Randall result?

(A) Trust income is payable annually to Lisa for life. Lisa has the power under the trust to cause the income to be paid to Randall. Lisa receives an annual distribution of income from the trust.

(B) Trust income is payable annually to Lisa for life. For a period of 10 consecutive years, Randall has the power to cause the trustee to distribute all trust principal to Lisa. Ten years pass by, and Randall never requests that the trustee distribute the trust principal to Lisa.

(C) Trust income is to be accumulated for a period of 10 years. During the 10-year period, Lisa has the power to cause the trustee to distribute accumulated income to herself. Ten years pass by, and Lisa never requests that the trustee distribute the accumulated income.

(D) Trust income is to be accumulated for a period of 10 years. For a period of 10 consecutive years, Lisa has the power to have the income distributed to her. Provided, however, that Lisa may only receive a distribution of income for reasons associated with her health, education, maintenance, or support (e.g., an ascertainable standard). Lisa never requests a distribution.

127. During 2006, Sharon transferred property to a trust for the benefit of her daughter Lisa. The terms of the trust provided that Lisa was to receive all trust income at least quarterly during each year. The trust also provided a special power of appointment to Lisa that authorized her to appoint trust assets to her daughter Taylor at any time during Lisa's life. Lisa exercises her power in 2006 by appointing half of the trust corpus to Taylor. Discuss whether Lisa has made a taxable gift in 2006.

ANSWER:

Except where otherwise indicated, the answers provided assume the donor is a U.S. citizen and resident, and any beneficiary also is a U.S. citizen and resident. Additionally, unless otherwise indicated, assume that the donor has no remaining gift or estate tax credit and that the donor and donor's spouse do not elect to split gifts. Further, assume there are no applicable deductions.

FACTS FOR QUESTIONS 128 THROUGH 135

IQ became a software magnate with a little financial help and legal assistance from his father. In a phenomenally short period of time, his net asset value grew into the millions. Among other assets, IQ currently has $2,000,000 of "excess" cash in his bank account. IQ has a wife plus four children under the age of eight. IQ also has two siblings, each of whom has four young children of their own. Realizing early on that the U.S. Treasury stands to take a substantial portion of his wealth upon his death, IQ comes to your office seeking advice in minimizing gift taxes payable during his life and estate taxes payable upon his death.

128. Assuming that IQ has approximately 40 years to live, under which of the following proposed plans is IQ most likely to minimize any transfer taxes?

    (A) IQ plans to give each of his four children $500,000 this year.

    (B) IQ plans to give each of his four children $20,000 every year for the next 20 years.

    (C) IQ plans to give each of his four children $12,000 every year for the next 40 years.

    (D) IQ plans to give it all equally to his four children upon his death.

129. After explaining to IQ that while each of the above plans suggested in Question 128 have their tax benefits and drawbacks, you indicate that none of the plans address the obvious problem of giving substantial sums of money to minor children outright. Indeed, young children probably lack the financial acumen needed to responsibly manage substantial sums of money. Being quick on the uptake, IQ recognizes the problem and suggests creating one or more trusts to manage the funds for the various beneficiaries. In an effort to address the problem, he makes four alternate gifting proposals. Which of the following proposals will result in minimizing gift taxes?

(A) Contribute $10,000 per year per beneficiary ($40,000 annually) with instructions to distribute all net income equally to his four children annually and distribute the remainder equally to the four children when the youngest of the children reaches 35 years of age.

(B) Contribute $10,000 per year per beneficiary ($40,000 annually) with instructions to distribute accumulated net income to the four children in such shares as the trustee in her discretion deems advisable, remainder to IQ's brother upon IQ's death.

(C) Contribute $10,000 per year per beneficiary ($120,000 annually) with instructions to accumulate net income and distribute all trust assets equally to IQ's four children and eight nieces and nephews when the youngest of the children reaches 35 years of age.

(D) Contribute $10,000 per year per beneficiary ($120,000 annually) with instructions to distribute net income and principal to IQ's four children and eight nieces and nephews for their maintenance, education, health, or support during their lives as necessary, remainder equally to the 12 children when the youngest of the children reaches 35 years of age.

130. Would your answer to Question 129, above, change if the trust provisions in answer options (B) and (C) provided that the trustee must equally distribute net income annually among the beneficiaries? Please explain your answer.

ANSWER:

131. IQ is now beginning to really understand the value of gifting. However, he notes that if only the income stream qualifies as a present gift, he is not utilizing the full amount of the annual exclusion. This is because the present value of the income stream is always less than the amount contributed to the trust. Moreover, IQ begins to focus on the amount of access his children, nieces, and nephews will have over assets distributed from the trust. He decides retaining control is as important as utilizing the maximum annual exclusion amount and that all of the children are too young to receive any of the money outright. In fact, IQ is adamant that his children, nieces, and nephews not receive any of the trust corpus until they are mature enough to manage the funds. He inquires as to what methods he has at his disposal that will allow him to limit or prevent the children from having any access to the trust income and principal. Of course, like all clients, IQ would still like to obtain the maximum tax savings. Which of the following plans is most likely to effectuate IQ's goals?

(A) Create 12 separate trusts today (one for the benefit of each child) and contribute $10,000 annually to each trust. Upon making each contribution, notify each of the 12 children that he or she has the option of withdrawing up to $10,000 within a 15-day period after contribution. The trust requires the trustee to distribute net income and principal to the beneficiary for his or her maintenance, education, health, or support during the beneficiary's life as necessary. The trustee is further directed to distribute any remaining income and principal to the beneficiary when the beneficiary attains the age of 40, or if the beneficiary dies before age 40, to the beneficiary's estate.

(B) Create 12 separate trusts today (one for each child) and contribute $10,000 annually to each trust. Upon making each contribution, notify each of the 12 children that he or she may request that the trustee distribute the $10,000 within a 15-day period after contribution, provided, however, that the trustee may deny the children's request for annual withdrawals and make distributions in his or her uncontrolled discretion as he or she deems advisable. The trustee is further directed to distribute any remaining income and principal to the beneficiary when the beneficiary attains the age of 40.

(C) Create 12 trusts today (one for each child) and contribute $10,000 annually to each trust. Each trust provides that the trustee may distribute net income and principal to the beneficiary for maintenance, education, health, or support during the life of the beneficiary. The trustee is further directed to distribute any income and principal to the beneficiary when the beneficiary attains the age of 21 or to the beneficiary's estate if the beneficiary dies prior to attaining the age of 21.

(D) Create 12 trusts today (one for each child) and contribute $10,000 annually to each trust. Each trust provides that the trustee may distribute net income and principal to the beneficiary for maintenance, education, health, or support during the life of the beneficiary. The trustee is further directed to distribute any remaining income and principal to the beneficiary when the beneficiary attains the age of 40 or to the beneficiary's estate if the beneficiary dies prior to attaining the age of 21, provided, however, that the beneficiary may elect to receive any trust income and principal upon attaining the age of 21.

132. IQ has come to respect you and now simply asks what alternative courses of action you might advise if he sets up a "*Crummey* Trust" for the benefit of each of his children and, as they get older, one or more of them exercises their right to withdraw one of the annual contributions that IQ makes to the trust. He indicates that this would thwart his goal of keeping the trust funds from the children until a later date when presumably the children are more mature. Do you have any advice for IQ?

ANSWER:

133. A couple of years have passed since you last met with IQ to discuss his lifetime gifting plans. He meets with you again and indicates that he continues to prosper

immensely from his software business. Due to his continued prosperity he is looking for another avenue to reduce his net worth (and ultimately his gross estate upon his death) by gifting additional amounts to his children, nieces, and nephews. He says that he has heard about these so called "529" college savings plans, and he would like to start one for each of his children, nieces, and nephews. He asks whether he can avoid additional gift taxes through use of such savings plans. Which of the following options would result in the most gift tax savings for IQ?

(A) IQ stops contributing to any other trusts for the benefit of the 12 minors. Instead, he contributes $50,000 this year ($600,000 total) to 12 separate IRC § 529 qualified tuition programs for the benefit of his children, nieces, and nephews.

(B) IQ contributes $120,000 per year to a *Crummey* trust for the benefit of his children, nieces, and nephews (12 total). In addition, for the next five years, he contributes $10,000 per year ($120,000 total annually; $600,000 over the next 5 years) to 12 separate IRC § 529 qualified tuition programs for the benefit of each of his children, nieces, and nephews.

(C) IQ contributes $120,000 per year to a *Crummey* trust for the benefit of his children, nieces, and nephews (12 total). In addition, he contributes $50,000 this year ($600,000 total) to 12 separate IRC § 529 qualified tuition programs for the benefit of his children, nieces, and nephews.

(D) IQ contributes $120,000 per year to a *Crummey* trust for the benefit of his children, nieces, and nephews (12 total).

134. Assume that IQ never met with you as described in Question 133, above. Instead, 10 years has now past since meeting with IQ as described in Question 128, above, and his children, nieces, and nephews are of the age where they are beginning to go to college. You meet with IQ again and he is both happy and frustrated. IQ is happy because his success has continued and he is now worth "untold" millions. He also informs you that he has continued (and will continue) to execute the gifting plan that you and he came up with a decade or so ago, which utilizes his full annual exclusion from year to year. However, being the computer wiz that he is, he became frustrated when he determined that in order to continue reducing his gross estate he needs to have another avenue of gifting to his four children and eight nieces and nephews. IQ graduated from Harvard and has made substantial contributions to his alma mater over the years. Assume that annual tuition at Harvard is $34,000 and room/board is $16,000 per year. He expects that all of his children, nieces, and nephews will be attending Harvard and proposes the following plans. He would like you to tell him which of the following plans results in the least amount of gift taxes.

(A) IQ will set up a trust for the benefit of each of the 12 children (12 trusts total) and contribute $50,000 to each trust in each year that the beneficiary attends Harvard. The trustee is required to use trust funds to pay each child's room, board, and tuition directly to Harvard.

(B)   IQ will directly pay Harvard $34,000 per year on behalf of each of the 12 children (total of $408,000 per year) to cover each child's tuition at Harvard (while in attendance).

(C)   IQ will set up a trust for the benefit of each of the 12 children (12 trusts total) and contribute $34,000 per year to each trust in which the beneficiary attends Harvard. The trustee is required to use trust funds to pay each child's tuition directly to Harvard.

(D)   IQ will give each of the 12 children $34,000 per year to enable the child to pay his or her tuition at Harvard (while in attendance).

135.   Several years have since past and you receive a phone call from IQ. He indicates that Paul, one of his business partners, has become seriously ill with a kidney disease. Paul undergoes weekly treatments and has undergone one kidney transplant operation that failed. He is currently scheduled to receive another transplant in a month. Paul's medical bills related to his diagnosis, treatments, and operations now exceed $600,000 and, unfortunately, Paul has no medical insurance. IQ wrote a check to Paul for $50,000 earlier this year to help cover the medical costs. IQ wants to give more but is concerned about adverse transfer tax consequences. What advice, if any, do you have for him in relation to the gift he has already made and any future transfers that he may make in relation to Paul's illness and medical bills? Please explain.

ANSWER:

David, a U.S. citizen, and his wife Antonia, a citizen of Mexico, were married when they were in their early twenties. They have been blessed over the last two decades with 10 children and, during the same period of time, David has built up a large landscaping business that he operates through his wholly owned U.S. Corporation located and headquartered in Denver, Colorado. In January of 2006, David decided to give $100,000 to each of the 10 children. Both David and Antonia appropriately consented to split gifts in the manner prescribed by Treas. Reg. § 25.2513. Further, unless otherwise instructed, assume that David and Antonia remained married throughout the year.

136. Assume both David and Antonia reside in Juarez, Mexico. What amount of taxable gifts will David and Antonia have to report in 2006?

    (A) David must report $1,000,000 in gifts; Antonia must report no gifts.

    (B) David must report $500,000 in gifts; Antonia must report $500,000 in gifts.

    (C) David must report $100,000 in gifts; Antonia must report no gifts.

    (D) Neither David nor Antonia must report any taxable gifts.

137. Assume instead that both David and Antonia reside in the United States. What amount of taxable gifts will David and Antonia have to report in 2006?

    (A) David must report $1,000,000 in gifts; Antonia must report no gifts.

    (B) David must report $500,000 in gifts; Antonia must report $500,000 in gifts.

    (C) David must report $100,000 in gifts; Antonia must report no gifts.

    (D) Neither David nor Antonia must report any taxable gifts.

138. Assume that both David and Antonia reside in the United States and David's business did extremely well during 2006. Due to his success, David made another $100,000 gift to each of the 10 children in December of 2006, but neither David nor Antonia filed a second consent to split gifts in relation to the December gifts. What amount of taxable gifts will David and Antonia have to report in 2006?

    (A) David must report $2,000,000 in gifts; Antonia must report no gifts.

    (B) David must report $1,000,000 in gifts; Antonia must report $1,000,000 in gifts.

(C) David must report $1,500,000 in gifts; Antonia must report $500,000 in gifts.

(D) Neither David nor Antonia must report any taxable gifts.

139. Assume the same facts as in Question 138, above. Assume further that Antonia divorced David on November 1, 2006. What amount of taxable gifts will David and Antonia have to report in 2006?

(A) David must report $2,000,000 in gifts; Antonia must report no gifts.

(B) David must report $1,500,000 in gifts; Antonia must report $500,000 in gifts.

(C) David must report $1,000,000 in gifts; Antonia must report no gifts.

(D) Neither David nor Antonia must report any taxable gifts.

140. Assume the same facts as in Question 138, above. In addition, assume that neither David nor Antonia made a gift in any prior year. Further, each of them had an applicable gift tax applicable exclusion amount of $1,000,000 and an IRC § 2503(b) annual exclusion of $12,000 that had not yet been used in relation to any of their children. What amount of taxable gifts will David and Antonia have to report in 2006?

(A) David must report $1,000,000 in gifts; Antonia must report $1,000,000 in gifts.

(B) David must report $880,000 in gifts; Antonia must report $880,000 in gifts.

(C) David must report $760,000 in gifts; Antonia must report $760,000 in gifts.

(D) Neither David nor Antonia must report any taxable gifts.

141. Assume the same facts as in Question 138, above, except that David made an additional gift of $200,000 (instead of $100,000) to each of the 10 children in December of 2006. Assume that neither David nor Antonia have used any of their applicable gift tax exemption amount of $1,000,000 and that neither had used any of their IRC § 2503(b) annual exclusion of $12,000 in relation to any of their children in 2006.

(a) Calculate the amount of gift tax, if any, that David and Antonia have to pay in 2006 if all consents to split gifts were properly filed.

ANSWER:

(b) Calculate the amount of gift tax, if any, that David and Antonia have to pay in 2006 if instead no consents to split gifts were ever filed.

ANSWER:

Except where otherwise indicated, assume the donor and any donee is a U.S. citizen and resident. Additionally, unless otherwise indicated, assume that the donor has no remaining gift tax credit and that all annual exclusions have been exhausted.

General Valuation Concepts

142. Uncle Benny is a miser and always has been. He is a workaholic who has saved all his life, and he is finally beginning to relax a little. After hearing that it never rained there, he purchased himself a condominium on the beach in southern California. His nephew, Joseph, has just turned 16, and Joseph has asked his Uncle Benny what he plans to do with his old car. Uncle Benny owns a 1964 ½ Ford Mustang convertible that he drove only on the weekends. After having spent a fine afternoon watching sets roll in and the sails blow by, Uncle Benny has a rare moment and tells Joseph that he can have the Mustang so long as he takes good care of it. Uncle Benny bought the car in 1964 and paid only $2,500 for it. Assuming Uncle Benny just transferred title and turned the keys over to Joseph today, what is the value of the Mustang for gift tax purposes?

    (A) $2,500, the price that Uncle Benny paid for the Mustang.

    (B) $18,000, the amount that a reputable local auto dealer offered to pay Uncle Benny for the Mustang.

    (C) $25,000, the amount that several auto dealers in town were selling other similar 1964 ½ Ford Mustang convertibles.

    (D) $10,000, the price that Benny sincerely believes that it is worth and the price that a passerby offered him earlier in the day for the Mustang.

143. Assuming the same facts as in Question 142, above, what would be Joseph's basis in the Mustang upon receiving the gift?

ANSWER:

144. Assume the same facts as in Question 142, above, except that instead of giving the Mustang to Joseph outright, Uncle Benny had shown his true colors and asked Joseph to pay him $7,000 for the car. Assume also that no gift taxes were paid on the transfer. What, if any, value must be reported as a gift from Benny to Joseph? What is Joseph's basis in the car?

ANSWER:

145. Assume that instead of purchasing the Mustang new in 1964, Uncle Benny had purchased the Mustang (as a used auto) a couple of years ago for $30,000. Assume further that Uncle Benny had driven the Mustang 50,000 miles and had not taken very good care of it in general. Uncle Benny now gifts the Mustang to Joseph, and the actual fair market value of the Mustang for gift tax purposes is currently $25,000. Several months later, Joseph damages the Mustang in an accident and just wants to sell it for what its worth. For purposes of calculating gain or loss (if any), what would Joseph's basis in the Mustang be if he sold it for $3,000?

    (A) $30,000.

    (B) $25,000.

    (C) $22,000.

    (D) $3,000.

146. Would your answer to Question 145, above, change if instead of selling the Mustang for $3,000, Joseph had not wrecked it and, instead, sold it for $35,000?

ANSWER:

147. Some weeks after gifting the Mustang to Joseph, Benny was feeling bad for his niece Katie who received nothing when she turned 16. He decided to give Katie a gift of some stock that he held in his brokerage account. He called his broker the next day, Tuesday, July 10, and instructed him to transfer 2,000 shares of ABC Corporation stock to an account in Katie's name. ABC Corporation stock is regularly traded over-the-counter on the New York Stock Exchange. At the end of trading on Tuesday, July 10, the highest quoted selling price was $10.25 and the lowest recorded selling price was $8.75. What is the value of the gift to Katie that Benny must report on his annual gift tax return for the year?

    (A) $9.50.

    (B) $1,900.

    (C) $9,500.

    (D) $19,000.

148. Assume the same facts as in Question 147, above, except assume instead that ABC Corporation stock was not so regularly traded and, in fact, there were no sales of ABC Corporation stock on Tuesday, July 10, the date of the gift. Assume

further that sales of ABC stock nearest the date of the gift were Friday, July 13, and Monday, July 9. On Monday, July 9, the lowest recorded selling price was $11.50 and the highest recorded selling price was $14.75. On Friday, July 13, the lowest recorded selling price was $7.00 and the highest recorded selling price was $13.00. What was the value of the gift to Katie that Benny must report on his annual gift tax return for the year?

(A) $19,000.

(B) $10.78.

(C) $21,562.

(D) $11.56.

149. Several years pass and one day Benny is out kite surfing for too many hours. He experiences the worst sunburn in his life, and his dermatologist indicates that he is beginning to show signs of first-stage skin cancer. Benny decides he has had enough of his beach house and the sun. The stock of his wholly owned corporation, his securities portfolio, and his other real estate investments have been performing excellently, and he figures that his brother's family would enjoy the beach house more than he would these days. He transfers title to the beach house to his brother and heads for Steamboat Springs, Colorado, to enjoy some snow skiing and fly fishing in the Yampa valley. Assuming Uncle Benny just transferred title to the house to his brother Brett today, what gift tax value should Benny report on his annual gift tax return?

(A) $700,000, the price that Uncle Benny originally paid for the home.

(B) $1,200,000, the amount that a reputable local real estate appraiser opined it was worth.

(C) $900,000, the assessed value of the home as reflected on the county tax rolls for purposes of determining local annual property taxes.

(D) $1,000,000, the price that Benny sincerely believes that it is worth and the price that an interested party offered him earlier that morning for the home.

Actuarial Concepts

150. Benny has fished the rivers of the Mountain West into virtual depletion. He has grown tired of the dry air and high altitude and yearns again for sunnier ocean climes. So he gives his Steamboat home to his brother Brett to live in for the duration of his brother's life and he gives the remainder equally to Joseph and Katie upon Brett's death. However, he is tired of paying professional appraisers and actuaries for their valuation services. Being a financial guru himself, Benny knows that between the life and remainder interests, he is giving 100 percent of the home away. However, he is confused about exactly what he should refer to

in order to determine the appropriate actuarial factor for calculating the value of the gifts. He called the IRS helpline and they kindly provided a copy of IRS Publication 1457, Actuarial Tables, curiously named "Book Aleph" (all 880 pages worth). He asks you which table in all of those pages is the most appropriate one to use for this purpose.

(A) Table B, Term Certain Factors.

(B) Table S, Single Life Remainder Factors.

(C) Table R(2), Two Life Last-to-Die Factors.

(D) Table K, Adjustment Factors for Annuities.

151. Benny locates the appropriate table and now realizes that he needs to determine his brother's age and the appropriate interest rate in order to cross-reference the appropriate factor. He knows his brother Brett is 52 years old, but he is clueless about which interest rate he should use. He again seeks your assistance and asks what the appropriate annual rate is. Assume that the date of the gift was July 15, 2007. What is the appropriate annual rate?

(A) 5.96 percent.

(B) 6.20 percent.

(C) 4.95 percent.

(D) 4.97 percent.

152. Having determined the appropriate actuarial table, his brother's age, and the applicable interest rate, what is the value of Brett's life interest in Benny's Colorado home? Assume the gift was actually made on July 15, 2007, and that on that date, the home had a fair market value of $2,000,000.

(A) $2,000,000.

(B) $255,840.

(C) $511,680.

(D) $1,488,320.

153. What is the value for gift tax purposes of Joseph and Katie's remainder interests?

(A) $2,000,000.

(B) $255,840.

(C) $511,680.

(D) $1,488,320.

154. Assume the same facts as in Question 150, above, except that instead of a life interest, Benny gave his brother Brett a 10-year term interest in the home. Assume further that after Brett's 10-year term interest has expired, the remainder interest in the home will go solely to Katie. What is the value of Brett's 10-year term interest for gift tax purposes?

(A) $2,000,000.

(B) $1,432,567.

(C) $883,210.

(D) $1,116,790.

Valuation Premiums and Discounts

155. Uncle Benny has now settled down in Sarasota, Florida, and has finally found new balance in his life. He spends his mornings practicing tai chi chuan on his own quiet stretch of beach on the Gulf of Mexico. His wholly owned corporation, the UB Corporation, has been prospering, and he expects the company to grow substantially over the next 15 to 20 years. In an effort to transfer some wealth with an eye toward minimizing estate taxes down the road, he has decided to start gifting shares of his corporation to Katie. Katie has now completed her undergraduate degree and is employed by UB Corporation as a CPA. Benny has engaged a reputable business appraiser who has just delivered an opinion to Benny indicating that the UB Corporation as a whole is worth $10,000,000. UB Corporation has 1,000,000 shares ($10 per share) outstanding. Benny gives Katie 150,000 or 1.5 percent of his shares in UB without any restrictions on her ability to sell the shares. Which of the following valuation adjustments is most likely to apply in valuing the 150,000 shares given to Katie?

(A) Blockage discount.

(B) Minority interest discount.

(C) Control premium.

(D) Subrogation discount.

156. Assume the same facts as in Question 155, above, except that instead of giving the UB Corporation shares to Katie outright, Benny gives the shares to Katie subject to an enforceable shareholder's agreement. The shareholder's agreement provides, among other things, that Katie's ability to sell the shares to third parties is restricted under certain circumstances. Which of the following valuation adjustments will most likely apply for purposes of valuing the 150,000

shares?

(A) Blockage discount.

(B) Control premium.

(C) Lack of marketability.

(D) Capital gains discount.

157. Assume the same facts as in Question 155, above. Assume further that the 150,000 shares that Benny is gifting to Katie qualify for a 20 percent minority discount and a 20 percent marketability discount, what is the value of the 15 percent interest in UB Corporation for gift tax purposes?

   (A) $1,500,000

   (B) $960,000

   (C) $900,000

   (D) $600,000

158. Assume the same facts as in Question 157, above. Continue to assume that 150,000 shares would qualify for a 20 percent minority discount and a 20 percent marketability discount. Assume that a total of three years have since passed and Uncle Benny has continued to gift additional shares of UB Corporation to Katie in each of the two years following the original gift. Katie now owns 4,500,000 (45 percent) of the 10,000,000 shares outstanding. Uncle Benny continues to be impressed with Katie's performance, and she has been promoted to vice president of the company. Benny is ready to turn the helm over to Katie. Uncle Benny wants to gift another 1,500,000 shares to Katie this year, bringing her interest up to a majority share of 60 percent. Would the value of these last 1,500,000 shares be any different than your answer to Question 157, above, consideration given to the fact that this additional 1,500,000 shares will result in Katie owning a majority or controlling interest in UB Corporation?

ANSWER:

159. Uncle Benny from Topic 19 just had his sixtieth birthday and is in great health. Uncle Benny is by most standards very wealthy now. His assets now consist of several large apartment buildings in downtown San Francisco, a home in Martha's Vineyard, and another home in Napa Valley. He also owns stocks and bonds that he holds in various investment accounts that he manages himself. All told, his net worth is around $50,000,000. Katie and Joseph, Benny's niece and nephew, have since met their respective spouses, married, and had three children each. In order to pool his resources with Katie and Joseph, consolidate the ownership of his assets, and make them easier to manage, Benny proposes to form a business entity and contribute some or all of his assets to the new entity. He is interested in creating a liability shield with the entity to minimize his legal and income tax exposure. Benny would like to maintain control over the entity and the assets held by the entity. Importantly, Benny plans to increase his lifetime gifting in order to minimize estate taxes and as part of the plan he intends to transfer portions of his ownership interest in the company to various family members as soon as the entity is formed. Which one or more of the following entities would you recommend to accomplish his goals and why?

   (A) Limited liability company ("LLC").

   (B) Limited partnership ("LP").

   (C) General partnership ("GP").

   (D) Subchapter C Corporation.

160. Assume the same facts as in Question 159, above, and that Uncle Benny has decided to form a limited partnership (LP). You have assisted Benny in filing an appropriate certificate with the Secretary of State to form the LP. Benny is now ready to make the initial contributions to the newly formed LP. He intends to contribute half of his assets, and he would like to gift a 5 percent ownership interest in the entity to Katie and Joseph each (10 percent total) as soon as possible. In order to maintain management control over the LP, Benny will receive all of the general partner units upon his contribution. Benny asks which of the following scenarios best suits his plans and is most likely to survive an IRS challenge?

   (A) Benny contributes his assets to the LP today with the LP issuing 90 percent of the limited partner units to Uncle Benny. Katie and Joseph are each allocated a 5 percent capital interest in the limited partnership upon Benny's initial contribution of assets. Katie and Joseph contribute no assets.

(B) Benny contributes his assets to the LP today, with the LP issuing 90 percent of the limited partner units to Uncle Benny. Katie and Joseph each contribute sufficient additional assets such that they each receive a 5 percent limited partner interest. One year later Benny gifts Katie and Joseph 5 percent each, leaving Benny with 80 percent of the LP units.

(C) Benny contributes his assets to the LP today, with the LP issuing 100 percent of the limited partner units to Uncle Benny. Upon issuance of the limited partnership units to Uncle Benny, he gifts 5 percent of the units each to Katie and Joseph.

(D) Benny contributes his assets to the LP today, with the LP issuing 90 percent of the limited partner units to Uncle Benny. Katie and Joseph each contribute sufficient additional assets such that they each receive a 5 percent limited partner interest.

161. Assume the same facts as in Question 160, above, except instead of contributing only half of his assets, Uncle Benny contributes 100 percent of his assets to the LP. How, if at all would your answer to Question 160 change?

ANSWER:

162. Again assume the same facts as in Question 160 (e.g., Benny only contributed half of his assets) and that some years have now passed. It turns out that Uncle Benny has become an incessant gambler and heavy drinker in his old age. He has lost all of the money and assets he set aside that were not contributed to the LP. Aside from his interest in the LLC, he is worth nothing. Due to the lack of funds to live on, he has recently indicated that he would like a substantial distribution from the LP to pay his gambling debts. His health is also beginning to decline, and he has some recent medical bills. He needs money fast. What advice do you give in relation to satisfying his debts from the proposed distributions from the LP?

(A) Uncle Benny should sell his LP units to either Joseph or Katie (or both), convert them to cash, and pay his debts.

(B) As the general partner, Uncle Benny should cause the LP to make a distribution to himself in an amount that provides sufficient funds to pay his debts.

(C) As the general partner, Uncle Benny should cause the LP to pay his debts.

(D) Uncle Benny should declare bankruptcy.

163. Again assume the same facts as Question 160, above. Assume further that Benny contributes his assets to the LP today, with the LP issuing 100 percent of the GP and LP units to Benny. Upon issuance of the units to Uncle Benny, Katie and Joseph are each credited 5 percent of the value of the assets to their respective capital accounts. (total of 10 percent of the LP units transferred to Katie and Joseph). Finally, instead of owning real estate, assume that Benny's assets now consist mainly of stocks and bonds held in a large portfolio of securities held in brokerage accounts. All told, his net worth is around $50,000,000. Four years after formation of the partnership, Benny passes away. What arguments might the IRS make in asserting that the value of all of the assets held by the LP should be included in Benny's gross estate?

ANSWER:

Except where otherwise indicated, assume the donor and any donee is a U.S. citizen and resident. Additionally, unless otherwise indicated, assume that the donor has no remaining gift tax credit and that all annual exclusions have been exhausted.

164. Dad is growing old and is concerned about his health. Mom passed away some years ago and, until recently, Dad has been able to go the bank and take care of his financial matters. Lately, Dad has been forgetting to pay his bills and has spent a lot of time at the hospital receiving treatments for his advanced emphysema condition. Under which of the following additional sets of facts will Dad make a taxable gift to Barry?

   (A) Dad stuffed some money into his bed mattress and said to Barry "If I get too sick, please use this money in my mattress to pay off my bills. Whatever is left over when I die is yours." Barry takes some of the money to pay one of Dad's hospital bills.

   (B) Dad handed some money to his son Barry and said, "I am giving you this money to hold for me in case I get too sick to pay my bills. From now on, please use the money to pay my bills." Barry uses some of the money to pay buy a new competition ski boat for himself.

   (C) Dad added Barry as a co-signatory to his bank account. He indicated to Barry that "If I get too sick, please use the money in my account to pay off my bills. And, if you get into financial trouble you are welcome to withdraw some of the money for yourself." Barry withdrew some of the money and paid Dad's hospital bills.

   (D) Dad added Barry as a co-signatory to his bank account. He indicated to Barry that "If I get too sick, please use the money in my account to pay off my bills. And, if you get into financial trouble you are welcome to withdraw some of the money for yourself." Barry withdrew some of the money to pay off the debt balance on his sports car.

165. Chuck has one daughter named Rhonda. Rhonda is 23 years old, and she has just graduated from college and started a new career as an accountant. She is shopping for a home, and Chuck wants Rhonda to have a nice place to live. On January 1, they went house hunting. Rhonda finds a home she likes, but the $300,000 cost of the home it is too expensive for her. Chuck decides to pay $60,000 as down payment for the purchase of the home, and he has title conveyed

in his and Rhonda's names as joint tenants with rights of survivorship. The property remains subject to a $240,000 mortgage, and the monthly payments (including principal and interest) are $4,000. Chuck makes 12 full monthly payments on the home during the year. Assume local law provides that either party may sever his or her half joint interest. What are the annual gift tax consequences of the above described transaction?

(A) $150,000 gift from Chuck to Rhonda.

(B) $30,000 gift from Chuck to Rhonda.

(C) $54,000 gift from Chuck to Rhonda.

(D) No gift from Chuck to Rhonda.

166. Would your answer to Question 165, above, change if instead of creating a joint tenancy with rights of survivorship, Chuck had created a tenancy in common?

ANSWER:

167. Would your answer to Question 165, above, change if Rhonda was Chuck's wife instead of his daughter?

ANSWER:

§ 2053: Expenses

168. Decedent was a rancher during his life. While lying in his hospital bed several days before his death, he requested that he be buried in his favorite truck, a beat-up old 1957 Ford pickup. In accordance with his last wish, the executor had the decedent's body inserted into the pickup and had the truck encased in cement. The executor then had truck (with the decedent inside) buried in a cemetery. While the truck was essentially worthless, it cost the executor $1,000 to encase the truck in cement, transport it to the cemetery, and have it buried. The executor then reported the $1,000 expense as a funeral deduction on the federal estate tax return. Under applicable state law, an executor may not expend estate funds on a burial receptacle (e.g., the truck in this case) unless the burial receptacle is "properly sealed." For federal estate tax purposes:

(A) The cost of the burial of the truck is fully deductible if the probate court ruled that the decedent could be buried in the cement-encased truck even though it might not be "properly sealed."

(B) The cost of the burial of the truck is fully deductible regardless of local law regarding the manner in which the truck was sealed.

(C) The cost of the burial of the truck is fully deductible if the state's highest appellate court had ruled that the decedent could be buried in the cement-encased truck.

(D) Even though the state's highest appellate court determined that the decedent could be buried in a cement-encased truck, the cost of the burial of the truck is not deductible because a federal court determined that it was not in fact properly sealed as required under state law.

169. Assume the same facts as in Question 168, above, except that the decedent was an automobile buff who collected cars and, instead of an old Ford Truck, the decedent requested that he be buried in a brand-new Ferrari. In accordance with his last wishes, the executor of the decedent's estate purchased a new Ferrari for $267,887, had the Ferrari "properly sealed" under state law for an additional $100,000, and had the decedent buried in it. The executor then reported the full $367,887 as a funeral expense on the federal estate tax return. Would the full amount of the expense be deductible for federal estate tax purposes?

ANSWER:

170. After decedent's funeral ceremony and burial at a local cemetery, a reception followed. The reception was held at a nearby hotel. The purpose of the reception was to show gratitude and thank the decedent's family, teachers, healthcare professionals, and others who rendered care to the decedent in her final years of life. The decedent's estate deducted $4,000, the estimated cost of the reception, from gross estate.

   (A) All $4,000 of reception expenses incurred are deductible as a funeral expense.

   (B) None of the reception expenses incurred are deductible as funeral expenses because the expenses were not connected with the decedent's funeral.

   (C) The cost of the reception is deductible as a funeral expense only to the extent that the expenditures substantiated by proof of such expenses.

   (D) The reception expenses are deductible only to the extent the exact amount is determined.

171. Decedent collected artistic paintings. By the end of his life, he had collected a large number of Picasso paintings. After consulting with qualified experts, the executor of the decedent's estate concluded that if she sold all the paintings at one time, the paintings would have brought substantially less proceeds than if the paintings were sold one at a time over several years. Flooding the market with the Picasso paintings would likely cause the price of the paintings to decline and therefore reduce the overall value of all the paintings on the market. In an effort to avoid flooding the market and with the goal of collecting more proceeds on behalf of the estate and its beneficiaries, the executor retained a well-known art gallery, which was instructed to sell the paintings over several years. The art gallery charged a commission for each painting sold and over several years the commissions totaled $1,500,000. Assuming the commission expenses are properly allowable under local law, would the full amount of the expense be deductible for federal estate tax purposes?

ANSWER:

172. Decedent passed away on June 30, 2008. Which of the following expenditures is deductible under § 2053?

   (A) Income taxes due on all income received by the decedent or his estate during the 2008 calendar year.

   (B) 2008 annual state personal property tax due on the decedent's automobile for the calendar year, all payable on January 1, 2008.

   (C) Income taxes due on income received after the decedent's death, payable on April 15 of the year following the decedent's death.

(D) Annual state real property taxes due and payable by the decedent on the decedent's home for the first half of the year but as yet unpaid.

173. Decedent was in a car accident on a dark night in bad weather conditions on an undivided rural highway. The decedent died when his car hit another car in a head-on collision. The driver of the other vehicle also died as a result of injuries from the accident. A state lawsuit was instituted by the other driver's estate against the decedent's estate, in which the other driver's personal representative sought damages of $1,000,000. The decedent was uninsured. Under which of the following circumstances will the decedent's estate be allowed to take a deduction under § 2053 for the claims or expenses incurred?

(A) Decedent's estate offers to settle the claim for $100,000, but the other driver's estate declines and counter-offers to settle for $400,000.

(B) Decedent's estate contests the claim but offers to settle the case for $300,000, and the offer is declined.

(C) Decedent's estate contests the claim and proves that the decedent was not negligent but incurs legal fees estimated by the executor of the decedent's estate to be approximately $20,000.

(D) Judgment is entered upon the jury's award of damages to the other driver's estate in the amount of $500,000.

174. Testator, at age 56, passed away when his wife was 50 years old. He executed a will that made bequests of remainder interests in all of his assets to a charity. The testator bequeathed a life estate in all his assets to his wife, giving her the right during her life to all of the income earned from such assets. On the date of his death, the testator's assets were properly valued at $1,000,000 total. Consideration given to his wife's long life expectancy, the actuarial value of the wife's life estate was calculated to be $900,000 and the value of the charity's remainder interest to be $100,000. In the first year after the testator's death, the assets produced $40,000 of income. However, before receiving any income payments, the testator's wife unexpectedly died seven months after the testator died. For deduction purposes, which of the following answer choices best describes how values should be assigned to the wife's and charity's claims against the decedent's estate?

(A) The value of the wife's claim should be redetermined based upon a seven-month life expectancy consistent with the wife's actual life span.

(B) Consistent with the actuarial determination and regardless of the fact that the wife lived for only seven months after the testator died, the wife's claim should still be valued at $900,000 and the charity's remainder interest claim valued at $100,000.

(C) Since the wife did not live her full life expectancy and did not receive any income from her life estate, and because the charity is in effect receiving the full value of the estate, the wife's claim against the estate should have no value and the charity's claim should be valued at $1,000,000.

(D) Since the wife died only seven months after the testator, the estate should set the value of the wife's life interest to $20,000 (one-half of the first year's income from the assets) and the value of the remainder interest to the charity to $980,000.

175. Decedent owned a home that was valued at $500,000 as of the date of the decedent's death. As of the date of death, the home had a recourse mortgage of $300,000 associated with it. For deduction purposes, which of the following statements most accurately reflects the value under § 2053 of the mortgage claim in relation to the home for estate tax purposes?

   (A) Decedent may deduct $500,000, the value of the home.

   (B) No deduction is allowed in relation to the mortgage. Rather, the decedent must include in gross estate $200,000, the net equity that the decedent had in the home as of the date of death.

   (C) Decedent must include in gross estate $500,000, and only then is the decedent allowed to deduct $300,000 from gross estate.

   (D) Decedent may deduct $200,000 from gross estate.

176. How, if at all, would your answer to Question 175, above, change if the mortgage was nonrecourse as to the decedent (e.g., the decedent was not personally liable for repaying the loan)?

ANSWER:

177. Under which of the following scenarios will the decedent's estate be allowed to deduct $50,000 for estate tax purposes?

   (A) Prior to the decedent's death, the decedent made a promissory note to his daughter in which he promised to pay her $50,000. Decedent received nothing in return for the promissory note. The balance of the note at the decedent's death was still $50,000.

   (B) Prior to the decedent's death, the decedent made a promissory note to his daughter in which he promised to pay her $100,000. In return for the note, the daughter transferred to the decedent a small parcel of land with a fair market value of $50,000. The balance of the note was still $100,000 at the decedent's death.

(C) Prior to the decedent's death, the decedent made a promissory note to his fiancée in which he promised to pay her $50,000 in return for her promise to marry him. The balance of the note was still $50,000 at the decedent's death.

(D) Prior to the decedent's death, the decedent co-signed a promissory note that his daughter made to a third party for $100,000. In return for the note, the daughter received a small parcel of land of equal value. The balance of the note was $50,000 at the decedent's death and the daughter continued to make payments to the third party consistent with the terms of the note.

§ 2054: Losses

178. Decedent purchased a home in Seattle, Washington, on June 30, 1980, for $75,000. Decedent passed away on December 31, 2007, and, at the time of her death, the home was valued at $250,000. Under which of the following circumstances may the decedent's estate claim a loss of $250,000 under IRC § 2054?

(A) Decedent's home completely burned down on June 15, 2008. Decedent was uninsured.

(B) On June 14, 2008, consistent with the terms of the decedent's will, the executor of the decedent's estate distributed the home to the decedent's brother. The home completely burned down on June 15, 2008, before the decedent's brother could obtain insurance on the home.

(C) On December 30, 2007, the decedent's home completely burned down. Decedent passed away from smoke inhalation the next day. Decedent was uninsured.

(D) Decedent's home completely burned down on June 15, 2008. Decedent's estate received $250,000 in insurance proceeds several months later.

179. Decedent purchased a home in Seattle, Washington, on June 30, 1980, for $75,000. Decedent passed away on December 31, 2007, and at the time of her death, the home was valued at $250,000. At the time of the decedent's death, she also owned 1,000 shares of stock in a Saudi Arabian oil company. The stock had a value of $500,000 on the date of the decedent's death. Which of the following sets of circumstances will result in either a "casualty" or "theft" under IRC § 2054?

(A) On June 15, 2008, during the period in which the decedent's estate was being settled, the Boeing, Starbucks, and Microsoft corporations each moved their business operations from Seattle to the Cayman Islands. As a result of an acute reduction in demand for homes in the region, the value of the decedent's home held by the decedent's estate fell from $250,000 to $100,000.

(B) On June 15, 2008, during the period in which the decedent's estate was being settled, the executor of the decedant's estate sold the 1,000 shares of Saudi Arabian oil company stock and invested the money in her own business venture, which completely failed.

(C) In early December of 2007, the decedent's stock broker had transferred the shares of stock to his own personal account, sold the stock, and lost all the proceeds gambling at the high rollers table in Las Vegas.

(D) On June 15, 2008, during the period in which the decedent's estate was being settled, an Iraqi army overran all the oil fields in Saudi Arabia and set them on fire. These actions caused the value of the decedent's stock holdings in the Saudi Arabian company to decrease substantially.

180. Decedent purchased a home in Seattle, Washington, on June 30, 1980, for $75,000. Decedent passed away on December 31, 2007, and, at the time of her death, the home was valued at $250,000. On March, 1 2008, during the period in which the decedent's estate was being settled, the home was partially destroyed by a storm. After the storm and damage occurred, the house had a value of $150,000. What amount of loss deduction may the decedent's estate take?

   (A) $75,000

   (B) $100,000

   (C) $150,000

   (D) $250,000

181. How, if at all, would your answer to Question 180, above, change if the decedent's estate had received $75,000 in insurance proceeds?

ANSWER:

§ 2055: Charitable Transfers

182. Decedent, an avid philanthropist during life, left a validly executed will in place. Which of the following bequests will qualify for a charitable deduction?

   (A) A bequest to a Catholic priest to purchase a car for himself.

   (B) A bequest to the University of Wyoming for educational use.

   (C) A bequest to the Democratic National Committee to fund a political campaign.

   (D) A bequest to a trust set up to fund a group that lobbies for stricter environmental laws.

183. Decedent passed away, leaving a validly executed will in place. Decedent was wealthy and always had a philanthropic mind-set. Which of the following alternative circumstances will most likely result in a $35,000 charitable deduction for the decedent's estate? Assume that applicable state law does not prevent any of the following sets of circumstances from qualifying as a charitable contribution.

(A) Decedent's will provided that "I give to my executor One Hundred Thousand ($100,000) Dollars, not subject to any trust, but in the hope that he will dispose of it at his absolute discretion, but giving due weight to any memoranda I may leave to him made during my life." Decedent left a memorandum indicating that he desired that $35,000 go to the United Way Charity. Consistent with the memorandum, the executor gave $35,000 to the United Way Charity.

(B) Decedent's will provided that "I give $35,000 to Yale University, but this bequest will become effective only to the extent that my wife gives her express consent in writing and in the absence of such express consent the bequest shall be and is hereby revoked." Within six months after the decedent's death, the decedent's wife properly gave her express consent and the executors paid $35,000 to Yale University.

(C) Decedent's will provided that "I give $35,000 to Mr. Byron T. Watson, a homeless person residing at the Helpful Homeless Shelter, 321 Skid Road, Los Angeles, CA." Within six months after the decedent's death, the executor of the decedent's estate paid $35,000 to Mr. Byron T. Watson.

(D) Decedent's will provided that "I give to my executor One Hundred Thousand ($ 100,000) Dollars to dispose of in part or whole at his absolute discretion to one or more of the following charitable institutions: Yale University, United Way Charity, or the Roman Catholic Church. Among other distributions, the executor gave $35,000 to the United Way Charity.

184. Decedent passed away, survived by a son and a daughter and leaving a validly executed will in place. His estate was valued at $100,000,000 on the date of his death. While the decedent was wealthy and always had a philanthropic mind-set, he cared deeply for his two children and their financial well-being. The provisions of his will left a specific sum for his son. The rest of his assets were governed by the residuary clause, which provided that all the assets be held for the benefit of his daughter, income to her annually for life, remainder to the Red Cross (a qualified charitable organization) upon his daughter's death. Under which of the following alternative circumstances will the decedent's estate be allowed a charitable deduction in excess of the remainder interest to which the Red Cross is otherwise entitled?

(A) Daughter instructed the executor to transfer to the Red Cross any income in excess of $1,000,000 that was due annually from her interest in the residuary assets.

(B) Son executed a qualified disclaimer with respect to the specific bequest he received from his father.

(C) Daughter instructed the executor of the decedent's estate that her share of income from the residuary should be paid to the Red Cross for the foreseeable future.

(D) Daughter executed a qualified disclaimer with respect to all the decedent's property. In gratitude for her actions, the Red Cross appointed the decedent's daughter as president of the organization.

185. Decedent, Rose Cuadrez, passed away with a validly executed will. She was a wealthy person during life and, among other things, she owned an original Bustamante sculpture. She had purchased the sculpture for $1,000,000 in 1980 and on June 1, 2008, the date of her death, the sculpture was valued at $2,000,000 and was included in her estate. Under the provisions of her will, the sculpture was to be donated to National Museum of Art, a qualified charitable institution. On September 30, 2008, six months after the decedent's death but prior to distribution of the sculpture to the museum, the value of the Bustamante sculpture declined to $1,500,000. What amount of charitable deduction may the decedent's estate claim? Assume no IRC § 2032 election was made.

(A) $2,000,000

(B) $1,500,000

(C) $1,000,000

(D) No estate tax deduction allowed for contributions in kind.

186. How, if at all, would your answer to Question 185, above, change if the executor of the estate determined that on the aggregate it would be best if the estate made a § 2032 alternate valuation date election?

ANSWER:

187. Assume that the facts are the same as in question 185, above, except that instead of dying on June 1, 2008, Rose Cuadrez remained alive and gifted the sculpture to the National Museum of Art on that date? Assume Rose was at all times during her life a citizen and resident of the United States. What amount of gift tax deduction may Rose take?

(A) $2,000,000

(B) $1,500,000

(C) $1,000,000

(D) No gift tax deduction allowed for a gift in kind.

188. Would your answer to Question 187, above, change if Rose was neither a citizen nor a resident of the United States?

ANSWER:

189. During life the decedent owned a parcel of real property with a building on it, which he referred to as the "rental property." Decedent leased the property to various tenants from time to time, and tenants paid monthly rent. Upon the decedent's death in 1980, which of the following sets of circumstances will result in a charitable deduction for the decedent's estate?

(A) In 1975, the decedent contributed the rental property to an irrevocable trust during his life, under which he was to receive the income during his life and upon his death the rental property would be distributed to a qualified charity.

(B) Decedent's will provides that his brother will receive a life estate in the rental property and the remainder will pass to a charity.

(C) Decedent's will provides that the rental property will be distributed to his brother if his brother survives him but if his brother is not then living, the property will pass to a qualified charity.

(D) Decedent contributed the rental property to a trust that is to pay income to his sister for her life remainder to the decedent's brother. Decedent's brother's will provides that all of his property will go to a qualified charity.

§ 2056: Marital Deduction

The following facts apply to Questions 190 through 191. Decedent died in July of 2008. Decedent had substantial wealth and was survived by his wife and two children, a son and a daughter. Answer the following questions, which contain additional supplemental facts.

190. Under which of the following answer options will the decedent's estate be allowed a $1,000,000 IRC § 2056 marital deduction?

(A) Decedent, a citizen of the United Kingdom and resident of the United States, bequeathed $1,000,000 to his wife, a citizen of the United Sates and a resident of United Kingdom.

(B) Decedent, a citizen and resident of the United States, bequeathed $1,000,000 to his wife, a citizen and resident of France.

(C) Decedent, a citizen of the United States and resident of Mexico, bequeathed $1,000,000 to his wife, a citizen and resident of Mexico.

    (D)   Decedent, a citizen and resident of Japan, bequeathed $1,000,000 to his wife, a citizen and resident of the United States.

191.   Assume instead that the decedent had not passed away and that he was a citizen and resident of the United States and that he came to you for advice on how to bequeath $1,000,000 to his wife, a citizen and resident of France. May the contribution to the trust qualify for the marital deduction? What advice would you give to the decedent? Would your advice allow the $1,000,000 to escape U.S. taxation completely?

ANSWER:

The following facts apply to Questions 192 through 196. Decedent died in July of 2008. Decedent had substantial wealth and was survived by his wife and two children, a son and a daughter. Unless otherwise directed, assume that Decedent and his wife are both citizens and residents of the United States. Answer the following questions, which contain additional supplemental facts.

192.   Under which of the following answer options will the decedent's estate be DENIED an IRC § 2056 marital deduction?

    (A)   Decedent died without a will. Under applicable state intestate succession law, the decedent's wife received one-half of the assets in the decedent's net estate.

    (B)   Decedent died with a will that left all of his assets to his first spouse, with whom he continued to have an extramarital relationship. Decedent's surviving spouse had no right to dower or an elective share under state law.

    (C)   Decedent's surviving spouse received nothing under the decedent's will but after his death, the decedent's surviving spouse elected for and received a substantial amount of the decedent's estate under a state law right to an elective share.

    (D)   Prior to marrying his surviving spouse and during life, the decedent set up a trust in which he received all trust income during his life and the remainder to his girlfriend. He later married his girlfriend, who became his surviving spouse, and she received the trust assets upon the decedent's death.

193.   Decedent died with a valid will that gave everything to his daughter. Assume that his surviving spouse had no right to dower or an elective share. Under which of the following answer options may the decedent's estate take an IRC § 2056 marital deduction in relation to his ownership interest in the piece of real property described in each answer option?

(A) At his death, the decedent's gross estate consisted of an interest in only one piece of property, which he and his wife owned as tenants in common.

(B) At his death, the decedent's gross estate consisted of an interest in only one piece of property, which he and his wife owned as community property.

(C) At his death, the decedent's gross estate consisted of an interest in only one piece of property, which he and his wife owned as joint tenants with right of survivorship.

(D) At his death, the decedent's gross estate consisted of an interest in only one piece of property, which he owned as joint tenants with rights of survivorship with his daughter.

194. Decedent's validly executed will contained no specific or general bequests of assets to any individual other than his wife. The residuary of his estate was also to be distributed to his wife. Under which of the following answer options will the decedent's estate be allowed an IRC § 2056 marital deduction?

(A) At the date of the decedent's death, he owned an insurance policy with respect to which he had designated his spouse as the sole beneficiary. Upon his death, the insurance company paid the policy proceeds to the decedent's surviving spouse.

(B) At the date of the decedent's death, he possessed a general power of appointment over certain valuable property, which he failed to exercise during his life. In default of his exercise of the power, his estate received the property.

(C) At the date of the decedent's death, the decedent's spouse owned a life insurance policy payable on the decedent's life. Upon his death, the insurance company paid the policy proceeds to the decedent's surviving spouse.

(D) At the date of the decedent's death, he possessed a special power of appointment over certain valuable property. Decedent's will exercised the power in favor of his surviving spouse.

195. Assume the same facts as in Question 194, above, except that the decedent's daughter is the residuary taker. Assume further that the decedent's estate was valued at $8,000,000 on his death in July of 2008 and that $7,500,000 goes by specific bequest to the surviving spouse and only $500,000 goes to the daughter via the residuary. Realizing that the decedent's estate is entitled to a $2,000,000 estate tax exemption equivalent in 2008, of which $1,500,000 will be lost, may the surviving spouse waive the application of IRC § 2056 in an effort to reduce the surviving spouse's gross estate?

ANSWER:

196. Decedent died with a validly executed will in place that gave none of his assets to his wife. Under which of the following circumstances will the decedent's estate receive a $20,000 marital deduction under IRC § 2056(a)?

    (A) Surviving spouse was paid $20,000 as executor's fees under state law.

    (B) Surviving spouse was paid $20,000 in satisfaction of a properly executed promissory note that wife made to the decedent during his life.

    (C) Executor paid $20,000 to surviving spouse in exchange for a cemetery lot in which the executor had the decedent buried.

    (D) Executor paid $20,000 to surviving spouse in settlement of a bona fide claim by surviving spouse for an elective share.

The following facts apply to Questions 197 through 204. Decedent died on January 1, 2008. Decedent had substantial wealth and was survived by his wife and two children, an adopted son and a daughter. Decedent's daughter was his genetic child from a prior marriage. Decedent's son was not his genetic child. Rather, his son was his surviving wife's child from a previous marriage. Assume for purposes of the following questions that both the decedent and his wife were U.S. citizens and residents. Unless otherwise instructed, assume that the property interest received by the surviving spouse would otherwise appropriately "pass" to the surviving spouse and that that the property bequeathed to the surviving spouse was included in the decedent's estate. Answer the following questions, which contain additional supplemental facts.

197. Under which of the following scenarios will the interest received by the surviving spouse NOT qualify as a terminable interest under IRC § 2056(b)?

    (A) Decedent devised real property to his surviving spouse for life, with the remainder to his son.

    (B) Decedent bequeathed the residue of his estate in trust with income to his surviving spouse for a term of 10 years, remainder to his daughter.

    (C) Decedent devised a residence to his son for life with remainder to surviving spouse if she survives the decedent's daughter. But if the surviving spouse predeceases the daughter, the property passes to the decedent's daughter.

    (D) Decedent devised a promissory note that he had received from his son to his surviving spouse. The note was payable for a term of 10 years.

198. Under which of the following scenarios will the interest received by the surviving spouse QUALIFY as a terminable interest under IRC § 2056(b)?

    (A) Decedent devised real property to his daughter for her life, remainder to his wife.

    (B) Decedent devised all of his interest in a patent to his surviving spouse.

(C) Decedent devised to his wife any interest that the decedent had as beneficiary under a trust that paid all trust income and principal to the decedent when the decedent reached 50 years of age. Decedent died after having lived 45 years.

(D) Decedent provided in his will that if his wife survived him, she was to receive $1,000,000.

199. Under which of the following sets of circumstances will the decedent's estate be denied an IRC § 2056(a) deduction for the value of the interest in the property?

(A) During his lifetime, the decedent purchased an annuity contract providing for payments to the decedent for life, then to his wife if she survives him. Upon surviving spouse's death, any remaining value in the annuity goes to the decedent's daughter.

(B) Decedent bequeathed amounts to his surviving spouse with instructions to his executor to use the amounts bequested for the purchase of an annuity for the benefit of the decedent's surviving spouse.

(C) During his lifetime, the decedent purchased an annuity contract providing for payments to the decedent for life, then to his wife if she survives him. Upon surviving spouse's death, any remaining value in the annuity goes to the estate of the survivor.

(D) Decedent devised an annuity he purchased during life with a term of 20 years to his wife for her life, remainder to his heirs.

200. Under which of the following sets of circumstances will the decedent's estate be denied an IRC § 2056(a) deduction for the value of the interest in the property?

(A) Decedent devised property to his surviving spouse, provided, however, that if the decedent and his wife die in a common disaster, the property then goes to his son.

(B) Decedent devised property in trust all income annually to his wife for life, remainder to the decedent's son. Decedent's will also provided that surviving spouse have a general power of appointment over the trust property exercisable by her alone.

(C) Decedent devised property in trust all income annually to his wife for life, remainder to the decedent's son. Decedent's will also provided that no other person has the power to appoint any part of the property to any person other than the surviving spouse.

(D) Decedent devised property to his surviving spouse for life, remainder to his son, provided, however, that the son must pay surviving spouse fair market value for the remaining interest in the property.

201. Decedent devises property to a trust income to his wife for life, remainder to his son. Assume that the bequest meets the requirements of qualified terminable interest property and the executor is instructed to and does make an appropriate election under IRC § 2056(b)(7)(B)(i)(III). Which of the following is LEAST likely to accurately describe the decedent's purpose for wanting to make such a bequest?

(A) Because although he loves his spouse, he wants to prevent her from controlling or benefiting from any of his assets after he dies.

(B) Because if he gives all of his assets to his surviving spouse outright, she may favor her son in her estate plan leaving the decedent's daughter with nothing.

(C) Because he loves his wife and his daughter and he wants his wife to have some access to his assets but does not want his wife to waste the assets in such a fashion that his daughter receives nothing.

(D) Because he fears that his wife may remarry after his death and due to intestate succession or otherwise, her next husband may get all of his assets.

202. Would your answer to Question 201, above, change at all if instead the decedent and his wife had married each other without having previously been married or divorced? Thus, assume instead that they had married each other as high school sweethearts, had conceived their two children as their own, and were married when the decedent passed away.

ANSWER:

203. Which of the following sets of circumstances describes the most access to the property held in trust that may be allowed to a surviving spouse when a QTIP election is made?

(A) The surviving spouse may only receive a fixed amount of income annually from the property that is the subject of a QTIP election.

(B) The amount that a surviving spouse may receive from property that is the subject of a QTIP election is limited to all income annually for life.

(C) The amount that a surviving spouse may receive from property that is the subject of a QTIP election is limited to all income annually for life and amounts from trust property needed for her health, education, maintenance, or support.

(D) In addition to annual income, the decedent may allow the surviving spouse to have access to the property that is the subject of a QTIP election for her own use without limitation.

204. Is there a practical difference between a life estate with a power of appointment as described under IRC § 2056(b)(5) and an election with respect to a life estate for the surviving spouse as described under IRC § 2056(b)(7)?

(A) No, they accomplish the same thing.

(B) Yes, the difference is that in a § 2056(b)(7) interest the first spouse to die can prevent the surviving spouse from having access to the remainder.

(C) Yes, the difference is that in a § 2056(b)(7) interest the first spouse to die can give an income interest to the surviving spouse and identify one or more persons who will take the remainder.

(D) No, there is only a technical difference that requires the executor to make an election in order to qualify under § 2056(b)(7). No such election is required under § 2056(b)(5).

Basic Principles

Hank Stern has reached his fifty-seventh birthday, and he has done well for himself financially over the last half century in the oil industry. He decides this is the year to loosen up his historically tight purse strings for his family and close friends. So, he invites everyone to his house for a big banquet. After dinner Hank stands up, dings one tine of his fork on his crystal wine glass, and begins to announce various gifts to the lucky recipients.

205. Hank announces that the following recipients will each receive $50,000, and sends his favorite niece out into the room to deliver the checks. Which of the following recipients is a "skip person" for purposes of the generation-skipping transfer (GST) tax?

    A. Hank's mother, who is now 75 years old.

    B. Hank's son's daughter Miley, who is now 18.

    C. Hank's grandfather, who is now 95 years old.

    D. Hank's daughter, who is now 40 years old.

206. Would your answer to Question 205, above, change if Hank had legally adopted his son and daughter and Hank's son had legally adopted his 18-year-old daughter?

ANSWER:

207. Assume the same facts as in Question 205, above. Which of the following recipients is a "skip person" for purposes of the GST tax?

    A. Hank's brother, who is now 56 years old.

    B. Hank's cousin, who is now 57 years old.

    C. Hank's niece, who is now 30 years old.

    D. Hank's niece's daughter, who is now seven years old.

208. Hank has a stepbrother named Harley. Hank announces that he will give $1,000,000 to Harley's grandson. Is Harley's grandson a skip person?

ANSWER:

209. Assume the same facts as in Question 205, above. Which of the following recipients is a "skip person" for purposes of the GST tax?

   A. Hank's friend, who is now 43 years old.

   B. Hank's third cousin, who is now 55 years old.

   C. Hank's second cousin, who is now 17 years old.

   D. Hank's friend's daughter, who is now 25 years old.

210. How, if at all, would your answer to Question 209, above, change if answer option (D) provided that Hank's friend's daughter was 17 years old and Hank was now married to her?

ANSWER:

211. Which of the following transfers to a trust is a transfer to a "skip person" for purposes of the generation-skipping transfer (GST) tax?

   A. Hank's will establishes a testamentary trust with income payable to his granddaughter for a period of 10 years, remainder to Hank's wife.

   B. During life, Hank establishes an irrevocable trust under which income is to be paid to Hank's son for life. On the death of Hank's son, principal is to be paid to Hank's granddaughter.

   C. Hank's will establishes a testamentary trust under which the income is to be paid to Hank's wife for life and the remainder is to be paid to Hank's granddaughter.

   D. During life, Hank establishes an irrevocable trust under which income is to be paid to his son for life, and he also gives his son power to appoint who takes the remainder. Son appoints the remainder to Hank's granddaughter.

Direct Skips

Hank Stern is now 60 years old. He has continued to prosper from his energy investments, and he continues to enjoy his wealth. He has transferred substantial amounts in the past to his children. Several of his children have children of their own, and Hank has begun to enjoy his relationships with his various grandchildren. For purposes of the following problems, assume that Hank is in the 45 percent gift and GST tax rate brackets and that he has exhausted his gift tax annual exclusion and gift and estate tax exemption amounts.

212. One of Hank's children, Mona, has a daughter named Miley. Hank makes an inter vivos gift of 500,000 to Miley. What amount, if any, transfer tax (gift tax and GST tax) would be due on the transfer?

ANSWER:

213. Which of the following persons would have to pay tax, if any, due under the facts of Question 212, above?

    A. Hank.

    B. Miley.

    C. Mona.

    D. No tax is due.

214. How much of the gift described in Question 212, above, if any, is retained by Miley?

Explain:

ANSWER:

215. Is the GST tax due on a direct skip from Hank to Miley during Hank's life an "inclusive" or "exclusive" tax?

ANSWER:

216. Assume that instead of Hank making a gift directly to Miley, Hank decides he has had enough of this expensive GST tax system and he makes a gift of $725,000 to Mona. Mona then makes a gift of $500,000 to Miley. Assume that both Hank and Mona have used up their annual gift tax exclusion and their gift tax exemption equivalent. What amount, if any, of GST and/or gift tax would be due on the transfer by both Hank and Mona?

ANSWER:

217. How much, if any, of the gift described in Question 216, above, is retained by Miley?

ANSWER:

218. Comparing Question 212 to Question 216, above, which method of transferring $500,000 from Hank to Miley results in the smallest tax liability?

ANSWER:

219. Assume the facts are the same as in Question 212, above, except that instead of giving the $500,000 to Miley during life, Hank dies and bequeaths the $500,000 to Miley via his will and that $500,000 was all that was left in Hank's estate after applicable expenses but before any estate or gift tax is paid. Assume further that Mona is alive at Hank's death. How much GST tax is due?

ANSWER:

220. Who of the following would have to pay tax due, if any, under the facts of Question 219, above?

    A. Hank's estate.

    B. Miley.

    C. Mona.

    D. No tax is due.

221. Is the GST tax due on a direct skip from Hank to Miley via Hank's will after his death an "inclusive" or "exclusive" tax?

ANSWER:

Taxable Terminations

Again, assume Hank is 60 years old and that he has transferred substantial amounts in the past to his children. Several of his children have children of their own, and Hank has begun to enjoy his relationships with his various grandchildren. For purposes of the following problems, assume that Hank is in the 45 percent gift and GST rate brackets and that he has exhausted his gift tax annual exclusion and gift and estate tax exemption amounts.

222. Hank creates a trust during life with income payable to his daughter Mona for life with the remainder to Miley, his granddaughter. Under which of the following circumstances, if any, will a taxable termination occur?

    A. Mona dies.

    B. Mona receives a distribution from the trust and transfers the distribution to Miley.

    C. During Mona's lifetime, Miley receives a distribution from the trustee of the trust.

    D. A taxable termination does not occur under any of the above situations.

223. Hank creates a trust during life with income payable to his daughter Mona for life and, upon Mona's death, Mona has the power to appoint the remainder to anyone, including her own estate. Mona's will provides that all of her assets go to Miley upon Mona's death. Under which of the following circumstances, if any, will a taxable termination occur?

    A. Mona dies.

    B. During Mona's lifetime, Mona receives a distribution from the trust and transfers it to Miley.

    C. During Mona's lifetime, Miley receives a distribution from the trustee of the trust.

    D. A taxable termination does not occur under any of the above situations.

224. During life, Hank transfers $1,000,000 into a trust, income payable to his daughter Mona for her life. Upon Mona's death, the remainder is payable to Miley. Assume that the value of the assets in the trust upon Mona's death is $1,500,000. How much, if any, GST tax is due upon Mona's death?

ANSWER:

225. Assume the same facts as in Question 224, above. Which of the following would have to pay the GST tax, if any, due on the transfer?

    A. Trustee of the trust.

    B. Miley.

    C. Mona.

    D. No tax is due.

226. Is the GST tax due on a taxable termination an "inclusive" or "exclusive" tax?

ANSWER:

Taxable Distributions

Again, assume Hank has transferred substantial amounts in the past to his children. Several of his children have children of their own. For purposes of the following problems, assume that Hank is in the 45 percent gift and GST rate brackets and that he has exhausted his gift tax annual exclusion and gift and estate tax exemption amounts.

227. Hank has decided his favorite child is Mona and his favorite grandchild is Miley. Under which of the following sets of circumstances will a taxable distribution occur?

    A. Hank creates a trust for Miley for her life, with the remainder to be paid to Mona when Miley dies. Miley passes away, and the remainder of the trust is distributed to Mona.

    B. Hank creates a trust, income payable to Mona for life, remainder to be paid to Miley when Mona dies. Mona passes away, and the remainder of the trust is distributed to Miley.

    C. Hank creates a trust, income payable to Mona for life. When Miley turns 18, she is to receive half of the trust principal. The remaining principal is to be distributed to Miley upon Mona's death. While Mona remains alive, Miley turns 18 and receives distribution of one-half of the principal.

    D. None of the above qualifies as a taxable distribution.

228. During life, Hank transfers $1,000,000 into a trust, income payable to his daughter Mona for 15 years. At the end of the 15-year term, the remainder is payable to Miley. During the 15-year term, the trustee of the trust has discretion to distribute amounts to Miley. Trustee distributes $50,000 to Miley for her to take a trip around the world during the summer after graduating from college. How much, if any, GST tax is due upon the distribution?

ANSWER:

229. Who of the following would have to pay the GST tax, if any, due on the transfer described in Question 228, above?

    A. Trustee of the trust.

    B. Miley.

    C. Mona.

    D. No tax is due.

230. Is the GST tax due on a taxable distribution an "inclusive" or "exclusive" tax?

ANSWER:

Additional GST Considerations

231. Hank's daughter Mona passed away last week. Hank feels sorry for Mona's daughter, Miley (Hank's granddaughter), and would like to give Miley a substantial sum of money. Hank asks you whether the GST tax will apply. How do you advise?

ANSWER:

232. Hank's father Frank decides that Hank is not being generous enough to his great granddaughter Miley. Frank decides to transfer $1,000,000 to Miley. Given that Miley is assigned to the third generation below her great grandfather Frank, does the estate tax get applied twice? Assume that Hank has exhausted his gift tax annual exclusion and his gift and estate tax exemption amounts.

ANSWER:

PRACTICE EXAMINATION QUESTIONS

1. Adeline annually made annual exclusion gifts of cash to her 10 grandchildren. By the time Adeline died she had transferred $1 million in annual exclusion gifts to her grandchildren. In addition she had made a taxable gift of $1 million in 2007 to an irrevocable trust. Adeline died in 2008 with a taxable estate of $1.7 million. Calculate federal estate tax owed by Adeline.

ANSWER:

2. Bill sold his business to an unrelated employee in exchange for a promissory note. The promissory note had a self-canceling feature that provided for cancellation of any balance owed on the note by the employee as of Bill's death. Indicate whether Bill's gross estate will include the value of the promissory note at death under IRC § 2033, and the reason for your conclusion.

   (A) Bill's gross estate includes the value of the note as of the date of his death because up until that time Bill was entitled to payments on the note.

   (B) Bill's gross estate includes the value of the note as of the date of his death because courts ignore any self-canceling feature on a promissory note.

   (C) The value of the promissory note avoids inclusion in Bill's gross estate because Bill may no longer transfer the canceled note as of his death.

   (D) The value of the promissory note avoids inclusion in Bill's gross estate because, as of his death, Bill no longer owned the business.

3. Indicate whether your answer to the immediately preceding question would change if the promissory note did not have a self-canceling feature, and instead Bill forgave the note in his will.

ANSWER:

4. Cassandra made a transfer of cash to an unrelated corporate trustee for the benefit of her minor child. The irrevocable trust agreement directed trustee to apply income as necessary for the support of her minor child. At such time as child attains age 18, the trust directs trustee to pay all income to child at least annually. Cassandra dies at a time when child is 16 years old. Indicate whether Cassandra's gross estate will include any portion of the trust property pursuant to IRC § 2036.

(A) Pursuant to IRC § 2036, Cassandra's gross estate includes the entire value of trust property because the trust property could be used to satisfy Cassandra's legal support obligation to her minor child.

(B) Pursuant to IRC § 2036, Cassandra's gross estate includes only that portion of the trust property necessary to produce the income needed to satisfy the legal support obligation.

(C) Cassandra's gross estate does not include any portion of the trust property because income was payable only for the support of Cassandra's child and not for the support of Cassandra.

(D) Cassandra's gross estate does not include any portion of the trust property because the time period during which income was payable to Cassandra's child was not based on Cassandra's life.

5. Discuss whether your answer to the preceding Question 4 would change if instead Cassandra had died at a time when her child was 22 years old.

ANSWER:

6. Doug made a gift to a corporate trustee for the benefit of his niece, and on her death, for the benefit of his niece's children. Trustee is directed to use principal for the support of Doug's niece during her life. Any principal remaining in the trust on the death of his niece shall pass to his niece's children. Doug retains the power to remove and replace the trustee with any one of his choosing, including himself. Doug dies survived by his niece and her children. Indicate whether IRC § 2038 applies to include any trust property in Doug's gross estate, and why.

(A) IRC § 2038 includes all trust property in Doug's gross estate because trust property may be used to support his niece.

(B) IRC § 2038 includes all trust property in Doug's gross estate because of his ability to remove and replace the trustee with himself.

(C) IRC § 2038 includes only that portion of the trust property in Doug's gross estate attributable to the value of the niece's life interest in the trust.

(D) IRC § 2038 does not include any portion of the trust property in Doug's gross estate because an ascertainable standard applies to distributions.

7. Ellen, who is in good health, transfers all of her rental real property into a family limited partnership, the "FLP." She retains her home and sufficient assets to support herself for the remainder of her expected life. One month after formation of the FLP, Ellen transfers her 2 percent general partnership interest one-half to each of her two sons. Ellen also transfers equal shares of limited partnership interests to her two sons up to her maximum $1 million applicable gift tax exclusion

amount. She retains only a 20 percent limited partnership interest. The terms of the FLP agreement indicate that distribution will be made in proportion to the value of partnership interests held be each partner. When Ellen's sons take over management of the limited partnership, they continue to annually distribute 100 percent of the partnership income and distributions to Ellen during her life. Ellen dies survived by her two sons. Indicate the extent to which the limited partnership interests and the FLP assets will be included in Ellen's gross estate.

(A) Ellen's gross estate will include 20 percent of the value of the limited partnership interests retained by Ellen.

(B) Ellen's gross estate will include 20 percent of the value of the assets held by the FLP.

(C) Ellen's gross estate will include 100 percent of the value of all limited partnership interests held by both Ellen and her two sons.

(D) Ellen's gross estate will include 100 percent of the value of the assets held by the FLP.

8. Fred transfers cash to a trust and retains for a 10-year term a $5,000 annuity interest equal to 5 percent of the trust's value on formation. At the end of 10 years any remaining trust assets pass to his friend Gary. Fred dies 12 years after the original transfer to the trust and two years following termination of his annuity interest. Indicate the amount of trust assets, if any, included in Fred's gross estate.

(A) None of the trust assets are includible in Fred's gross estate because he held no interest in the trust as of his date of death.

(B) 5 percent of the trust assets are includible in Fred's gross estate because at the time of transfer he retained an annuity equal to 5 percent interest of the trust assets.

(C) The value of the assets necessary to produce the $5,000 annuity interest at the time of his death are includible in Fred's gross estate.

(D) 100 percent of the trust assets are included in Fred's gross estate because Fred died less than three years from termination of the annuity interest in trust.

9. Heidi and her sister Ingrid each paid 50 percent of the purchase price for a rental property. At the time of purchase, they took title as joint tenant with right of survivorship on the deed. Heidi dies in 2008 and is survived by Ingrid. Ingrid dies 30 days later. What portion of the rental property is included in Heidi's gross estate, and what portion is included in Ingrid's gross estate?

(A) Fifty percent of the rental property value is included in each of Heidi's and Ingrid's gross estates.

(B) Fifty percent of the rental property value is included in Heidi's gross estate and 100 percent of the rental property value is included in Ingrid's gross estate.

(C) Fifty percent of the rental property value is included in Heidi's gross estate and 75 percent of the rental property value is included in Ingrid's gross estate.

(D) Fifty percent of the rental property value is included in Heidi's gross estate and none of the rental property value is included in Ingrid's gross estate.

10. Assume the same facts as in Question 9 preceding. Also assume that both Heidi and Ingrid die with a taxable estate. After required adjustments under IRC § 2013, the portion of Heidi's estate tax attributable to inclusion of 50 percent of the rental property value in her gross estate equals $50,000. Also, after required adjustments under IRC § 2013, the portion of Ingrid's estate tax attributable to inclusion of the 50 percent rental property interest received from Heidi equals $30,000. Indicate the amount of tax on prior transfers credit, if any, allowable to Ingrid's estate.

   (A) None.

   (B) $30,000.

   (C) $50,000.

   (D) $60,000.

11. Kyle is trustee of a trust created by his mother. As trustee, Kyle may use trust property for his support in reasonable comfort. On his death, Kyle may appoint any remaining property held in trust among his surviving descendants. In the absence of an exercise of the power of appointment, the remaining trust property passes to named charities. Kyle dies without exercising the power of appointment to direct property at death to his surviving descendants. Will Kyle's gross estate include any of the trust property, and why or why not?

   (A) Yes, Kyle's gross estate will include trust property because Kyle may use property to satisfy a legal obligation of support to himself.

   (B) Yes, Kyle's gross estate will include trust property because Kyle holds a general power of appointment to distribute trust property at his death among his descendants.

   (C) No, Kyle's gross estate will not include trust property because Kyle did not exercise the power of appointment held at his death.

(D) No, Kyle's gross estate will not include trust property because Kyle's lifetime power was subject to an ascertainable standard, and at death Kyle could not direct property to his estate or his creditors.

12. In 2008, Lannie purchases $1,000,000 of life insurance on her own life, and names her child as beneficiary of the policy. The policy is a whole life policy. Later that year Lannie transfers ownership of the policy to her child at a time when the policy's cash surrender value is $15,000 and the policy's terminal interpolated reserve value is $12,000. Lannie does not retain any rights to the policy following its transfer. Lannie dies in 2009. Indicate whether any portion of the policy proceeds will be included in Lannie's gross estate, and why.

   (A) None of the policy proceeds will be included in Lannie's gross estate because the proceeds are not payable to her estate, and Lannie could not exercise any incidents of ownership over the policy proceeds at her death.

   (B) $3,000 of the proceeds are included in Lannie's gross estate because the value of taxable gifts made within three years of Lannie's death must be included in her gross estate.

   (C) $15,000 of the proceeds are included in Lannie's gross estate because the full value of gifts made within three years of Lannie's death must be included in her gross estate.

   (D) $500,000 of the proceeds are included in Lannie's gross estate because Lannie transferred the policy within three years of her death, and in absence of the transfer the proceeds would have been included in her gross estate.

13. Discuss whether Lannie could have avoided application of IRC § 2035 by structuring the purchase of the policy in a different manner.

ANSWER:

14. The following claims and expenses were incurred following Marvin's death. Indicate which of the following claims and expenses are deductible by Marvin's estate.

   (A) Expenses incurred for a reception held one month after Marvin's death to thank friends for their efforts in assisting Marvin during his bout with cancer.

   (B) The maximum statutorily allowed personal representative fee allowable under state law, even though Marvin's brother, who was personal representative of Marvin's estate, declined to take the full allowable fee.

(C) Claim timely filed against the probate estate by Marvin's child for payment of an outstanding $5,000 promissory note, payable by Marvin to child in exchange for child's promise to attend college.

(D) Past due property tax that had become due and payable by Marvin prior to his date of death on property owned by him and included in his gross estate.

15. Nancy owned patent rights that paid substantial royalties, but were scheduled to expire under federal law in 10 years. On Nancy's death, the patent rights passed to a trust for the benefit of her spouse Omar if he survived her by 30 days. Pursuant to the trust, Omar was to receive all trust income at least annually. On Omar's death, any remaining trust property was to pass as Omar appoints among Nancy's children, and in absence of appointment, to a named charity. Can Nancy's estate claim a marital deduction for the $1 million value of the insurance proceeds passing to the trust for the benefit of Omar, and, if so, how?

(A) Yes, Nancy's estate can claim a marital deduction for the value of property passing in trust for the benefit of Omar by electing to treat the trust as a qualified terminable interest property (QTIP) trust.

(B) Yes, Nancy's estate can claim a marital deduction for the value of property passing in trust for the benefit of Omar by electing to treat the trust as a general power of appointment trust.

(C) No, Nancy's estate cannot claim a marital deduction for the value of property passing in trust because Omar's interest is dependent on whether or not he survives Nancy for 30 days.

(D) No, Nancy's estate cannot claim a marital deduction for the value of property passing in trust because the property is a nondeductible terminable interest.

16. Indicate which of the following constitutes a taxable gift by Peter:

(A) Peter transfers $7 million of property to an irrevocable trust for his four nieces, and retains the right as trustee to make discretionary distributions of income and principal among his nieces as he sees fit.

(B) Peter transfers $7 million of property to an irrevocable trust for the benefit of his nephew. The nephew is to receive all income from the trust until he attains age 25, at which time remaining trust property is to be paid to the nephew, or if he is not then living, to his estate. Peter retains discretion to pay income to nephew prior to the date that the nephew attains age 25.

(C) Peter transfers $7 million of property to his revocable trust. The trust directs trustee to pay income and principal, in its discretion, for the benefit of Peter and his children.

(D) Peter names his child as beneficiary of a $7 million life insurance policy.

17. Will Quincy have made a completed gift if Quincy transfers property to an irrevocable trust, and retains the power as trustee to pay income and principal to his friend Opal for her support, with any remaining trust property passing to Opal's children upon her death? Explain your answer.

ANSWER:

18. On November 10, 2008, Penelope transfers $10,000 to Bank as trustee of an irrevocable trust. The trust terms grant her 25-year-old son Rylan the right to annually withdraw up to the lesser of the annual transfer to the trust or $10,000. Rylan's withdrawal right terminates 30 days following the date that Penelope makes the transfer to the trust. The trust terms require Bank to notify Rylan of his withdrawal right immediately upon receipt of any transfer to the trust. To the extent Rylan does not exercise his withdrawal right, the trust requires Bank to hold the property for the benefit of Rylan for his life, and upon his death to terminate the trust and distribute remaining trust property to Rylan's then-living descendants, per stirpes. During Rylan's life, Bank has discretion to pay income and principal for Rylan's support in reasonable comfort. Is the $10,000 transfer by Penelope to the trust a taxable gift, and why or why not?

(A) Yes. The $10,000 transfer to the trust is a taxable gift by Penelope because Rylan's withdrawal right exceeds the greater of $5,000 or 5 percent of the trust assets.

(B) Yes. The $10,000 transfer to the trust is a taxable gift because a substance-over-form analysis negates the availability of an annual exclusion where it is anticipated the power holder will never exercise the withdrawal right.

(C) Perhaps. The $10,000 transfer to the trust is a taxable gift by Penelope only if Rylan fails to exercise his withdrawal right because the property subject to the lapsed withdrawal right would then be a future and not a present interest in Rylan's hands.

(D) No. The $10,000 transfer to the trust is not a taxable gift because the withdrawal right, regardless of its exercise, provides Rylan a present interest in the transferred money sufficient to qualify for the gift tax annual exclusion.

19. Assume the same facts as in the preceding Question 18. If Rylan allows the withdrawal right to lapse, will Rylan make a taxable transfer, and, if so, in what amount?

(A) Yes. Rylan will be deemed to make a taxable transfer of $10,000.

(B) Yes. Rylan will be deemed to make a taxable transfer of $5,000.

(C) Yes. Rylan will be deemed to make a taxable transfer of $500.

(D) No. Rylan will not be deemed to make a taxable transfer.

20. Jerry, who is 37 years old, gives $20,000 to each of the below listed persons. Which of the following recipients is a "skip person" for purposes of the generation-skipping transfer (GST) tax?

(A) Jerry's mother, who is now 55 years old.

(B) Jerry's nephew's son Jason, who is now 27.

(C) Jerry's grandfather, who is now 75 years old.

(D) Jerry's daughter, who is now 20 years old.

21. Mary is 60 years old. Mary creates a trust during life with income payable to her daughter Nancy for life with the remainder to Judy, her granddaughter. Under which of the following circumstances, if any, will a taxable termination occur?

(A) Nancy receives a distribution from the trust and transfers the distribution to Judy.

(B) During Nancy's lifetime, Judy receives a distribution from the trustee of the trust.

(C) Nancy dies.

(D) A taxable termination does not occur under any of the above situations.

22. Frank seeks to set up a trust for the benefit of his daughter, Martine, and his grandson Einer. Under which of the following sets of circumstances will a taxable distribution occur?

(A) Frank creates a trust for Martine for her life with the remainder to be paid to Einer when Martine dies. Martine passes away and the remainder of the trust is distributed to Einer.

(B) Frank creates a trust income to Einer for life, remainder to be paid to Martine when Einer dies. Einer passes away and the remainder of the trust is distributed to Martine.

(C) Frank creates a trust income payable to Martine for life. When Einer turns 18, he is to receive half of the trust principal. The remaining principal is to be distributed to Einer upon Martine's death. While Martine remains alive, Einer turns 18 and receives distribution of one-half of the principal.

(D) None of the above qualifies as a taxable adistribution.

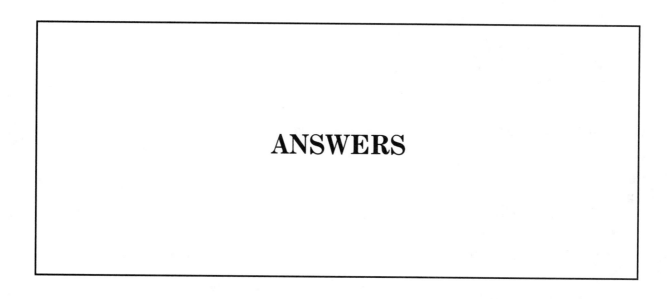

ANSWERS

Except where otherwise indicated, the answers provided assume the donor or decedent is a U.S. citizen or resident, and any beneficiary also is a U.S. citizen. Subject to applicable treaties, federal wealth transfer taxes apply to all property owned worldwide by a U.S. citizen. Separate wealth transfer tax rules apply to nonresident aliens.

1.   **Answer (D) is correct.** The federal estate tax focuses on the transfer of property owned by the decedent. The tax is imposed on the transfer of the "taxable estate" of a deceased U.S. citizen or resident. IRC § 2001(a). Taxable estate is the aggregate value of all property less applicable deductions passing from decedent to others. IRC § 2051. The federal estate tax applies only in the event the aggregate value of property transferred by decedent both during life and at death exceeds a specified amount, called the applicable exclusion amount. The maximum estate tax rate of 45 percent (beginning in 2007) applies to all property transferred (during life or at death) in excess of $2 million. It, thus, is a wealth transfer tax or a tax on the transfer of property or wealth of the decedent. Answer (D) is the best answer.

        Answers (B) and (C) are incorrect. An inheritance tax, also sometimes called a succession tax, focuses instead on the right to receive property by a beneficiary. The rate of inheritance tax depends on the relationship of a beneficiary to decedent, and the amount of property received by the beneficiary. Typically, inheritance tax exempts property received by a surviving spouse. It taxes at a lower rate that property received by children, and at a higher rate that property received by more remote relatives and friends. Inheritance, legacy, and succession taxes are often imposed by the various states and the District of Columbia. *See* IRC § 2011.

        Answer (A) is incorrect. Although politicians who favor repeal of the federal estate tax refer to it as a "death tax," the reference misleads. The calculation of federal estate tax derives from the value of property as of the decedent's death. It also applies to transfers occurring as a result of death. It is not, however, a tax on death.

2.   **Answer (C) is correct.** Currently the applicable exclusion amount for federal gift tax remains at $1 million, or, in other words the federal gift tax is calculated based on an applicable credit amount of $345,800. IRC §§ 2505(a)(1), 2001(c). The applicable exclusion amount for federal estate tax purposes tops out at $3.5 million in 2009, which translates to an applicable credit amount of $1,455,800. IRC §§ 2010, 2001(c). Thus, the applicable exclusion amounts and the applicable credit amounts for the federal estate and gift tax differ. Note that practitioners often refer to the

applicable exclusion amount as the "credit shelter amount" or the "exemption equivalent."

With the Tax Reform Act of 1976, P.L. 94-455, Congress unified certain aspects of the federal estate and gift taxes, including the rate structure and the unified credit amount (now referred to as the applicable credit amount). As a result, lifetime and deathtime transfers are cumulated and subject to the same rate schedule and applicable credit amount. Unification curtailed the ability to make lifetime transfers at lower gift tax rates formerly applicable to lifetime transfers. Prior to the 1976 Act, federal estate and gift taxes were calculated separately. They were subject to different rate schedules and different exemption amounts.

The Economic Growth and Tax Relief Reconciliation Act of 2001, P.L. 107-16, brought sweeping changes to the federal estate and gift tax. In anticipation of repeal of the estate tax beginning in 2010, the 2001 Act froze the federal gift tax applicable exclusion amount at $1 million of assets. The 2001 Act, however, incrementally increases the applicable estate tax exclusion amount (and as a result the corresponding credit amount) for the federal estate tax to a maximum of $3.5 million in 2009. The Act continued to apply the same rate schedule to both calculation of the federal estate tax and the gift tax. The highest applicable rate, however, eventually decreases in 2007 to 45 percent. While the tax rate continues to be marginal and increases from 41 percent to 45 percent (beginning in 2007) for gifts in excess of $1 million, the estate tax rate for transfers by U.S. citizens remains fixed at a flat 45 percent rate (beginning in 2007).

Summary of applicable exclusion amounts, applicable credit amounts, and tax rates:

The *gift tax* applicable exclusion amount equals $1 million, and the corresponding gift tax applicable credit amount equals $345,800, for years following 2001. IRC §§ 2505(a), 2001(c).

The *estate tax* applicable credit amount pursuant to IRC § 2010, increases based on the following applicable exclusion amounts:

Year of Death	Applicable Exclusion Amount	Applicable Credit Amount
2002 and 2003	$1,000,000	$345,800
2004 and 2005	$1,500,000	$555,800
2006, 2007 and 2008	$2,000,000	$780,800
2009	$3,500,000	$1,455,800

Note that the applicable credit amount is determined based on the applicable exclusion amount. IRC §§ 2010(c), 2505(a)(1). Essentially the applicable credit amount equals the tax imposed under IRC § 2001(c) on the applicable exclusion amount.

During the same period of time that the applicable exclusion amount increases from $1 million to $3.5 million, the top federal estate tax rate decreases from 50 percent to 45 percent. IRC § 2001(c)(2). This rate also applies to determination of the federal gift tax.

Calendar Year	Maximum Rate
2003	49%
2004	48%
2005	47%
2006	46%
2007, 2008, 2009	45%

Answers (A), (B), and (D) are incorrect. For the reasons stated above, none of these answers is entirely correct.

3. Questions 3 through 5 demonstrate the interaction between the federal estate and gift tax. The federal gift tax applies on an annual basis. Section 2502(a) provides the formula for calculation of federal gift tax. Based on 2002 taxable gifts of $1 million, Allan does not owe any gift tax for 2002 gifts. Note that taxable gifts do not include transfers subject to the gift tax annual exclusion amount of $10,000, as that amount is indexed for inflation. The 2002 federal gift tax is determined as follows:

Taxable gifts for current year:	$1,000,000	
Plus, Sum of taxable gifts for all preceding years:	0	
Equals, Sum of all taxable gifts:	$1,000,000	
Tentative tax on aggregate taxable gifts based on IRC § 2001(c) rates:		$345,800
Sum of taxable gifts for all preceding years:	$0	
Less, Tentative tax on sum of taxable gifts for all preceding years:		$0
Equals, Tentative gift tax for current year:		$345,800
Applicable Gift Tax Credit:	$345,800	
Less: Amount of credit used against prior year gifts:	0	
Equals: Allowable credit for current year:	$345,800	
Less, Allowable credit for current year:		$345,800
Equals, Gift tax owed for current year:		$0

Explanation of Calculation: IRC § 2502(a) first computes a tentative tax on all taxable gifts, including the current-year gifts and all prior-year gifts. It then computes a tentative tax only on all prior-year gifts. The difference between the two amounts is the tentative gift tax prior to application of the gift tax applicable credit. This calculation ensures the current year's gift bears tax at the highest applicable tax rate based on cumulative lifetime transfers. Note that tax rate schedule set forth under IRC § 2001(c) applies to determine the gift tax.

The gift tax calculation also keeps track of the amount of credit used in prior years, so that only the amount of unused credit available to offset current year's gift tax. IRC § 2505(a). The maximum gift tax credit allowable equals the amount of tax that would be imposed on the transfer of $1 million. IRC § 2001(c) indicates that amount is $345,800. By allowing a credit of $345,800, a donor may transfer up to $1 million of property free of federal gift tax. IRC § 2505(a) limits the credit allowable for a calendar year to $345,800 less the amount of that credit used against gift tax in all prior years. This prevents a double benefit from the applicable credit amount.

Note on Payment of Gift Tax: Taxpayers determine any gift tax owed on an annual basis. Gift tax returns must be filed by April 15 following the calendar year for which the gift tax is due. IRC § 6075(b)(1). An extension of time to file may be granted for up to six months. IRC § 6081. The donor bears liability for the tax. IRC § 2502(c). However, if the donor fails to pay the tax, the donee becomes liable for payment under a theory of transferee liability. IRC § 6324(b).

4. Determine the 2003 gift tax liability for Allan based on the same formula. Allan's gift tax liability for 2003 equals $210,000, as follows:

Taxable gifts for current year:	$500,000	
Plus, Sum of taxable gifts for all preceding years:	1,000,000	
Equals, Sum of all taxable gifts:	$1,500,000	
Tentative tax on aggregate taxable gifts based on '2001(c) rates:		$555,800
Sum of taxable gifts for all preceding years:	$1,000,000	
Less, Tentative tax on sum of taxable gifts for all preceding years:		$345,800
Equals, Tentative gift tax for current year:		$210,000
Applicable Gift Tax Credit:	$345,800	
Less, Amount of credit used against prior year gifts:	345,800	
Equals, Allowable credit for current year:	$0	
Less, Allowable credit for current year:		$0
Equals, Gift tax owed for current year:		$210,000

5. IRC § 2001(b) provides the formula for calculating federal estate tax. Based on that formula, Allan's estate owes $480,000.

The formula aggregates lifetime and deathtime transfers for the purpose applying the progressive rate schedule. Specifically, the calculation aggregates the "taxable estate" and "adjusted taxable gifts." IRC § 2001(b). Section 2051 defines "taxable estate" as the gross estate less the deductions allowable against the estate tax. "Adjusted taxable gifts," pursuant to IRC § 2001(b), means the taxable gifts made by decedent after December 31, 1976, other than those gifts includible in the gross estate.

Amount of taxable estate:	$2,000,000	
Plus, Amount of adjusted taxable gifts:	1,500,000	
Equals, Aggregate transfers:	$3,500,000	
Tentative tax on aggregate transfers (2006, 46% top rate):		$1,470,800
Amount of adjusted taxable gifts:	$1,500,000	
Less, aggregate tax on adjusted taxable gift which based on tax rates		
applicable in year of death:		$210,000
Equals, Tentative estate tax:		$1,260,800
Less, Estate tax applicable credit amount for year of death:		780,800
Equals, federal estate tax owed:		$480,000

Explanation of Calculation: IRC § 2001(b) again requires a determination of tentative tax. The tentative estate tax is based on the aggregate of lifetime and deathtime transfers. The tentative tax is based on aggregate transfers in order to be sure the appropriate progressive rates of tax apply. Subtracted from the tentative tax is the tax that would have been paid on adjusted taxable gifts had the rate schedule as of decedent's death applied at the time of the gifts. By subtracting the amount of gift tax paid, the calculation gives the estate credit for the gift tax previously paid at currently applicable rates. Finally, the applicable credit amount is subtracted. Note that the full applicable credit amount applies because just as the equation adds back in the total amount of adjusted taxable gifts, it must correspondingly add back in the full applicable credit amount. The cumulative nature of the calculation make it appear that the credit applies in full at death, but remember that the taxpayer in fact may only use the applicable credit amount once.

Note on Payment of Estate Tax: The estate tax return is due the date that is nine months after the date of decedent's death. IRC § 6075(a). Generally, payment is also due at that time. IRC §§ 6075, 6151. A personal representative may bear personal liability for unpaid tax if she distributes any assets of the estate before payment of the federal estate tax due. *See* Treas. Reg. § 20.2002-1. The beneficiaries of the estate may also bear liability for the tax up to the amount of property received. IRC § 6324(a)(2). An extension for filing the estate tax return may be granted for up to six months. IRC § 6081. An extension to pay the tax may be granted under limited circumstances. *See* IRC §§ 6161 (upon showing of reasonable cause), 6163 (tax attributable to remainder or reversionary interests), and 6166 (tax attributable to closely held businesses).

6. **Answer (B) is correct.** A donor may make present interest gifts of up to the annual gift tax exclusion amount per person per year. The gift tax annual exclusion equals $10,000, as that amount is indexed for inflation. IRC § 2503(c). In 2008, the indexed amount equaled $12,000. The direct transfer to child and grandchild qualifies as a present interest. Thus, Debra may transfer a maximum amount of $24,000 (i.e., 2 × $12,000) to child and grandchild, and not use any of Debra's applicable credit amount. Effective use of transfers subject to the gift tax annual exclusion can lead to considerable gift and estate tax savings in light of its "per person per year" feature.

    Answer (A) is incorrect. The amount of the gift tax annual exclusion is no longer $10,000.

    Answers (C) and (D) are incorrect. Excluded from taxable gifts are those amounts transferred directly to a qualified educational organization for tuition (and those amounts transferred to a qualified medical care provider for medical care). If Debra had chosen to transfer $12,000 directly to child and to grandchild, and an additional $50,000 to the accredited college for grandchild's tuition, then Answer (D) would have been correct. However, because Debra contemplated transfers directly to child and grandchild, as contrasted from direct payments to the college, Answer (D) is incorrect. For similar reasons, Answer (C) is incorrect.

7. **Answer (C) is the best answer.** When advising a client to make a gift, several factors impact the client's decision.

    Likelihood of Appreciation: Answer (C) is the best answer because the lake home is likely to appreciate more than the other assets and for that reason will likely result in the greatest estate tax savings. Once donor transfers an asset, assuming donor does not retain any further interest in the transferred asset, the asset will escape further wealth transfer taxation in donor's hands. Thus, all appreciation will transfer free of any federal estate tax. A primary estate planning goal is to pass as much value free of estate or gift tax as possible.

Answer (B) should be avoided for several reasons. The stock value is falling. As discussed more extensively below, adverse income tax consequences can arise in relation to devalued assets transferred either by gift or at death. IRC § 1014 requires that property passing from a decedent obtains a fair market value basis upon transfer. Where property has decreased in value and has a basis higher than its fair market value, the basis is reduced at death to fair market value. Thus, it generally makes more sense for the grantor to sell the loss property during life, thereby freeing up the losses to be offset against any income that the grantor may have in the year of sale. Transferring loss property at death will result in a permanent inability to use the losses experienced during life.

Future Needs of Donor: The donor should give only those assets the donor does not need to use in the future. The donor needs to continue to use both the apartment building and the residence in the future for donor's support. The lawyer will have an unhappy client if the donor transfers either of these assets without being counseled about the inability to further use the assets once transferred. For this reason, **avoid choosing Answers (A) or (D).**

Balancing Income and Wealth Transfer Tax Consequences: The lawyer should also consider the income tax consequences of the transaction. When donor makes a gift, the asset transferred takes the same basis in the hands of the donee that it had in the hands of the donor. IRC § 1015. Thus, any gain inherent in the asset at the time of the gift is preserved and taxable in the hands of the donor. Contrast the income tax consequences of a gift, with the income tax consequences of retaining the property until death. Property passing from a decedent at death generally obtains a "step up" or increase in basis equal to the fair market value of the asset at decedent's death. IRC § 1014. This "stepped-up" basis assumes the asset appreciated in the hands of the decedent. Any inherent income tax cost disappears if the asset is held until death. This benefit is particularly acute with respect to Answer (A) in this case. Assuming Barbara has been renting the apartment building for a prolonged period of time (see also Answer (D) indicating that Barbara intends to reside in her home for a long time), the apartment building is likely to be depreciated to a very low or zero basis upon Barbara's death. A transfer of the apartment building during life would result in the recipient taking a very low transfer basis, which would trigger very high capital gains upon sale by the recipient.

The income tax cost needs to be balanced against the potential estate tax savings. Often this comparison leads to the conclusion that a gift will result in greater tax savings once the 15 percent income tax cost of gifting the asset is balanced against the potential 45 percent estate tax cost of retaining the asset. This comparison is especially appropriate when the asset is appreciating rapidly and the asset is transferred without paying a gift tax because the value of the asset falls within the applicable exclusion amount or the gift tax annual exclusion.

8.   **Answer (B) is correct.** The Code allows an exemption against generation-skipping transfer ("GST") tax similar to that provided with respect to the federal estate and gift taxes. The amount of GST tax exemption has varied since enactment of the GST tax. Currently, the GST exemption equals the applicable exclusion amount for federal estate tax purposes. IRC § 2631(c). Thus, the maximum amount Charles may pass free of GST tax is the estate tax applicable exclusion amount at the time of the transfer. For that reason, **Answers (A), (C), and (D) are incorrect.** Note that because the transfer will be in trust for the benefit of all grandchildren, no portion of the gift will qualify for an exclusion from the gift tax, and as a result in order to avoid GST tax the amount of the gift may not exceed the GST exemption allocable to the gift. IRC §§ 2611(b), 2642(c).

Note on GST Tax Rate and Payment: The Code imposes GST tax at a flat rate equal to the maximum federal estate tax rate on generation-skipping transfers. IRC § 2641(a). The amount of GST tax depends on allocation of the GST exemption. The attorney must carefully consider when and how to allocate the GST exemption. The person liable for payment of GST tax depends on the type of GST transfer (i.e., taxable distribution, taxable termination, or direct skip). IRC § 2603(a). Generally, GST tax is paid out of the property that constitutes the generation-skipping transfer. IRC § 2603(b).

Note on History of GST Tax: The current version of the GST tax, enacted as part of the Tax Reform Act of 1986, Pub. L. No. 99-514, applies only to generation-skipping transfer occurring after certain dates. Generation-skipping transfers occurring before those dates are "grandfathered," and escape application of the GST tax. In very general terms, Section 1433 of the Tax Reform Act of 1986, applies the GST tax to all generation-skipping transfers made after October 22, 1986, and all lifetime transfers made after September 25, 1985. The Act, however, also employs different effective dates for transfers pursuant to certain trusts.

9.   The gift tax is said to work as a "backstop" to the estate tax because, absent a gift tax, taxpayers who are able to anticipate the moment of death could transfer all assets during life and completely avoid payment of estate tax. The GST tax also works as a "backstop" to the estate tax by ensuring that transfer of property in excess of the GST exemption will incur transfer tax at each generational level. It is designed to avoid the ability to skip a "generation" of tax. Absent the GST, tax assets could be held in trust for many generations and escape any type of transfer tax following taxation of the initial transfer to trust. These taxes also work as a "backstop" to the income tax by discouraging transfers to persons in lower income tax brackets.

10.   **Answer (C) is the best answer.** The Economic Growth and Tax Relief Reconciliation Act of 2001, Pub. L. No. 107-16, repeals the estate tax during the year 2010. In 2011, the Act resurrects the federal estate tax. Congress has

addressed several attempts to bring certainty to the estate tax. Current negotiations among the two political parties indicate the final compromise on the estate tax will reflect an applicable exclusion amount of $5 million, and a maximum estate tax rate of 35 percent. In the meantime, one of the best planning techniques for moderately wealthy clients may be to take all steps necessary to survive until 2010 (and then die in 2010? — just kidding. . . .) **Answers (A), (B), and (D) are all possible but uncertain.**

11. **Answer (B) is correct.** IRC § 2033 includes in decedent's gross estate "the value of all property to the extent of the interest therein of the decedent at the time of his death." Thus, for IRC § 2033 to apply, decedent must own an "interest in property." In *Helvering v. Safe Deposit & Trust Co.*, 316 U.S. 56 (1942), the United States Supreme Court distinguished powers of appointment from interests in property, and held that IRC § 2033 did not apply to include in the gross estate an unexercised general power of appointment. (At that time the counterpart to IRC § 2041 did not include in the gross estate, as it does now, unexercised general powers of appointment.) The practical importance of *Safe Deposit & Trust Co.* today is that the court narrowly construed IRC § 2033 to include only "interests in property." It left the issue of whether the gross estate includes a power of appointment to an analysis of IRC § 2041, discussed later.

Answers (A) and (D) are incorrect. IRC § 2033 includes in the gross estate property owned by decedent, and partial interests in property owned by decedent, such as tenant-in-common interests and community property interests. The term "interest" in property clarifies that not only does IRC § 2033 include an entire parcel of land owned by decedent, but also lesser interests in property. Note that the gross estate includes a decedent's one-half interest in community property regardless of how title is held as between the spouses. The surviving spouse's corresponding community interest in the property is vested in the surviving spouse. As such, the surviving spouse's share is not included in the gross estate of the deceased spouse under IRC § 2033. Whether property amounts to community property is a matter of state law.

Answer (C) also is incorrect. Treasury Regulation § 20.2033-1(a) specifically characterizes the estate tax as an excise tax, and indicates that provisions like those exempting interest earned on bonds from income taxation do not extend to the estate tax. Thus, tax-exempt bonds owned by decedent represent interests in property subject to estate taxation. Similarly, in *United States v. Wells Fargo Bank*, 485 U.S. 351 (1988), the Congressional declaration that certain "project notes" issued by municipalities for housing projects were exempt from "all taxation" by the United States did not protect the notes from estate taxation.

Note on Scope of Gross Estate: As noted above, IRC § 2033 includes "all property to the extent of the interest therein of the decedent at the time of his death." This section reaches property subject to probate or, in other words, that property owned by decedent prior to death and passing pursuant to decedent's will (or in the absence of a will, pursuant to the intestacy statutes). In addition, IRC § 2033 applies broadly enough to include certain nonprobate transfers; for example, bank accounts of decedent passing by beneficiary designation. To the extent property is not included in the gross estate under IRC § 2033, it may be included under IRC §§ 2034 through 2044. These other sections extend the reach of the estate tax to include most property over which decedent retained an interest in or power over even though ownership and title prior to death was not in the name of the decedent.

12. **Answer (C) is correct.** Essentially a two-part test applies to determine inclusion under IRC § 2033: (1) decedent must hold a beneficial interest in property immediately prior to death, *see Helvering v. Safe Deposit & Trust Co.*, 316 U.S. 56 (1942) (must own beneficial interest in property); *Connecticut Bank & Trust Co. v. United States*, 465 F.2d 760 (2d Cir. 1972) (interest must arise prior to death), and (2) decedent's interest in property must be capable of transfer at death, *see Rev. Rul. 75-145*, 1975-1 C.B. 298 (decedent "must . . . possess rights that he can transmit to a survivor.") Fred's vested remainder interest meets both parts of this test. Fred's remainder interest amounts to a beneficial interest in property. Keep in mind that the controlling factor in part (2) of the test is not dependent on whether the interest in property is vested, but on whether the beneficial interest is transmissible at death.

   Answers (A) and (B) are incorrect. These interests terminate as of death. Because Fred could not transmit the interests at death, IRC § 2033 does not apply, and these interests avoid inclusion in Fred's gross estate.

   Answer (D) is also incorrect. A trustee holds bare legal title, and must administer trust property for the benefit of those with beneficial interests in the trust. Treas. Reg. § 20.2033-1(a). Bare legal title does not confer a property interest capable of taxation. Thus, the gross estate does not include the property of which Fred was trustee under IRC § 2033.

13. **Answer (C) is correct.** Again, analysis under the two-part test outlined in the answer to the immediately preceding question applies. Damages from pain and suffering arise from injuries sustained and suffered during Geri's lifetime. The action for such damages accrues during decedent's life. The answer indicates that Geri's personal representative succeeds to Geri's interest, and brings the action on behalf of the estate. Thus, recovery would pass pursuant to Geri's will or, in the absence of a will, pursuant to state intestacy statutes. The two-part test is met. *See Connecticut Bank & Trust Co. v. United States*, 465 F.2d 760 (2d Cir. 1972).

   Answer (A) is incorrect. Answer (A) outlines the type of action specifically at issue in *Connecticut Bank & Trust Co. v. United States*, 465 F.2d 760 (2d Cir. 1972). The court distinguished the wrongful death recovery from an action based on pain and suffering on the basis that the right to the wrongful death recovery does not accrue until the moment after the time of death. The court reasoned that what the estate tax "taxes is not the interest to which the legatees and devisees succeeded on death, but the interest which ceased by reason of the death." The court concluded: "Where, as here, there was no property interest in the decedent which passed by virtue of his death, but rather one which arose after his death, such an interest is not property owned at death and not part of the gross estate under § 2033." The court also looked to *state law* for affirmation that, pursuant to

Connecticut statutes, a person has no right to bring an action for damages resulting from the person's death.

Note on Importance of State Law: Courts look to state law to determine the property rights accorded to decedent. Based on those property rights and interests, courts apply federal estate tax law to determine whether to subject those rights and interests to tax. The United States Supreme Court in *Commissioner v. Est. of Bosch*, 387 U.S. 456 (1967) addressed whether "a federal court or agency in a federal estate tax controversy is conclusively bound by a state trial court adjudication of property rights or characterization of property interests when the United States is not made a party to such proceeding." In Revenue Ruling 69-285, the Service interpreted the holding of *Bosch* to mean: "A state court decree is considered to be conclusive in the determination of the Federal tax liability of an estate only to the extent that it determines property rights, and if the issuing court is the highest court in the state." The Service's reading of *Bosch* limits the controlling effect of lower state court holdings. With regard to the determination of estate tax consequences, only "proper regard" need be given the holdings of lower state tribunals. Where, however, a final and conclusive state court order binding the parties and adjudicating property rights is entered prior to the event causing a tax to be owed, the order does control determination of property rights for purposes of determining estate tax. Rev. Rul. 73-142, 1973-1 C.B. 405.

Answers (B) and (D) are also incorrect. Similar reasoning applies to exclude recoveries outlined in Answers (B) and (D) from inclusion as part of the gross estate under § 2033. The Service in Rev. Rul. 54-19, 1954-1 C.B. 179, ruled that recovery under a statute similar to Answer (B), where the survivor may bring the wrongful death recovery, avoids inclusion in the gross estate on the basis that "nothing 'passed' from the decedent to the beneficiaries" because decedent held no right of action as of death. *See also*, Rev. Rul. 75-127, 1975-1 C.B. 297 (addresses both answers (A) and (B)). Similarly, in Rev. Rul. 82-5, 1982-1 C.B. 131, the Service ruled that a survivor's benefit paid under a no-fault insurance policy required by state law in order to maintain a driver's license was not includible in the gross estate of decedent who died from a car accident. In that ruling, the Service indicated: "Since the loss for which the benefits are designed to compensate for did not accrue until after the decedent died, the right of the decedent's spouse to the benefits also did not arise until after the decedent died."

14.   **Answer (C) is correct.** The facts of this question mirror those of *Estate of Barr v. Commissioner*, 40 T.C. 227 (1963). The Tax Court focused on the IRC § 2033 requirement that decedent own "interests in property . . . at the time of his death." The court held decedent did not own any interest in the death benefits until those benefits were approved by the company's board of directors. It found: "[D]ecedent had no more than a hope or expectancy that his surviving spouse might receive a . . . death benefit." The court distinguished those cases where employees held enforceable vested rights to death benefits as of death. *See also Bogley v. United States*, 514 F.2d 1027 (Cl. Ct. 1975) (The court contrasted corporate resolutions that permissively allowed payment of death benefits to an employee and avoided gross estate inclusion, and with those that contractually

obligated the corporation and were included in the gross estate, but did so under IRC § 2037, discussed in depth below.)

Answers (A) and (B) are incorrect. For the same reasons that Answer (C) is correct, Answers (A) and (B) are incorrect. Although property may pass pursuant to the probate estate, for IRC § 2033 to include the amount passing, the decedent must have acquired an interest in the property prior to death. If in fact decedent acquires an enforceable property interest in the death benefit prior to death, courts find the second prong of the two-part test for application of Section 2033 met on the basis that decedent consented to employment. The tax court has cited "[t]he decedent's previous and continued employment with the Company" as the source of the death benefits, and the transfer resulted therefrom. *Est. of Levine v. Comm'r*, 90 T.C. 723 (1988).

Answer (D) is also incorrect. As noted *Estate of Barr v. Commissioner*, 40 T.C. 227 (1963) on which this problem is based, courts can apply IRC § 2033 to include employee death benefits in decedent's gross estate. Section 2039 applies to include certain types of annuities. When companies pay death benefits in the form of an annuity, IRC § 2039, discussed in detail below, may apply.

15.   **Answer (A) is correct.** Using the now familiar analysis of determining whether decedent held a beneficial interest in property at death that was capable of transfer, the promissory note held by Kathy satisfied both requirements for IRC § 2033 inclusion. Treasury Regulation Section 20.2033-1(b) specifically includes "[n]otes or other claims held by decedent . . . even though they are canceled by the decedent's will."

Answers (B) and (D) are incorrect. Answer (B) sets forth an analysis appropriate to IRC §§ 2036 and 2038. It does not reflect the analysis used to determine inclusion under IRC § 2033. Answer (D) likewise sets forth an analysis irrelevant to application of IRC § 2033, as it does not matter whether Kathy received adequate consideration.

Answer (C) is incorrect. As the correct answer (A) indicates, forgiveness of the promissory note by will in fact resulted in a transfer of a property interest. If instead, however, the promissory note itself contained a self-canceling feature forgiving repayment on death of Kathy, as did the note in *Estate of Moss v. Commissioner*, 74 T.C. 1239 (1980), it would not result in IRC § 2033 inclusion of the promissory note in the gross estate. The court found that termination of the note prevents a transfer. The holding in *Moss* rested on the fact that the parties stipulated that full and adequate consideration was paid in the form of a premium for the self-canceling feature. The Service carefully scrutinizes self-canceling installment notes between family members. The estate must rebut a presumption that the self-canceling note is a gift. In *Costanza v. Commissioner*, 320 F.3d 595 (6th Cir. 2003), the taxpayer successfully rebutted the presumption by demonstrating the debtor actually made payments on the note, the note was secured by a mortgage, and the father was not expected to die prematurely (although in fact he did). These facts indicated a bona fide transaction. *Compare, Est. of Frane v. Comm'r*, 98 T.C. 341 (1992), *aff'd in part and rev'd in part*, 998

F.2d 567 (8th Cir. 1993).

Note Regarding Inclusion of Other Payments Due at Death: Treasury Regulation § 20.2033-1(b) specifically includes income earned but not yet collected at death. It gives as specific examples rent due and owing at death, accrued interest, and dividends declared and payable to the shareholder of record. If these items were not included in decedent's income prior to death, the items become income in respect of a decedent ("IRD"), and taxable to the decedent's estate (or to a beneficiary if passed through) pursuant to IRC § 691. Because items of IRD become subject to both income tax and estate tax following decedent's death, IRC § 691(c) provides an income tax deduction to the extent of estate taxes paid with respect to the IRD. Pursuant to IRC § 1014(c), items of IRD also do not receive a step up in basis at death, thus, preserving the reportable income.

16.   The vehicle should be included in the gross estate at its date of death value. IRC § 2031 provides: "The value of the gross estate . . . shall be determined by including . . . the value at the time of death of all property, real or personal, tangible or intangible, wherever situated." Treasury Regulation § 20.2031-1(b) sets "fair market value" as the standard, and defines it as "the price at which the property would change hands between a willing buyer and a willing seller, neither being under any compulsion to buy or to sell and both having reasonable knowledge of relevant facts." The value should reflect the price that a vehicle of approximately the same description, age, and condition could be purchased by the general public, as opposed to a dealer. Fair market value is a question of fact. Typically an appraisal is obtained. For vehicles, publications can provide retail value, for example, *Kelley Blue Book* value. Value is a key factor in determining the amount of the gross estate.

17.   **Answer (B) is correct.** Treasury Regulation § 20.2031-2(b)(1) requires that publicly traded stocks and bonds generally should be valued at the mean of the lowest and highest reported trading price for the date of death. In this example, $75 equals the mean ((50 + 100)/2). Thus, **Answers (A), (C), and (D) are incorrect.** The regulation also provides for a weighted average of mean selling prices in the event the stock or bond was not traded on the date of death.

Note on Valuation of Closely Held Business Interests: Often the stock of a closely held family business has never been sold prior to death. In that event, an appraisal should be obtained from a person qualified to appraise businesses. *See Furman v. Comm'r*, T.C. Memo. 1998-157. Treasury Regulation § 20.2031-3 and Revenue Ruling 59–60, 1959-1 C.B. 237, as it has been modified and amplified, outline factors that should be taken into account in valuing closely held businesses. Arriving at a value depends on the appraisal methodology used by the appraiser. The appraiser may use a method that (1) compares the closely held business to similarly situated businesses, (2) bases the value on a sum of the value of the assets held by the business, or (3) determines value based on the income and cash flows of a business. Typically an appraiser uses a weighted average of all three of these methods. In arriving at value, discounts or premiums may also apply. For example a discount for minority interest or a premium for a controlling interest may apply. Also, a lack of marketability discount may be appropriate to reflect the lack of an actual market for the shares. Business valuation is highly technical and typically requires special expertise.

18.   Certain life interests, remainders, and terms of years may be valued pursuant to actuarial tables. Treasury Regulation § 20.2031-7(d)(1) requires these interests to be valued pursuant to the IRC § 7520 regulations. Treasury has promulgated a series of factors for each applicable federal rate, and published them in tables. Treasury Regulation § 20.2031-7(2)(ii) specifies the manner for valuing an ordinary remainder interest. Applying that regulation, determine value by multiplying the present value of the trust property ($100,000) by the actuarial factor corresponding to the applicable federal rate for a life income beneficiary age 60, as indicated on Table S (.21196). Following this formula, the remainder interest is valued at $21,196.

Note on Use of Actuarial Tables, in General: Actuarial tables generally apply to value life interests, terms of years, remainders, and reversionary interests. The tables, however, may not be used if the interest being valued is subject to certain limitations or restrictions such as a power to withhold, withdraw, or accumulate income. Treas. Reg. § 20.7520-3(b)(2). If the person, who serves as the measuring life, is terminally ill, the tables also may not be used (with some minor exceptions). Treas. Reg. § 20.7520-3(b)(3). Depending on the circumstances, the Service may issue a special factor, if use of the standard factor is precluded.

Estate planners must focus on the estate planning ramifications to all individuals involved in the estate plan. The objective for the estate planner is to minimize federal wealth transfer tax for the donor, and to avoid any adverse consequences to the other parties involved. The following questions assist you in understanding which sections should be used to analyze the estate tax consequences of the various players typically involved in estate planning techniques. Keep in mind that at times more than one section may apply to include property in decedent's gross estate. The following answers, however, have been designed to result in one best answer for purposes of illustration.

19.   **Answer (B) is correct.** When the question presented focuses on the gross estate of the person who transferred the interest in property (the *donor*), of the choices provided, only IRC §§ 2033, 2036, and 2040 remain viable. In this fact pattern Laura transfers property to a trust and retains rights and interests to the trust property. IRC § 2036 specifically applies to determine whether retained rights to income or use and possession of the property previously transferred by donor cause the inclusion of the underlying trust property in the gross estate. Thus, (B) is the best answer.

     Answer (A) is incorrect. IRC § 2033 will not apply to include the value of the all trust property at death and held by the trustee. (Note that Laura transferred the property prior to death, and may have incurred a federal gift tax liability as a result of the transfer.) Because at death, Laura does not hold a beneficial interest in the entire interest in trust property previously transferred, IRC § 2033 does not apply to include the value of the trust property at death in the gross estate of Laura. Keep in mind, however, that depending on the type of interest retained, IRC § 2033 could apply to include in the gross estate the value of the retained interest in the property transferred, as opposed to the trust property itself. For example, if Laura had retained the remainder interest (or a reversion), IRC § 2033 might apply to include the value of the remainder/reversionary interest at death. Other sections that might apply to include the value of the trust property at Laura's death in Laura's gross estate include IRC §§ 2035, 2037, and 2038.

     Answer (C) is incorrect. IRC § 2040 applies only to joint tenancy with right-of-survivorship interests or tenancy-by-the-entirety interests. Any time either of those interests is at issue, apply IRC § 2040 to determine inclusion in the gross estate. Neither of these interests are involved in this question.

     Answer (D) is incorrect. IRC § 2041 applies to determine inclusion of powers of appointment held by persons other than the donor of the power. Treasury Regulation § 20.2041-1(b)(2) specifically indicates: "[T]he term 'power of appointment' does not include powers reserved by the decedent to himself within the concept of sections 2036 to 2038. . . . The power of the owner of a property interest already possessed by him to dispose of his interest, and nothing more, is not a power of appointment, and the interest is includible in his gross estate to the extent it would be includible under section 2033 or some other provision. . . ." Here the question focuses only on the donor.

20.   **Answer (D) is correct.** IRC § 2041 specifically addresses powers held by persons *other than* the donor of the power. The facts indicate Oscar holds the power to determine who receives trust principal on termination of the trust. This amounts to a power of appointment. Treasury Regulation § 20.2041-1(b) defines power of appointment for purposes of IRC § 2041 as including "all powers which are in substance and effect powers of appointment regardless of the nomenclature used in creating the power and regardless of local property law connotations." For example, the right of a beneficiary to withdraw trust property amounts to a power of appointment. *Id.* Also, for example, the power to alter, amend, or terminate the trust held by a beneficiary, who is not the donor, amounts to a power of appointment. A general power of appointment will be included in the gross estate, and a nongeneral power will not be included under IRC § 2041.

   Answer (A) is incorrect. A power of appointment does not amount to an interest in property. The United States Supreme Court in *Helvering v. Safe Deposit & Trust Co.*, 316 U.S. 56 (1942), specifically held that a general testamentary power of appointment over trust property did not amount to an interest in property. Thus, IRC § 2033 does not apply. In order for IRC § 2033 to apply, decedent must have held an interest in property at death.

   Answers (B) and (C) are also incorrect. IRC §§ 2036 and 2038 apply only to interests and powers retained by the donor with respect to property transferred by the donor. By their terms, these sections do not apply to powers held by a person other than the donor of the property.

21.   **Answer (D) is correct.** The trustee in this fact pattern is not the donor, and for purposes of analyzing whether the trustee's powers will cause inclusion in the gross estate of the trustee, the analysis is the same as in the immediately preceding question. The trustee Max will be taxed, if at all, under IRC § 2041, and only if the power is a general power of appointment.

   Answers (A), (B), and (C) are incorrect. Refer to the analysis in the immediately preceding question for an explanation as to why these answers are incorrect.

22.   **Answer (C) is correct.** The best answer is IRC § 2040 because it specifically addresses joint tenancy interests with right of survivorship. It applies to joint tenancy with right of survivorship as between spouses, and as between others.

   Answer (A) is incorrect. Treasury Regulation § 20.2040-1(b) clarifies that IRC § 2040, and not IRC § 2033, applies to determine gross estate inclusion of joint-tenancy-with-right-of-survivorship property. It provides: "Section 2040 specifically covers property held jointly by the decedent and any other person (or persons), property held by the decedent and spouse as tenants by the entirety, and a deposit of money, or a bond or other instrument, in the name of the decedent and any other person and payable to either or the survivor. The section applies to all classes of property, whether real or personal, and regardless of when the joint interests were created."

Answers (B) and (C) are incorrect. Answers (B) and (C) are incorrect. Neither IRC § 2034 nor § 2044 address the type of property interest in the question. IRC § 2034 applies to include dower and curtesy interests. This problem does not involve dower or curtesy interests. For that reason, (B) is not the best answer. Dower is an interest held by a widow in her deceased husband's property. Curtesy is an interest held by a widower in his deceased wife's property. These interests protected the surviving spouse from complete disinheritance. The vast majority of states have abolished such interests. Elective share rights, which must be elected by the survivor, have replaced the concepts of dower and curtesy. IRC § 2044 only includes in the gross estate of the surviving spouse that property for which an estate tax marital deduction pursuant to IRC § 2056(b)(7) was taken in the estate of the first spouse to die.

23.   **Answer (A) is the correct answer.** Lucy owns a property interest — a life insurance policy. As owner of the life insurance policy, Lucy may transfer ownership of the policy at death. Thus, because Lucy owns a property interest transferable at death, IRC § 2033 applies to include the value of the life insurance policy in Lucy's gross estate.

Answer (B) is incorrect. IRC § 2036 addresses interests in income and rights to possession or use of property transferred by a decedent during life. These facts indicate Lucy owned the life insurance policy at death, and had not previously transferred it. Thus, IRC § 2036 does not apply.

Answer (C) is incorrect. IRC § 2042 applies only to policies of insurance on decedent's life. It does not apply to ownership of insurance policy on the life of someone other than decedent.

Answer (D) is incorrect. IRC § 2044 applies to include in the gross estate of the surviving spouse only that property for which an estate tax marital deduction pursuant to IRC § 2056(b)(7) was taken in the estate of the first spouse to die.

24.   **Answer (A) is correct.** The focus of IRC § 2034 is on the property owned by decedent that is subject to a surviving spouse's dower or curtesy interest, or estate in lieu of dower or curtesy. IRC § 2034 specifically includes in the gross estate the "value of all property to the extent of any interest therein of the surviving spouse, existing at the time of the decedent's death as dower or curtesy, or by virtue of a statue creating an estate in lieu of dower or curtesy." Barry's right to an elective share should fall within IRC § 2034. Dower and curtesy provided the surviving widow or widower, respectively, an enforceable interest in the property of the deceased spouse. For example, dower often gave the widow a life estate in one-third of the husband's real property. Most states have statutorily abolished dower and curtesy in favor of a right of election. The inchoate interests of dower and curtesy in common law states generally have been replaced by the concept of an elective share. As indicated by the facts of this problem, an elective share also protects the surviving spouse, and ensures that the surviving spouse obtains a certain amount of a couple's assets.

Whether an elective share right is "in lieu of dower or curtesy" requires an examination of state law. The fact that the right of election differs in character from dower or curtesy interests does not matter. Treas. Reg. § 20.2034-1. *See also, Est. of Johnson v. Comm'r*, 718 F.2d 1303 (5th Cir. 1983) (Court found Texas homestead interest held by surviving spouse to be an interest in lieu of dower or curtesy). IRC § 2034, thus, ensures that property held by decedent and subject to the right of election does not escape taxation in decedent's estate.

Answers (B), (C), and (D) are incorrect. Answer (B) is incorrect as it is a red herring. **Answers (C) and (D) are incorrect.** Congress enacted IRC § 2034 to preclude any argument that the potential ability of the surviving spouse to control disposition of the property or to enforce a claim against the property caused the property to escape inclusion in decedent's gross estate. *See Est. of Johnson v. Comm'r*, 718 F.2d 1303 (5th Cir. 1983); Priv. Ltr. Rul. 8651001. Answer (C) is also incorrect because the answer focuses on Barry's rights, as opposed to Anna's interest in the property. Answer (D) is also incorrect for a similar reason.

25.   This question addresses the flip side of the issue addressed by IRC § 2034 in the previous question. Rather than focusing, as does IRC § 2034, on the property subject to the elective share, this question focuses on the elective share right itself.

The right to an elective share is not included in Barry's gross estate as surviving spouse. The Service in Revenue Ruling 74-492 directly addressed this issue. It ruled that IRC § 2033 does not apply to cause inclusion because the right of election terminates on Barry's death, and as a result Barry does not own a property interest transferable by Barry on death. It also ruled that IRC § 2041 does not serve to cause inclusion. It reasoned: "Under the Federal estate tax scheme enacted in the Internal Revenue Code for the implementation of widows' right of election laws, an unexercised right during the statutory period does not come within the taxable scope of section 2041 on the basis that the failure to assert the inchoate right constitutes a complete and effective disclaimer or renunciation of a power of appointment by operation of law." IRC § 2034 has no application because it is Barry's right of election that is at issue here, and not the property held by Anna, the predeceased spouse.

26.   This question focuses on the final issue that often arises regarding estate tax implications of marital rights. Specifically, the issue becomes whether a surviving spouse's claim against a decedent's estate pursuant to a premarital agreement in which the consideration was a waiver of marital rights may be deducted pursuant to IRC § 2053. The requirements of IRC § 2053 are addressed later. This question narrowly addresses whether a waiver of marital rights amounts to "full and adequate consideration" as set forth in IRC § 2043(b). IRC § 2053 generally allows as an estate tax deduction only those claims based on full and adequate consideration.

Answer (C) is correct. This fact pattern is based on *Estate of Herrmann v. Commissioner*, 85 F.3d 1032 (2d Cir. 1996). The Second Circuit in *Herrmann* relied upon IRC § 2043(b)(1), which states that "a relinquishment or promised relinquishment of dower or curtesy, or of a statutory estate created in lieu of dower or curtesy, or of other marital rights in the decedent's property or estate shall not be considered to any extent a consideration 'in money or money's worth.'" The court reviewed the purpose underlying this rule: "Section 2043(b)(1) was designed to prevent a husband and wife from entering into agreements that use consideration that is valid under state contract law to transform nondeductible marital rights — such as dower — into deductible contractual claims against the estate thereby depleting the taxable estate." *See also, Merrill v. Fahs*, 324 U.S. 308 (1945) (Based on similar facts, finds a release of marital rights does not amount to adequate consideration for gift tax purposes.)

Answers (A) and (B) are incorrect. For purposes of federal estate and gift tax, it is irrelevant whether a release of marital rights amounts to adequate consideration, and whether in fact the surviving spouse can enforce a claim under the premarital agreement.

Answer (D) is incorrect. There are exceptions to the rule that a release of marital rights does not amount to full and adequate consideration. IRC § 2043(b)(2) indicates that if the requirements of IRC § 2516(1) are met, a release of marital rights will amount to full and adequate consideration if the release is incident to divorce. Specifically, if spouses enter into a written agreement regarding marital and property rights "and divorce occurs within the 3-year period beginning on the date 1 year before such agreement is entered into . . . , any transfers of property or interests in property made pursuant to such agreement . . . shall be deemed to be transfers made for a full and adequate consideration in money or money's worth." The facts of this problem, however, do not fall within this exception because the agreement was not made incident to divorce.

Also note two other exceptions to the general rule. For gift tax purposes, the Supreme Court in *Harris v. Commissioner*, 340 U.S. 106 (1950), held that property transferred in the manner specified in a postnuptial agreement and pursuant to a judicial decree does not need to be supported by consideration for gift tax purposes. This includes agreements that become part of the judicial decree if the court possessed the ability to modify the agreement. Also, if transfers are made in consideration of a release of support rights of a former spouse or for a donor's child, the transfer is deemed made for adequate consideration. Rev. Rul. 68-379, 1968-2 C.B. 414. In order to avoid gift tax consequences, the value of the support rights surrendered must equal the value of the property transferred in exchange. Rev. Rul. 77-314, 1977-2 C.B. 349.

ADJUSTMENTS FOR CERTAIN GIFTS MADE WITHIN THREE YEARS OF DECEDENT'S DEATH, IRC § 2035

27. **Answer (B) is correct.** One of the purposes of IRC § 2035 is to act as a stop-gap to IRC §§ 2036 through 2038 and 2042. It prevents a donor from retaining an interest in transferred property for the better part of the donor's life and then relinquishing the power or interest within three years of death without tax consequence. To restate this rule in terms of requirements, IRC § 2035 triggers inclusion in the gross estate when —

   (1) Decedent transferred property during life and retained a power over or interest in the transferred property that could cause inclusion pursuant to IRC § 2036, 2037, 2038, or 2042,

   (2) Decedent then transfers the retained interest or relinquishes the retained power so that decedent no longer possesses the interest or power,

   (3) Decedent transfers the retained interest or relinquishes the retained power during the three-year period ending on the date of decedent's death, and

   (4) Decedent does not make the transfer subject to a bona fide sale for money or money's worth.

   The amount included in the gross estate is the amount of property that would have been included had decedent not transferred the retained interest or relinquished the power within three years of death.

   In this question, Alice retains a power to determine who is to receive the income from the trust for a period that does not end prior to Alice's death. Thus, if Alice died retaining this power, the trust assets would be included in Alice's gross estate under IRC §§ 2036 and 2038. Alice relinquishes this power when Alice irrevocably resigns as trustee. However, Alice does not relinquish the power during the three-year period ending on the date of her death. Thus, the requirement that the transfer of the retained interest or relinquishment of the power must occur during the three-year period ending on date of death is not met.

   The Service issued Private Letter Ruling 200432016, clarifying application of the three-year time period with respect to the inclusion of gift tax under IRC § 2035. The ruling begins counting on the date of death, and counts backward three years. Thus, in this example the three-year period begins on the date of death or March 6, 2008, includes that date, and counts backwards to March 7, 2005. The transfer in this question was made on March 6, 2005, and thus does not fall within the three-year rule.

Answers (A), (C), and (D) are incorrect for the reasons stated above. Alice initially retained an interest prohibited by IRC §§ 2036 and 2038, thus, **Answer (A) is incorrect**. Also, Alice relinquished the power more than three years prior to her death as required to trigger the statute, thus **Answers (C) and (D) are incorrect**.

28. In this case, IRC § 2035 would apply to include the trust property in Alice's gross estate because (1) Alice retained a power to determine who receives trust income that would have caused inclusion under IRC §§ 2036 and 2038, (2) Alice relinquished the power by irrevocably resigning as trustee, and (3) did so within the three-year period ending on her date of death. The value included in the gross estate is the value in the trust as of date of death. *See Estate of DeWitt v. Commissioner*, T.C. Memo. 1994-552.

29. **Answer (D) is correct.** Based on Barney's retained power to revoke the trust, IRC 2038 causes inclusion of the $900,000 trust property held at decedent's death. Although Barney directed $100,000 of the trust property to be transferred to Barney's child during the three-year period ending before death, IRC § 2035(e) steps in and deems the transfer to be made directly by decedent and not from the revocable trust (that was subject to income taxation in Barney's hands pursuant to IRC § 676). Because, pursuant to IRC § 2035(e), the transfer is deemed to be made directly by decedent, IRC § 2035(a) becomes inapplicable.

   Answers (A), (B), and (C) are incorrect for the reasons stated above.

30. **Answer (C) is correct.** IRC § 2035 also serves as a stop-gap to IRC § 2042, which includes certain life insurance policies on decedent's life. With respect to life insurance policies, the gross estate includes the value of the insurance proceeds paid at death if:

   (1) Decedent transferred an insurance policy owned by him on his life, or relinquished any incidents of ownership with respect to a policy on his life, and

   (2) Had decedent not made the transfer or relinquished incidents of ownership, the policy would have been included in decedent's gross estate, and

   (3) The transfer or relinquishment occurred during the three-year period ending on the date of decedent's death, and

   (4) Decedent did not transfer the policy subject to a bona fide sale for adequate consideration in money or money's worth.

   In this question Collin owned a life insurance policy that would have been included in Collin's gross estate under IRC § 2042 had he not transferred it during the three-year period ending on the date of his death.

   Answers (A), (B), and (D) are incorrect for the reasons stated above.

   The amount included in Collin's gross estate is the amount that would have been included had Collin not transferred the policy or relinquished incidents of ownership within three years of death. This amount would have been the $1 million in policy proceeds, and for that reason answers (A), (B), and (D) are incorrect.

Note that had Collin instead transferred $20,000 cash to his child, and had the child purchase the policy on Collin's life, neither IRC § 2035 nor § 2042 would have applied to cause inclusion in Collin's gross estate because Collin would never have owned the policy in the first place.

31.   **Answer (A) is correct.** Dorthea did not retain any power over or interest in the property transferred to Dorthea's children. Thus, IRC § 2035(a) does not apply to include any portion of the property in Dorthea's gross estate.

IRC § 2035(b) applies to increase the gross estate by the amount of any gift tax paid by decedent on transfers made by decedent or decedent's spouse during the three-year period ending on decedent's date of death. Because the amounts transferred by Dorthea fell within the annual gift tax exclusion amount, no gift tax was payable with respect to the transfers, and for that reason IRC § 2035(b) also would not apply.

Answers (B), (C), and (D) are incorrect for the reasons stated above.

32.   **Answer (A) is correct.** As discussed above, IRC § 2035(a) generally does not apply to include outright transfers. This is because an outright transfer of property would never have caused the transferred property to be included in decedent's gross estate under IRC §§ 2036 through 2038. Thus, the amount of the cash gift is not included in Elise's gross estate. Because the cash gift was made more than three years prior to decedent's date of death, IRC § 2035(b) does not apply to gross up the estate by the amount of gift tax paid. Only if the gift was made within the three-year period ending on the date of decedent's death does IRC § 2035(b) kick in to include in the gross estate the amount of any gift tax paid by decedent on a gift made by decedent or decedent's spouse.

Answers (B), (C), and (D) are incorrect for the reasons stated above.

Note, however, that if the facts were changed so that the gift had been made within the three-year period ending on the date of Elise's death, the $50,000 gift tax paid by Elise would be included in Elise's gross estate pursuant to IRC § 2035(b). This result prevents the taxpayer from taking advantage of the tax-exclusive nature of the gift tax by making what is essentially a death-bed transfer. Gift tax is not paid on the amount of property used to pay gift tax owed, but estate tax is paid with respect to property used to pay the estate tax. Thus, the gift tax is tax-exclusive, and the estate tax is tax-inclusive. Absent application of IRC § 2035(b), a donor/decedent would pay less tax by transferring all property during life and paying a gift tax. IRC § 2035(b) precludes this result for transfers made during the three-year period ending on the date of decedent's death by grossing up the estate by the amount of gift tax paid during that time.

33.   In an effort to prevent "death-bed" manipulation of assets for purposes of qualifying for special-use valuation under IRC § 2032A, in determining the applicability of that section, IRC § 2035(c) includes in the gross estate all taxable transfers by decedent (other than transfers of an insurance policy and other than

those for which a gift tax marital deduction is allowed) made within the three-year period ending on decedent's date of death. Thus, Fred's transfer would be deemed to be included in the gross estate for the sole purpose of determining whether the estate may make the special-use valuation election.

A similar rule applies for determining applicability of the special election for redemption of stock to pay death taxes, the special election to defer payment of estate tax related to certain closely held businesses, and the application of certain liens for taxes.

Congress enacted IRC § 2036, and its sister sections IRC §§ 2035, 2037, and 2038, to protect the integrity of the estate tax. Absent these sections, a taxpayer could transfer title to property, and yet retain all the important attributes of ownership without triggering estate tax. IRC §§ 2036 through 2037 step in and require inclusion in decedent's gross estate of any property transferred where decedent retains an important attribute of property ownership as specified in those sections. IRC § 2035 provides a safety net where within three years of decedent's death, decedent relinquishes a prohibited retained right or interest in property under those sections. IRC § 2035 thus protects against death-bed manipulation of IRC §§ 2036 through 2038.

34.   **Answer (C) is correct.** In order for IRC § 2036 to include property in the gross estate, the following requirements must be met: (1) decedent must have transferred an interest in property, (2) decedent must have retained either the right to income, possession, or enjoyment of the property, or the right to designate who receives the income, possession, or enjoyment of the property, and (3) the property interest must be retained for decedent's life, a period not ascertainable without reference to decedent's death, or a period that does not in fact end before decedent's death. IRC § 2036, thus, focuses on the important property rights or income and possession and enjoyment of property.

While Alyssa meets two of the IRC § 2036 requirements (she transferred an interest in her home and retained the right to possess and enjoy her home), she did not retain the interest for the requisite period of time. IRC § 2036 applies only when decedent retained the right to possess the property for "life or for any period not ascertainable without reference to his death or for any period which does not in fact end before his death." If decedent survives the period during which decedent retained the right to possess the property, as did Alyssa, none of the transferred property is included in the gross estate.

This leads to an important planning strategy — the qualified personal residence trust, where taxpayer may transfer a residence pursuant to the requirements of IRC § 2702 at a reduced federal gift tax cost, and avoid estate tax if taxpayer survives the term of the trust.

Answers (A) and (B) are incorrect. IRC § 2036 does not focus on when the donor's retention of the interest begins, but only whether the interest was retained for life, for any period not ascertainable without reference to decedent's death, or for a period that does not end before decedent's death.

Answer (D) is also incorrect. The requisite time period for application of IRC § 2038 differs from that of IRC § 2036. IRC § 2038 focuses on whether decedent retained a power to alter, amend, or revoke an interest "where the enjoyment thereof was *subject at the date of his death* to any change through the exercise of a power. . . ." (emphasis added). The answer in (D) incorrectly focuses on a time period not ascertainable without reference to decedent's death.

35.   The answer to the prior Question 34 would change. Alyssa's gross estate would include the value of the trust property at her death because under these facts she has retained the right to possess the home transferred to trust for a period that does not in fact end before her death.

36.   **Answer (A) is correct.** Barry's gross estate will include the trust property pursuant to IRC § 2036 because Barry retained the right to income from the trust property that Barry transferred to the trust, and Barry retained the interest for life. As noted above, retention of a "life interest" falls within the requisite time period for application of IRC § 2036. Barry thus met all three requirements of IRC § 2036 for inclusion in the gross estate. (Note that the answer would not change if instead what Barry retained was a life estate interest with remainder to Barry's child.)

Answers (B) and (C) are incorrect. IRC § 2038 applies in those instances where decedent transfers an interest, and holds at death the "power" to "alter, amend, revoke or terminate" the interest. In this fact pattern, Barry does not retain any "power" over the property transferred, and for that reason IRC § 2038 would not apply. IRC § 2037 applies under certain circumstances where decedent retains a reversionary interest in property transferred. Barry has not retained such an interest. Also, Treasury Regulation § 20.2039-1(e) indicates that in this situation IRC § 2036 is the appropriate section for inclusion in the gross estate, and not IRC § 2039.

Answer (D) is incorrect. Answer (D) is incorrect for the reason that IRC § 2036 does include the property in Barry's gross estate. The focus of these sections is on the retained rights and powers of Barry with respect to transferred property, and not the rights of others.

37.   Barry's gross estate will also include the trust property despite the changed fact. IRC § 2036(a)(2) includes the trust property in the gross estate, where as in this problem, decedent retained "the right, either alone or in conjunction with any person, to designate the persons who shall possess or enjoy the property or the income therefrom." Your answer also would not change even if Barry shared this power with Cassie.

38.   **Answer (C) is correct.** Although Cory transfers property to trust and retains a right to an annuity, or in other words, a portion of the income (and perhaps principal) of the trust for a period of years, Cory does not retain any interest as of his death. For that reason he has not retained the prescribed interest for the requisite time period — for life, for a period not ascertainable without reference to her death, or for a period that does not end before her death.

This fact pattern highlights an important planning strategy used with grantor-retained annuity and unitrusts. A taxpayer may transfer to taxpayer's family a remainder interest in property at a reduced gift tax cost by retaining a qualified annuity or unitrust interest as specified in IRC § 2702, and avoid estate tax inclusion if the taxpayer survives the term of the trust.

Answer (D) is incorrect. Answer (D) is incorrect because an annuity interest can cause inclusion under IRC § 2036. If taxpayer retains an annuity interest, it is as though taxpayer retained a right to at least a portion of the trust's income. Treasury Regulation § 20.2036-1(c) specifies how to determine the amount included in the gross estate when an annuity or unitrust interest is retained, and decedent dies during the term of the trust.

Answers (A) and (B) are incorrect. As indicated above, there is no gross estate inclusion because Cory has survived the term of the trust. The time periods referenced in these answers are irrelevant to a determination of whether IRC § 2036 applies.

39.   **Answer (A) is correct.** Although Daisy does not retain the right to income or to possess or enjoy the trust property pursuant to the trust terms, it can be inferred that the child and Daisy in reality agreed Daisy would retain such possession based on the objective fact that Daisy continued to live in the home rent-free, and that a portion of the trust income was used to pay Daisy's personal living expenses.

If an implied agreement can be shown that taxpayer intended to retain a prescribed interest for life, as here, courts generally apply IRC § 2036 to include the trust property in taxpayer's gross estate. *See Est. of Linderme v. Commissioner*, 52 T.C. 305 (1969); Rev. Rul. 78-409, 1978-2 C.B. 234. Note, however, that the Service does not argue implied agreement where the transfer of a home (as opposed to home and other income-producing assets) is between spouses, and the transferor spouse continues to co-occupy the home with the transferee spouse, as indicated in Rev. Rul. 70-155, 1970-1 C.B. 189. The implied agreement argument may be avoided if fair rental value is paid for the home, but not if after taking into account the entire transaction a fair rent is not in fact paid. *See Est. of Maxwell v. Commissioner*, 3 F.3d 591 (2d Cir. 1993). Similarly, use of trust income for the benefit of the donor, although not technically allowed, requires inclusion of the income-producing property in the gross estate. *See Est. of Paxon v. Commissioner*, 86 T.C. 785 (1986); *Est. of Hendry v. Commissioner*, 62 T.C. 861 (1974); *Est. of McCabe v. United States*, 475 F.2d 1142 (Ct. Cl. 1973); *Est. of McNichol v. Commissioner*, 265 F.2d 667 (3d Cir. 1959).

Answers (C) and (D) are incorrect. Answers (C) and (D) are incorrect for the reasons stated above. An implied agreement to retain a prescribed interest in transferred property for life will cause inclusion in decedent's gross estate regardless of the legally enforceable terms of the trust or retention of rights as a trustee.

Answer (B) also is incorrect. Answer (B) is incorrect because there generally is no duty of support owed to an adult child.

40.   **Answer (B) is correct.** Eva retained a prescribed interest in property because trustee was required to satisfy Eva's legal obligation of support to her child. Thus,

Eva retained a right to income and to enjoy the trust property. Had the trustee failed to provide for child's support, Eva would have had to spend her own money to do so. Treas. Reg. § 20.2036-1(b)(2). Eva also retained the interest for a period that in fact did not end before her death, thus meeting the requisite time requirement.

Answers (A), (C), and (D) are incorrect. For the same reason that Answer (B) is correct, the other answers are incorrect.

41.   **Answers and Scenarios (A), (C), and (D) all cause inclusion in Frank's gross estate.** IRC § 2036(a)(2) includes in the gross estate of the transferor all property over which transferor retained the right to designate the person or persons who shall enjoy the income from the transferred property. In each of these scenarios, the trustee can choose whether daughter or grandchild will enjoy the income from the trust property. In Scenario A, if trustee pays principal to grandchild, then grandchild will thereafter be entitled to any income from the distributed principal, and not daughter. In Scenario C, trustee may choose who receives the income. In Scenario D, if trustee accumulates income and adds it to principal, then grandchild and not daughter will enjoy the accumulated income. *See* Treas. Reg. § 20.2036-1(b)(3), and *United States v. O'Malley*, 383 U.S. 627 (1966).

    Answer and Scenario (B) will avoid inclusion in Frank's gross estate under IRC § 2036(a)(2). Treasury Regulation § 20.2036-1(b)(3) provides that the phrase " 'right . . . to designate the person or persons who shall possess or enjoy the transferred property or the income therefrom'. . . . does not include a power over the transferred property itself which does not affect the enjoyment of the income received or earned during the decedent's life. (See, however, section 2038 for the inclusion of property in the gross estate on account of such a power.)" If trustee invades principal for the benefit of daughter, daughter will continue to receive all income from the distributed principal. Thus, trustee does not have discretion to change who receives income from the trust, and for that reason IRC § 2036(a)(2) does not apply to include trust property in Frank's gross estate. Note, however, that IRC § 2038 will apply to include the trust property in Frank's gross estate because daughter has the power to impact timing of distribution of principal.

42.   The transferor is deemed to have the powers of decedent if transferor has the unrestricted power to remove or discharge a trustee at any time and appoint herself as trustee. Greg has such a right. Thus, because trustee has the right to designate who will receive trust income, and Greg is deemed to hold that right, IRC § 2036(a)(2) causes trust property to be included in Greg's gross estate. Treas. Reg. § 20.2036-1(b)(3). This result may be avoided by limiting the person who may replace trustee to one who is not the transferor or related or subordinate to transferor. Rev. Rul. 95-58, 1995-2 C.B. 191.

43.   **Retained Voting Rights with Respect to Transferred Stock.**

    Answer (B) is correct. Called the anti-*Byrum* provision, IRC § 2036(b) was passed in an effort to overrule *United States v. Byrum*, 408 U.S. 125 (1972), where the Court held retention of the right to vote transferred stock did not trigger application of IRC § 2036. Now, Section 2036(b)(1) deems the retention of the right to vote, directly or indirectly, transferred stock of a controlled corporation as retention of the enjoyment of the transferred stock. Thus, Julius retained a power prohibited by IRC § 2036. Not only must Julius retain the right to vote the stock that was transferred, but the corporation also must be a controlled corporation. IRC § 2036(b)(2) defines a controlled corporation as one where at any time after the transfer and during the three years immediately prior to decedent's death, decedent owned *or* had the right to vote, alone or with another, at least 20 percent of the total combined voting power of all classes of the corporation stock. Immediately prior to his death, Julius owned or had the right to vote 25 percent of the stock, which exceeds 20 percent. Thus, both requirements of IRC § 2036(b) are met, and Julius's gross estate includes the stock transferred to his son.

To answer this question it is not necessary to apply the IRC § 318 ownership attribution rules to determine whether the definition of "controlled corporation" is met because Julius directly owns or has the right to vote more than 20 percent of the stock. If the 20 percent requirement had not been met, it would have been necessary to apply the IRC § 318 ownership attribution rules to definitively determine whether the definition had been met.

Answer (A) is incorrect. Answer (A) incorrectly focuses on the percentage of the stock transferred, as opposed to the focus of IRC § 2036(b)(2), which is on the percentage of stock the donor owned or had the right to vote after the transfer and within three years of transferor's death.

Answer (C) and (D) also are incorrect. IRC § 2036(b)(2) does not focus only on ownership to determine control, but also includes stock that transferor had the right to vote. It also is not limited to transfers in trust.

44. In Revenue Ruling 81-15, 1981-1 C.B. 457, the Service ruled that transfer of nonvoting stock with concurrent retention of voting stock in a controlled corporation did not trigger inclusion of the transferred stock in the gross estate under IRC § 2036(b). This ruling provides an easy strategy for a donor to avoid application of IRC § 2036(b) and still retain the same right to vote as before the transfer.

It should be noted that it is unclear whether the Service would issue the same ruling under the facts of Revenue Ruling 81-15 in light of recent cases in the area of family limited partnerships. Recent cases have held that retention of a general partner interest after transfer of limited partnership interests triggers inclusion under IRC § 2036(a). *See Est. of Strangi v. Commissioner*, T.C. Memo. 2003-145, *aff'd* 417 F.3d 468 (5th Cir. 2005).

45. **Answer (A) is correct.** At first glance it appears that Lacey's gross estate should not include any trust assets because Lacey did not retain any benefits with respect to assets Lacey transferred to trust. Before IRC § 2036 can apply to include assets in a decedent's gross estate, the decedent must retain a benefit from the property transferred. Courts, however, look to the substance of the transaction to determine who transferred the property. The Court in *United States v. Grace*, 395 U.S. 316

(1969), held "that application of the reciprocal trust doctrine requires only that the trusts be interrelated, and that the arrangement, to the extent of mutual value, leaves the settlors in approximately the same economic position as they would have been in had they created trusts naming themselves as life beneficiaries." Applying the reciprocal trust doctrine, the Court uncrossed the trusts, and deemed the decedent to be the transferor of the trust held for decedent's benefit. The Court included in decedent's gross estate the value of the trust held for the benefit of decedent. The facts of this problem are similar to that of *Grace*, and should lead to application of the reciprocal trust doctrine.

Answers (B), (C), and (D) are incorrect. These answers are incorrect because they fail to uncross the trusts and deem Lacey to be the transferor of the trust for Lacey's benefit.

46. **Answer (B) is correct.** One-half the value of the trust assets is includible in Nels' gross estate. Treasury Regulation § 20.2036-1(a) indicates that if decedent retained an interest to only a portion of the property, then only a corresponding portion is included in decedent's gross estate. Nels retained an interest in one-half the income of the trust, so one-half is included. Nels meets the other requirements of IRC § 2036 — Nels transferred the property to the trust, and Nels retained a right to the income of the trust for life.

Answers (A) and (D) are incorrect for the same reasons as indicated above.

Answer (C) also is incorrect. If decedent retains an interest in trust for life, the entire proportionate value of the trust property is included in the gross estate, and not just the value of decedent's life estate. Were this not the result, taxpayer could avoid estate tax on the value of the remainder simply by transferring property to trust and retaining all the attributes for life.

47. **Answer (D) is the best answer.** If decedent sold property for "adequate consideration in money or money's worth" and the sale was bona fide, an exception applies to prevent inclusion of the property in decedent's gross estate. This makes sense because presumably the proceeds from the sale equal to the value of the property have already been included in decedent's gross estate under IRC § 2033, and it would be unfair to cause double inclusion by adding the value of the property over which decedent retains an interest. Thus, Answer (D) is the best answer because Olivia received cash equal to the fair market value of the home when she made the sale to her son.

Answer (A) is incorrect. Even though Olivia transferred property and in fact retained possession or enjoyment of the property for a period not ending before her death, decedent's gross estate does not include the property for the reasons stated above. The bona fide sale exception applies.

Answer (B) also is incorrect. The bona fide sale for adequate consideration exception has two prongs: (1) the sale must be bona fide, and (2) it must be for adequate consideration in money or money's worth. While the answer states one of the tests for determining if the sale is bona fide, the facts do not raise this issue. There are no facts demonstrating the sale is not bona fide.

Answer (C) also is incorrect. The focus should be on adequate consideration paid for the home, and not on whether a fair rental value is paid.

48.   **Answer (C) is correct.** Because, given the changed facts, Olivia sold her home for less than an adequate consideration in money or money's worth, the bona fide sale exception does not apply. Thus, a court would likely include the value of the home as of Olivia's date of death less the amount of consideration actually paid in Olivia's gross estate. IRC § 2043 specifies that the amount included equals the fair market value at date of death less the amount of consideration paid. Thus, the gross estate would include the full amount of any appreciation in the home between the date of sale and the date of death.

Answers (A) and (B) are incorrect. As indicated above, in order to capture the full appreciated value of the home in the gross estate, and yet not double count any consideration paid, IRC § 2043 includes the full fair market value as of date of death less actual consideration paid, and not a proportionate amount of the value or the full value.

Answer (D) also is incorrect. IRC § 2036 will include the value of the home in Olivia's gross estate because Olivia continued to live in the home and paid less than full fair market value rent. Thus, a court would find an implied retention of the right to possess and enjoy the home. For that reason Answer (D) is incorrect.

49.   The issue is whether the bona fide sale exception for adequate consideration applies to avoid application of IRC § 2036. There is a split of authority among the courts. The Third, Fifth, and Ninth Circuits have held that the exception applies when consideration received equals the value of the remainder interest. *See D'Ambrosio v. Commissioner*, 101 F.3d 309 (3d Cir. 1996); *Wheeler v. United States*, 116 F.3d 749 (5th Cir. 1997); *Est. of Magnin v. Commissioner*, 184 F.3d 1074 (9th Cir. 1999). The Federal Circuit and the Tax Court have held that the exception only applies if the person receiving the remainder interest pays consideration equal to the full fair market value of the entire property as of the date of the gift. *Gradow v. United States*, 897 F.2d 516 (Fed. Cir. 1990); *Est. of Gregory*, 39 T.C. 1012 (1963).

Note also that the Tenth Circuit in *United States v. Allen*, 293 F.2d 916 (10th Cir. 1961), addressing the sale of a life estate, reached a similar conclusion as that reached in *Gradow*. Note also that Congress has attempted to resolve this issue at the time of the transfer by enacting IRC § 2702, which addresses the value of any gift when a transfer of a partial interest is made to a *family member* (as defined in that statute).

50.   **Answer (A) is correct.** IRC § 2038 includes in the gross estate the value of any interest in property transferred by decedent and subject as of the date of decedent's death to a power to "alter, amend, revoke, or terminate." It also includes property interests that were subject to such a power that was relinquished within the three-year period ending on decedent's date of death. In this fact pattern, Andy meets all three requirements of IRC § 2038 — Andy transferred the property to the trust, Andy held the power to revoke the entire trust, and the property was subject to the power as of Andy's date of death. Note that the relevant time period focuses only on whether decedent held the power as of date of death. Because the power of revocation extended to all trust property, IRC § 2038 includes the entire value. Also, there are no facts indicating that the property was transferred subject to a bona fide sale for full and adequate consideration, so that exception does not apply.

> *Note:* Revocable trusts similar to this one are often used as the primary vehicle to pass property at death. These trusts serve several non-tax purposes including the ability to avoid probate with regard to assets owned by trustee. While the power to alter or revoke the trust allows the transferor to change the dispositive terms of the trust in much the same way that a will may be changed, revocable trusts do not necessarily provide any estate tax savings.

    Answer (B) is incorrect. The entire value of the trust will be subject to tax under IRC § 2038, and not just the value of the remainder interest, because in this fact pattern both the income and principal were subject to the power to revoke. Pursuant to IRC § 2038 the gross estate includes the value of any interest subject to the power to alter, amend, revoke, or terminate. This causes IRC § 2038 to overlap with the reach of IRC § 2036(a)(2). While IRC § 2036(a)(2) includes property subject to retained powers over income interests, IRC § 2038 applies to include property subject to powers over both income and principal. Property, however, is only included once, and under the section that includes the greatest value.

    Answer (C) also is incorrect. It is sufficient that decedent held a power to alter, amend, revoke, or terminate as of the date of decedent's death. No requirement exists regarding exercise of the power.

    Answer (D) also is incorrect. IRC § 2038(b) specifically prohibits easy avoidance by providing that a power will be deemed to exist as of date of death even though it is "subject to a precedent giving of notice" or even if it "takes effect only on the expiration of a stated period after exercise." Thus, the fact that the revocation cannot occur until after 60 days notice does not serve to avoid application of the statute based on the time requirement.

51. **Answer (A) is correct.** Becca holds the power to "alter" the timing of when the beneficiary receives income and principal. The Supreme Court in *Lober v. United States*, 346 U.S. 335 (1953), held the power to impact timing of income sufficient to cause inclusion under IRC § 2038.

Answers (B) and (C) are incorrect. For the same reasons that (A) is correct, (B) and (C) are incorrect.

Answer (D) is incorrect. IRC § 2038 *includes* powers to alter, amend, revoke, and terminate held at decedent's death regardless of whether the power is held "by decedent alone or in conjunction with any other person. . . ." It does not matter whether the person has an adverse interest. It also does not matter in what capacity decedent may exercise the power, and even though decedent is a co-trustee, IRC § 2038 may apply to trustee powers held by Becca. Thus, Answer (D) is incorrect.

52. **Answer (D) is correct.** IRC § 2038 does not include in the gross estate powers subject to a determinable external standard. Generally, determinable external standards are those that allow distribution in terms of maintenance, education, support, and health. (A determinable external standard is similar to, but a bit broader than, an ascertainable standard.) The court in *Jennings v. Smith*, 161 F.2d 74 (2d Cir. 1947), determined that such powers become "a duty enforceable in a court of equity . . ." Powers subject to determinable external standards compel a trustee to distribute pursuant to the standard, and eliminate discretion. Generally, standards that base distribution on a beneficiary's happiness or comfort, without more, fail to meet the definition of determinable external standard because of the broad discretion remaining with trustee.

Answers (A), (B), and (C) are incorrect. Just as with IRC § 2036, under IRC § 2038, if a transferor has the power to remove and replace a trustee with herself, the transferor will be deemed to hold the powers of the trustee. Here, however, the powers of the trustee are insufficient to cause inclusion in the gross estate in light of the determinable external standard, and for that reason Answer (A) is incorrect. IRC § 2038 applies to powers, and not the retention of income or the possession and enjoyment of property as indicated in Answer (B). In addition, Cindy generally will not owe a duty of support to her adult child. However, IRC § 2038 does apply to powers over both income and principal, and for that reason Answer (C) is incorrect.

53. IRC §§ 2038 and 2036(a)(2) overlap to a certain extent. Both include powers that impact the possession and enjoyment of income from property transferred by decedent, as is the case here. Just as with IRC § 2038, under IRC § 2036(a)(2), courts hold that decedent has not retained sufficient power to cause inclusion when the power is subject to a determinable external standard. Also, just as with IRC § 2038, when decedent can replace and remove trustee with himself or herself,

decedent is deemed to hold the powers of trustee. The only difference between the answers is that IRC § 2036 applies only to income interests, as opposed to interests in or powers over corpus.

54. **Answer (A) is correct.** While both IRC §§ 2036 and 2038 cause inclusion in the gross estate because Demetra held a power to alter enjoyment of the trust income as of her death, only IRC § 2036 includes the value of "all" trust property in Demetra's gross estate. IRC § 2038 includes in the gross estate only the value of the trust property subject to the power, and here that would equal the value of the income interest for Demetra's life. Demetra retains no power over the remainder interest.

Answers (B), (C), and (D) are incorrect for the reasons stated above.

55. **Answer (D) is correct.** In order for IRC § 2036 to trigger inclusion in Hanson's gross estate, Hanson would have to retain an interest in the income of the property transferred or a power over the income from the property transferred. In order for IRC § 2038 to trigger inclusion, Hanson would have to hold a power at death to alter, modify, revoke, or terminate the trust. In this problem, Hanson does not retain any interest in or hold any power over the trust property. Thus, the trust property is not includible in Hanson's gross estate under either IRC §§ 2036 or 2038.

Answers (A), (B), and (C) are incorrect for the reasons stated above.

56. **Answer (A) is correct.** This problem mirrors the facts of *Est. of Farrel v. United States*, 77-1 U.S. Tax Cas. (CCH) ¶ 13,185 (Ct. Cl. 1977). Under both IRC § 2036 and § 2038, a transferor is deemed to hold the powers held by the trustee if the transferor may replace the trustee with a trustee of transferor's choosing. This result is avoided only where transferor's discretion is limited to naming a trustee who is not related or subordinate to transferor. Rev. Rul. 95-58, 1995-2 C.B. 191. However, IRC § 2038 applies only to those powers decedent holds as of date of death. Decedent did not hold any power to replace a trustee as of date of death. IRC § 2036(a)(2) leads to a different result because it includes property to the extent that transferor retains a power over enjoyment of income for "for life or for any period not ascertainable without reference to his death or for any period which does not in fact end before his death. . . ." Here Jaime retained a power to replace trustee for life, and, because of the replacement power, is deemed to hold trustee's discretionary power over income.

Answers (B), (C), and (D) are incorrect for the reasons stated above.

57. **Answer (B) is correct.** IRC § 2037 includes an amount of trust assets in Anderson's gross estate because Anderson's interest in the trust meets all the requirements of IRC § 2037. Specifically, IRC § 2037 requires:

    (1) Decedent transfer property,

    (2) possession or enjoyment of the transferred property by someone other than decedent could only be obtained by surviving decedent (the "survivorship" requirement),

    (3) decedent retained a possibility that the property (and not just the income interest in the property) would return to decedent or would be subject to a power of disposition by decedent (called a "reversionary interest"),

    (4) the value of the reversionary interest immediately before decedent's death was greater than 5 percent of the entire value of the transferred property (the "5 percent test"), and

    (5) decedent did not transfer the property subject to a bona fide sale for adequate consideration in money or money's worth.

    Treas. Reg. § 20.2037-1(a). Applying these requirements to the facts of the problem, (1) Anderson transferred property, (2) Anderson's child could obtain possession of the property only by surviving Anderson, (3) Anderson retained the possibility the property would return to Anderson if he survived his spouse, or in the words of the statute, Anderson retained a reversionary interest, and (4) these questions assume the reversionary interest meets the 5 percent test. Treas. Reg. § 20.2037-1(e), example 3. In order to determine whether the reversionary interest exceeds 5 percent of the value of the transferred property, the valuation tables promulgated by Treasury apply. Treas. Reg. § 20.2037-1(c)(3). Also, there are no facts to indicate that the exception for a bona fide sale for adequate consideration in money or money's worth should apply.

    Answer (A) is incorrect. Any interest Anderson retained with respect to trust property terminates upon Anderson's death. For that reason, IRC § 2033 does not apply. In order for IRC § 2033 to apply there must be a property interest capable of transfer by decedent as of decedent's death.

    Answers (C) and (D) are also incorrect for the reasons discussed above.

58. IRC § 2037 includes in the gross estate the value of the transferred property to the extent of the reversionary interest. IRC § 2037(a). Anderson's gross estate thus includes the value of the property transferred less the value of Anderson's spouse's outstanding life estate. Treas. Reg. § 20.2037-1(e), example 3.

59. **Answer (A) is correct.** Recall that IRC § 2033 applies to include property in the gross estate when decedent holds a beneficial interest in property, and can transfer the beneficial interest at death. Bob holds a reversionary interest in property that Bob could transfer. Thus, IRC § 2033 would include the reversionary interest in Bob's gross estate. *See* Treas. Reg. § 20.2037-1(e), example 1.

    Answer (B) is incorrect. IRC § 2037 does not apply to include Bob's retained interest in the gross estate because the retained interest does not meet the "survivorship requirement." Each beneficiary (the sister and sister's children) can enjoy the property without surviving Bob.

    Answers (C) and (D) also are incorrect for the reasons stated above.

60. **Answer (D) is correct.** IRC § 2033 does not apply because Cynthia gave away all interest and control over the property transferred on the date of the gift, even though the property does not actually pass outright to Cynthia's descendants until Cynthia's death. Cynthia did not retain any interest that could be transferred by Cynthia at death. IRC § 2037 does not apply because Cynthia did not retain any reversionary interest. *See* Treas. Reg. § 20.2037-1(e), example 2.

    Answers (A), (B), and (C) are incorrect for the reasons stated above.

61. **Answer (A) is correct.** Answer (A) is the best answer and states the requirements of IRC § 2037 in the most accurate manner. Retention of the possibility that the trust property will be subject to a power over both income and principal, retained by Ellen, falls within the definition of "reversionary interest." Thus, Ellen retained a reversionary interests, as required by IRC § 2037. Ellen's niece could possess the property only by surviving Ellen, thus meeting the survivorship requirement of IRC § 2037. Finally, the problem assumes that the value of the reversionary interest immediately before Ellen's death exceeded 5 percent of the value of the trust property.

    Answers (B), (C), and (D) are incorrect for the reasons stated above. Answer (B) does not clearly state the test for IRC § 2037. Answer (C) is wrong because Ellen has retained a reversionary interest as defined by the statute. Answer (D) does not properly focus on whether Ellen retained any interest in the transferred property.

62. **Answer (C) is correct.** IRC § 2037(b) specifies that decedent's gross estate will not include transferred interests in property "if possession or enjoyment of the property could have been obtained by any beneficiary during the decedent's life through the exercise of a general power of appointment . . . which in fact was exercisable immediately before the decedent's death." The question poses the fact pattern addressed by this statement. *See* Treas. Reg. § 20.2037-1(e), example 6. This fact pattern fails the survivorship requirement because on exercise of the power of appointment the appointee may enjoy the property without surviving Frances.

    Answers (A), (B), and (D) are incorrect for the reasons stated above. Generally, powers of appointment are not attributed as between spouses. In addition, the exception does not require exercise of the power, only that it be held immediately before decedent's death.

63.   IRC § 2037 includes in the gross estate only reversionary interests retained by a decedent that exceed 5 percent of the trust property immediately before decedent's death. Here Greg's reversionary interest will be compared to the value of the trust property without any deduction for the value of niece's outstanding life estate. Actuarial tables will apply to determine the value of the reversion. The value is determined without regard to the fact of decedent's death, and without regard to whether the estate elects alternate valuation. Treas. Reg. §§ 20.2037-1(c)(3), (4).

64. **Answer (C) is correct.** Congress enacted IRC § 2039 specifically to deal with the survivor annuity under an employer-funded retirement plan. Litigation had raised an issue as to whether a decedent's gross estate included the value of a survivor annuity where decedent did not contribute to the fund. IRC § 2039 clarifies Congress' intent to include these types of plans. Thus, Answer (C) is correct. Prior to enactment of IRC § 2039, the Service successfully litigated some cases on the basis of IRC § 2033, and some on the basis of IRC §§ 2036 through 2038.

    Answer (A) is incorrect. Answer (A) is incorrect because IRC § 2039 specifically does not apply to benefits payable under a life insurance contract. It states: "The gross estate shall include the value of an annuity or other payment receivable by any beneficiary by reason of surviving the decedent under any form of contract or agreement . . . (*other than as insurance under policies on the life of the decedent*). . . ." IRC § 2039(a). Whether a contract amounts to a life insurance contract has been litigated. In those cases, courts ask whether underwriting for the contract shifts or spreads risk of premature death. The life insurance contract, thus, takes into account more than just "investment risk." *See All v. McCobb*, 321 F.2d 633 (2d Cir. 1963). Courts may apply the integrated transactions doctrine to determine whether the contract is one of life insurance where a series of contracts are involved. *See Montgomery v. Commissioner*, 56 T.C. 489 (1971), *aff'd* 458 F.2d 616 (5th Cir. 1971).

    Answer (B) is incorrect. The Service has issued regulations indicating it will not apply IRC § 2039 to include assets held in a grantor-retained annuity trust in the estate of decedent. Treas. Reg. § 20.2039-1(e)(1). Rather, the treasury regulations specify the amount to be included in the gross estate under IRC § 2036, and generally include that amount of trust assets necessary to generate the annuity payment received by decedent under that section.

    Answer (D) also is incorrect. Generally, IRC § 2039 does not apply to government benefits on the basis that a federal act does not constitute a "contract or agreement" as required by IRC § 2039. Rev. Rul. 60–70, 1960–1 C.B. 372, *as modified*, Rev. Rul. 73-316, 1973-2 C.B. 318. *See also* Rev. Rul. 2002-39, 2002-2 C.B. 33 (indicating inapplicability of IRC § 2039 with regard to annuities payable to New York City firefighters and police who die from injuries sustained while performing duties). The Service, however, indicates that such benefits may be includible in the gross estate pursuant to IRC § 2033 if decedent may designate the beneficiary.

65. **Answer (A) is correct.** IRC § 2039 applies broadly to include more than just employer-sponsored annuities. It includes commercial annuities, private annuities,

and other annuities payable under agreements or plans if the following requirements are met:

(1) A beneficiary receives an annuity or other payment by reason of surviving decedent,

(2) The annuity or other payment is made under a contract or agreement other than a life insurance policy on decedent's life,

(3) An annuity or other payment was also payable to decedent or decedent possessed the right to receive such payment, either alone or with another, under the terms of such contract or agreement, and

(4) Decedent received the annuity or other payment or possessed the right to do so for decedent's life, for a period not ascertainable without reference to decedent's death or for a period that does not in fact end before decedent's death.

The amount included in the gross estate equals the value of the annuity or amount of other payment that is proportionate to the total amount of the purchase price contributed by decedent.

In this question, pursuant to the terms of the agreement with the lottery agency, Alice was in fact receiving an annuity for a period that did not end before her life, and Alice's descendants were entitled to receive the annuity upon surviving Alice. Because Alice paid 100 percent of the price of the lottery ticket, Alice's gross estate must include 100 percent of the value of the annuity as of Alice's death.

Answer (B) is incorrect. The estate in *Estate of Shackleford v. United States*, 1998 U.S. Dist. LEXIS 12442 (E.D. Cal.), *aff'd* 262 F.3d 1028 (9th Cir. 2001), argued that only a minute portion of the value of the annuity should be included in decedent's gross estate because decedent was only one of millions of people who bought lottery tickets to provide the winner the annuity benefits. The Court easily dispensed of this argument, and included the full value of the annuity as of decedent's death in his estate. Decedent's purchase of $1 resulted in receipt of the winnings in the form of an annuity.

Answers (C) and (D) are also incorrect. Answer (C) is incorrect because it does not matter whether or not the decedent could direct who is to receive the annuity payments following decedent's death. *See* Treas. Reg. § 20.2039-1(b)(2), example 2. Although the annuity was for a term of years, decedent was receiving the annuity at the time of death. Thus, decedent was paid the annuity for a period that did not in fact end before his death. IRC § 2039(a).

66. **Answer (D) is the best answer.** IRC § 2039 requires the annuity or other payment following decedent's death be made pursuant to a contract or agreement. Much litigation has occurred in an attempt to determine the parameters of this requirement. Here the employer was not required to make the payment to the designated beneficiary pursuant to the contract because Bill did not live to age 65 as required under the contract. Public Company made the lump sum payment voluntarily, and the facts indicate it did not do so as a matter of course (i.e., it was

an "unusual" move). *See* Treas. Reg. § 20.2039-1(b)(2), example 4. *See also Courtney v. United States*, 1984 U.S. Dist. LEXIS 16439 (Cl. Ct.), *Barr v. Commissioner*, 40 T.C. 227 (1963). These facts contrast with the holding in *Estate of Neely*, 613 F.2d 802 (Cl. Ct. 1980), where decedent and decedent's family controlled the employer corporation and as a result it was highly unlikely that the "voluntary" payment would not be made on decedent's death.

Answer (A) is incorrect for the reason indicated above.

Answers (B) and (C) also are incorrect. Answer (B) is incorrect because IRC § 2039 includes both "the value of an annuity or other payment." The lump sum amount falls under the broad umbrella of "other payment." Thus, because of the reason given in Answer (B), it is not the best option. Answer (C) is incorrect because IRC § 2039 does not require that Bill in fact receive a payment under the contract, but considers it sufficient that Bill have "the right to receive" the payment. Thus, the reason given in Answer (C) is also not the best answer.

67.   **Answer (A) is correct.** The question here is whether the form of "separate" plans should be respected so that IRC § 2039 does not apply to either plan. Based on these facts, Treas. Reg. § 20.2039-1(b)(2), example 6, takes the position that "[t]he scope of section 2039(a) and (b) cannot be limited by indirection." It indicates that IRC § 2039 does include the value of the annuity payable by reason of Clarice's death to Clarice's spouse in the gross estate. The regulation focuses on the substance and interconnectedness of the agreements. To find otherwise would create a simple way in which to avoid application of IRC § 2039 in every situation. When considered together, these two plans meet all the requirements of IRC § 2039 for inclusion in the gross estate.

In contrast, note that if the facts were changed so that Plan 1 did not pay decedent an annuity, but instead, for example, paid decedent a salary for consulting services or provided a disability plan, then even were the contracts to be construed together, the requirement that decedent be paid an annuity or other payment would not necessarily be met if the payment to the employee was not of the same type as the payment to the beneficiary. *See Estate of Schelberg v. Commissioner*, 612 F.2d 25 (2d Cir. 1979), *Kramer v. United States*, 406 F.2d 1363 (Ct. Cl. 1969),

Answer (D) is incorrect. For the reasons stated above, Answer (D) is incorrect.

Answers (B) and (C) are incorrect. Answer (B) is incorrect because the fact that the beneficiary could forfeit the payments does not preclude inclusion. It would, however, impact the value to be included in Clarice's gross estate. Treas. Reg. § 20.2039-1(b)(2), example 2. Answer (C) is incorrect because Clarice was in pay status and in fact received annuity payments prior to death so that the condition of forfeiture based on Clarice reaching a specific age no longer applied.

68.   **Answer (A) is correct.** The full value of the annuity as of Dani's date of death is included in Dani's gross estate because payments by Dani's employer are treated as being made by Dani. IRC § 2039(b) states: "any contribution by the decedent's employer or former employer to the purchase price of such contract . . . shall be considered to be contributed by the decedent if made by reason of his

employment." *See also* Treas. Reg. § 20.2039-1(c), example 2. Because of the attribution of the employer's payments to Dani, the entire value of the annuity is included in Dani's gross estate.

Answer (B) is incorrect for the reason stated above. Note, however, that if the facts were changed so that Dani's spouse (and not Dani's employer) had contributed one-half of the payments for the joint and survivor annuity, only one-half of the annuity would be included in Dani's gross estate per Treas. Reg. § 20.2039-1(c), example 1.

Answers (C) and (D) are incorrect. Answer (C) is incorrect because it does not matter if Dani was in pay status because Dani had "the right" to receive payments had Dani lived. Answer (D) is incorrect because IRC § 2039 includes the annuity if decedent had the right to receive the annuity "either alone or in conjunction with another for his life. . . ." The facts indicate that Dani had the right to an annuity for her life. Dani's spouse also had the requisite right to receive payments "by reason of surviving the decedent. . . ." The test is *not*, as the answer states, limited to those situations where the beneficiary's right to receive any benefits begins only after decedent's death.

69.   **Answer (D) is correct.** IRC § 2040 specifically indicates that it applies to property held as joint tenants with right of survivorship and that held as tenants by the entirety. IRC § 2040. Treasury Regulation § 20.2040-1(b) clarifies that IRC § 2040 applies to all classes of property, including real property, bank accounts, and bonds. Property owned as joint tenants with right of survivorship allows either joint tenant to enjoy the entire property subject to the interest of the other joint tenant. The characteristic that sets joint tenancy with right of survivorship apart from other types of tenancies is that on the death of a joint tenant, the interest of the predeceased joint tenant in the property passes by operation of law to the surviving joint tenant or joint tenants. Tenancy-by-the-entirety property is property held only between a husband and wife, and similarly, on the death of a spouse, the entire interest in the tenancy-by-the-entirety property passes to the surviving spouse. The primary differences between tenancy-by-the-entirety property and joint-tenancy-with-right-of-survivorship property are that the former (1) is held only between spouses, and (2) both spouses must consent to a termination of the tenancy by the entirety. In contrast, a joint tenant may unilaterally terminate the joint tenancy with right of survivorship by conveyance or by a request for partition.

      Answers (A), (B), and (C) are incorrect. As indicated above, IRC § 2040 specifies the extent of its application. It does not apply to tenancies in common or community property. Neither of those tenancies carries with it a survivorship interest. A tenant in common may pass the tenancy-in-common interest by will. Likewise, a spouse can pass his or her community property interest by will.

70.   **Answer (C) is correct.** An exception to the general rule applies for qualified joint interests. When the only two joint tenants are spouses, and the spouses hold title as joint tenants with right of survivorship, or when the spouses hold property as tenants by the entirety, the jointly held property meets the definitional requirements of a "qualified joint interest." IRC § 2040(b) includes in the gross estate one-half the value of the qualified joint interest regardless of the amount contributed by each joint tenant. Congress enacted this straightforward 50 percent inclusion rule to avoid the need to trace contributions by spouses.

      Answers (A), (B), and (D) are incorrect due to the 50 percent inclusion rule applicable to qualified joint interests.

71.   **Answer (B) is correct.** An exception to the general rule applies for joint-with-right-of-survivorship property received by decedent and the other joint tenants by gift, inheritance, devise, or bequest. IRC § 2040(a); Treas. Reg. § 20.2040-1(a)(1). In the event that decedent and the other joint tenants received the joint-tenancy-with-right-of-survivorship interests by gift, inheritance, devise, or bequest, decedent's gross estate includes a fractional share of the jointly held property. Here, Ellie owned the land with Carl and David, so Ellie's fractional share is one-third. As a consequence, Ellie's gross estate includes one-third the fair market value of the land. *See* Treas. Reg. § 20.2040-1(c)(8).

Answers (A), (C), and (D) are incorrect. Where property is received by the joint tenants as a result of a gift, inheritance, devise, or bequest, tracing rules do not apply to determine gross estate inclusion. Instead, a simple rule requiring inclusion of a fractional share equal to decedent's fractional interest in the property applies.

72. **Answer (D) is correct.** For the reasons stated below, because neither the qualified joint interest exception nor the exception for property received by gift, inheritance, devise, or bequest applies, the general rule of IRC § 2040(a) applies to avoid inclusion in Gavin's gross estate. The general rule of IRC § 2040 includes the entire value of the jointly held property in a decedent's gross estate, unless the estate can demonstrate that a portion of the consideration for the property was supplied by the other joint tenants. In the event the other joint tenants provided a portion of the consideration, the gross estate includes the value of the jointly held property less the portion attributable to consideration supplied by the other joint tenants. Treas. Reg. § 20.2040-1(a)(2). Here, the other joint tenant Fred supplied all of the consideration. Thus, Gavin's gross estate does not include any of the jointly held property. Treas. Reg. § 20.2040-1(c)(3). Note that if instead Fred had died before Gavin, Fred's estate would include the entire value of the jointly held property because he provided all of the consideration. Treas. Reg. § 20.2040-1(c)(1).

Answers (A) and (C) are incorrect. Neither Gavin's ability to access the account during life nor the amount of income received by Gavin during life impact the amount included in the gross estate under IRC § 2040. Gross estate inclusion under that section focuses only on the consideration, if any, provided by the deceased joint tenant.

Answer (B) is incorrect. The exception applicable to property received by joint tenants by gift, inheritance, devise, or bequest applies only where all joint tenants so received the property. Where one of the joint tenants provided consideration for the property, the general rule of IRC § 2040(a) applies instead.

73. **Answer (A) is correct.** Because all consideration contributed toward the purchase of the land and home held as joint tenants with right of survivorship originated from Heidi, her gross estate includes the entire date-of-death value of the land and home. It does not matter that the land appreciated in value from the time of the gift to Heidi's daughter until the time the land and home were placed in joint tenancy. Treas. Reg. § 20.2040-2(c)(4).

Answers (B), (C), and (D) are incorrect for the reasons noted above.

74. These facts reflect the facts of *Estate of Goldsborough v. Commissioner*, 70 T.C.

1077 (1978), *aff'd* 673 F.2d 1310 (4th Cir. 1982). Because Heidi's daughter sold the property, and reinvested the sales proceeds prior to investing in the jointly owned property, courts hold that the $50,000 of appreciation realized by Heidi's daughter as income is her property. Thus, the amount excluded from Heidi's gross estate is calculated as follows:

Amount Excluded	=		Date-of-Death Value
		×	(survivor's consideration)
			(entire consideration paid)
or,			
Amount Excluded	=		$200,000
		×	($50,000/$200,000)
	=		$50,000

Thus, Heidi's gross estate includes $150,000 or the date-of-death value of $200,000 less the $50,000 amount excluded attributable to consideration deemed furnished by Heidi's daughter and attributable to the income realized on the original gift.

The answer would be different if instead Heidi's daughter simply exchanged the land originally received from Heidi for the condominium. In that event, the entire value would be included in Heidi's gross estate. The key factual difference was the realization of income. *See also Estate of Kelley v. Commissioner*, 22 B.T.A. 421 (1931); *Harvey v. United States*, 185 F.2d 463 (7th Cir. 1950).

75.　**Answer (B) is correct.** The Service in Revenue Ruling 76-303, 1976-2 C.B. 266, takes the position that, on the simultaneous deaths of joint tenants where property owned by right of survivorship passes one-half to each of their gross estates, the gross estate of the contributing joint tenant, here Ingrid, includes the entire value of the property, and the gross estate of the noncontributing joint tenant, here Joan, includes one-half the value. Essentially the Service applies the general rule of IRC § 2040(a) to the one-half of the property passing by survivorship from the contributing joint tenant to the noncontributing joint tenant; and applies IRC § 2033 to the one-half of the property passing by state law under the contributing joint tenant's estate. Based on this reasoning the entire value of the apartment building is included in Ingrid's gross estate. The noncontributing joint tenant's estate includes one-half the value of the jointly held property passing pursuant to the noncontributing joint tenant's estate under IRC § 2033.

Answers (A), (C), and (D) are incorrect for the reasons stated above.

76. **Answer (A) is correct** because Alison can appoint trust property by will to her estate or the creditors of her estate. IRC § 2041(b)(1) defines a general power of appointment as a power "exercisable in favor of the decedent, his estate, his creditors, or the creditors of his estate. . . ." The definition reads in the disjunctive so the fact that the power is only exercisable at death to Alison's estate or the creditor's of her estate still satisfies the definition. This type of general power of appointment, if held at death, is subject to federal estate taxation. Taxation makes sense because, although Alison does not own the property subject to the power, Alison exercises control over the property in the same manner as if she owned it, in light of the fact that she can pay it to her estate and the property can pass under her will. Alternatively, she can use the property to satisfy her legal obligations by appointing the property to a creditor of her estate. A power exercisable by will, such as the one held by Alison, is sometimes referred to as a "testamentary" power.

   Answer (B) is incorrect for the reasons stated above.

77. **Answer (A) is correct** because Bob can use trust property to pay his taxes or the taxes of his estate. Payment of taxes is payment of a creditor, and a general power of appointment includes the power to appoint to his creditors or the creditors of his estate. Treas. Reg. § 20.2041-1(c)(1). The fact that Bob can appoint property only to pay creditors and not to himself or his estate again makes no difference under the statutory definition provided by IRC § 2041(b)(1). A power exercisable during life is often referred to as an inter vivos or lifetime power of appointment, and Bob's ability to appoint to his creditors falls within this category. He holds both an inter vivos and a testamentary power of appointment.

   Answer (B) is incorrect for the reasons stated above.

78. **Answer (A) is correct.** Carl as trustee may appoint trust property to himself. A power to appoint to oneself falls within the definition of general power of appointment. IRC § 2041(b)(1), Treas. Reg. § 20.2041-1(c)(1). It does not matter that the power held by Carl was not labeled as a power of appointment. It also does not matter whether the power is held individually or in a fiduciary capacity. Treas. Reg. § 20.2041-1(b)(1).

   Answer (B) is incorrect for the reasons stated above.

79. **Answer (B) is correct.** The Code excepts from the definition of general power of appointment "[a] power to consume, invade, or appropriate property for the benefit of the decedent which is limited by an ascertainable standard relating to the health,

education support or maintenance of the decedent. . . ." IRC § 2041(b)(1)(A). This is sometimes referred to as a MESH [Maintenance-Education-Support-Health] standard. The regulations clarify: "A power is limited by such a standard if the extent of the holder's duty to exercise and not to exercise the power is reasonably measurable in terms of his needs for health, education, or support (or for any combination of them)." By inserting an ascertainable standard and allowing a trustee to take into account the ascertainable standard, the drafter builds in flexibility.

Answer (A) is incorrect for the reasons stated above.

80.   **Answer (A) is correct.** Treasury regulations clarify that, if a holder of a power may use property to satisfy the holder's legal obligations, the power qualifies as a general power of appointment. Treas. Reg. § 20.2041-1(c)(1). Generally, a parent has a legal obligation to support minor children. In this problem, Elise may appoint trust property to satisfy her legal obligation of support to her minor children.

Answer (B) is incorrect for the reasons stated above.

81.   **Answer (B) is correct.** The power held by Frank is subject to an ascertainable standard. The regulations enumerate a series of standards that meet this definition of ascertainable standard, and they include: "support in reasonable comfort," "maintenance in health and reasonable comfort," and "support in his accustomed manner of living," among other standards. Thus, Frank's power falls squarely within these examples. Drafters generally should try to use one of the ascertainable standards enumerated in the regulations if the client's goal is to avoid classification as a "general power of appointment" and the client prefers to avoid the need to obtain a court order addressing the ability of the state court to enforce or ascertain the standard.

Answer (A) is incorrect for the reasons stated above.

82.   **Answer (B) is correct.** Treasury regulations specify that Gary does not hold a general power of appointment. Treas. Reg. § 20.2041-1(c)(1). The power specifically prohibits appointment to Gary, his estate, his creditors, or the creditors of his estate. This is the broadest limited power of appointment that a transferor may confer. Use of such a standard avoids estate tax in Gary's estate as the power holder, yet still allows Gary substantial flexibility to change the default dispositive provisions of the trust. Note, however, that if the power was drafted to leave out one of these four categories of appointees, the answer would change because then property could be appointed for the power holder's benefit.

Answer (A) is incorrect for the reasons stated above.

83.   The issue focuses on whether the ability of Hans to distribute property "in the event of emergency or illness" qualifies as an ascertainable standard. If it does, courts find Hans holds a special power of appointment; and, if it does not, courts find Hans holds a general power of appointment. Treasury regulations do not include "emergency or illness" within the standards acknowledged as being reasonably measurable in terms of support, health, maintenance, or education. In

analyzing this issue, courts look to state law to determine if a state court would enforce the standard as one that was ascertainable. At least one court, *Sowell v. Comm'r*, 708 F.2d 1564 (10th Cir. 1983), has held the standard ascertainable. *Contra* Tech. Adv. Mem. 8339004.

The courts are likewise divided based on application of state law as to whether "comfort" or "happiness" is an ascertainable standard. Treasury regulations, however, clearly state the Service's position that a standard based on "comfort" or "happiness" fails to qualify as an ascertainable standard. Note that the concept of "ascertainable standard" as developed under IRC §§ 2036 and 2038 differs from that under IRC § 2041 to the extent that ascertainable standards under those sections need not be measurable in terms of support, health, or education.

84.   **Answer (A) is correct.** IRC § 2041(a)(2) includes in the gross estate those general powers of appointment that "decedent has at the time of his death." The analysis must find (1) a general power of appointment, and (2) possession of the general power of appointment by decedent as of death. In this problem, Jacob held a general power of appointment because he could appoint trust property to his estate. He possessed the power as of death because he was allowed to exercise the power in a will. Thus, IRC § 2041(a)(2) would include the trust property in Jacob's gross estate.

Answer (B) is incorrect because Jacob did not "retain" any interest in the trust. The trust was created by Jacob's parent and not Jacob. Retention of an interest is essential for application of IRC §§ 2036 through 2038 but is not an element of IRC § 2041 where the power has not been exercised or released as here.

Answers (C) and (D) are incorrect because failure to exercise a power no longer avoids inclusion in the gross estate. With respect to powers created prior to October 22, 1942, failure to exercise a general power of appointment avoids inclusion. In addition, it does not matter whether any beneficial interest of the power holder in the trust is ascertainable. It only matters whether the power is ascertainable.

85.   **Answer (A) is correct.** The issue presented by this problem is whether Jacob holds the general power of appointment as of his death, even though state law precludes him from exercising the power once the court places him under a guardianship. The court in *Estate of Alperstein v. Comm'r*, 613 F.2d 1213 (2d Cir. 1979), held that the incapacity of a power holder was irrelevant to the determination of whether the power holder held the general power at death. The *Alperstein* court relied on legislative history and prior case law in arriving at its conclusion that IRC § 2041(a)(2) intended to reach all powers granted a decedent. It also cited the prior Supreme Court case, *Noel v. Comm'r*, 380 U.S. 678 (1965), stating: "It would stretch the imagination to think that Congress intended to measure estate tax liability by an individual's fluctuating, day-to-day, hour-by-hour capacity to dispose of property. . . ." Likewise, a child's minority does not impact application of IRC § 2041(a)(2) to general powers held by a minor.

Answer (B) is incorrect because the power has not lapsed. If Jacob recovered from his incapacity, Jacob would be able to exercise the power.

Answers (C) and (D) are incorrect because the exercise of the power is irrelevant to an application of IRC § 2041(a)(2). Even in the absence of an exercise of the power, the gross estate will include a general power of appointment deemed held at death.

86. **Answer (B) is the best answer.** Although Kathy's lifetime general power of appointment terminated the moment prior to her death, courts have included property subject to the power in the holder's gross estate. *Jenkins v. United States*, 428 F.2d 538 (5th Cir. 1970). To not include general powers exercisable up to the moment of death would be to elevate form over substance in light of the fact that decedent's power is terminated only by death. Up until the moment of death, Kathy could have distributed the entire trust corpus to herself and directed its passage under her will, or by doing so to her intestate takers.

Answer (A) is incorrect because it does not necessarily matter that the power holder is a beneficiary or a trustee. The gross estate includes a general power of appointment regardless of the capacity, beneficiary or trustee, in which the power is held. Treas. Reg. § 20.2041-1(c).

Answers (C) and (D) are incorrect. For the reasons indicated above, courts deem a power terminating on the death of a power holder to be held as of the date of death. Thus, the fact that Kathy's power terminated the moment before death does not cause the trust property to escape inclusion in the gross estate.

87. **Answer (C) is correct.** Two issues present themselves in this problem: (1) does Monty hold a general power of appointment at death; and, (2) does the power fall within the exception provided by IRC § 2041(b)(2) excepting taxation of the lapse of certain powers limited to no more than the greater of $5,000 or 5 percent of the trust assets. With regard to the first issue, the court in *Estate of Kurz v. Comm'r*, 101 T.C. 44 (1993), found the taxpayer under similar facts "held" the general power of appointment as of death. The court acknowledged that Treasury Regulation § 20.2041-3(b) recognizes contingencies that preclude exercise of the power, and that based on the contingency the power escapes gross estate inclusion. The court, however, distinguished contingencies within the control of the decedent. It noted that "any illusory or sham restriction placed on a power of appointment should be ignored." With regard to the second issue, the $5,000 or 5 percent exception of IRC § 2041(b)(2) applies to taxation of lapsed powers. As of Monty's death, the 5 percent general power of appointment had not lapsed. Instead, Monty had sufficient control as of his death over both trusts to exercise the 5 percent general power of appointment over the credit shelter trust. Treasury Regulation § 20.2041-1(b)(3) includes in the gross estate only the portion of trust assets over which the decedent could exercise the power; thus, 5 percent of the trust assets are included in Monty's gross estate.

Answer (A) is incorrect. The court in *Estate of Kurz, supra*, cited Treasury Regulation § 20.2041-3(b), which states: "[A] power which by its terms is exercisable only upon the occurrence during the decedent's lifetime of an event or a contingency which did not in fact take place or occur during such time is not a power in existence on the date of the decedent's death." Nevertheless, the court distinguished the condition imposed by this problem from the example of the condition in the regulations where the decedent could not exercise the power until attaining a certain age. In this problem, decedent had control over whether the condition precluded exercise of the 5 percent general power of appointment at death, where in the regulation example the beneficiary had no control over whether she died before attaining a certain age.

Answers (B) and (D) are incorrect. The $5,000 or 5 percent exception only applies to the lapse of certain powers. As noted above, the 5 percent power held by Monty had not lapsed as of Monty's death. Only the lapse of the 5 percent general power of appointment over the credit shelter trust *in prior years* may fall under the protection of the exception. Whether the gross estate includes property subject to the lapse of the general power of appointment depends on the type of interests the beneficiary held in the trust, as discussed below.

88.   **Answer (B) is correct.** Nancy's gross estate includes only the property subject to the general power of appointment held as of the date of her death. On the date of her death, Nancy held the power to appoint to herself up to $5,000. Thus, her gross estate includes $5,000. Although IRC § 2041(a)(2) includes in the gross estate property "with respect to which the decedent has at any time exercised or released [a general] power of appointment by a disposition which is of such nature that if it were a transfer of property owned by the decedent, such property would be includible in the decedent's gross estate under section 2035 to 2038 inclusive," this inclusionary rule does not apply to Nancy. The "5 and 5" exception precludes application of the general rule. IRC § 2041(b)(2) treats the lapse of a power as a release, but only if the lapse "exceeded in value, at the time of such lapse, the greater of" $5,000 or 5 percent of the assets subject to the power at the time of the lapse. Because the trust instrument limited the annual general power of appointment to $5,000, the lapse of Nancy's power during years 1 and 2 fall within the "5 and 5" exception. Thus, Nancy's gross estate does not include any portion of the property over which she could have exercised a power of appointment prior to its lapse. Treas. Reg. § 20.2041-3(d)(3).

Answers (A), (C), and (D) are incorrect for the reasons stated above.

89.   **Answer (C) is correct.** The gross estate includes property subject to a general power of appointment held by decedent at death. IRC § 2041(a)(2). At death, Oscar held a general power of appointment over $10,000 of trust assets because he could pay that sum to himself. Thus, at least $10,000 is includible in Oscar's gross estate. The gross estate also includes property with respect to which decedent (1) exercised or released a power of appointment and (2) following the exercise or release of the power decedent retains an interest in the property such that, had decedent instead owned and transferred the property, it would have been included in decedent's gross estate under IRC §§ 2035 through 2038. IRC § 2041(a)(2); Treas. Reg. § 20.2041-3(d)(1). A lapse of a power is deemed a release to the extent the lapse exceeds the greater of $5,000 or 5 percent of the property subject to the

power as of the date of the lapse. IRC § 2041(b)(2). Thus, Oscar is deemed to release the power of appointment to the extent of $5,000 (i.e., $10,000 withdrawal power less $5,000). [Note that $5,000 is greater than 5 percent of $60,000 or $3,000.] Under the terms of the trust, Oscar continues to receive all income from the $5,000 of property over which Oscar previously released a general power of appointment for each of years 1 through 3. Treasury regulations direct that the portion of trust assets deemed to be retained each year following the release should be aggregated to determine the fraction of trust assets at death subject to inclusion in the gross estate under IRC § 2041(a)(2). Oscar retained $5,000/$60,000 or one-twelfth of the assets each year. Thus, an additional three-twelfths of $60,000, or $15,000, is included in Oscar's gross estate. Treas. Reg. § 20.2041-3(d)(4). The total amount included in Oscar's gross estate equals $25,000 or the $10,000 of assets subject to his general power of appointment at death, plus the aggregate of the proportions of trust property over which Oscar was deemed to release a power but retain a prohibited interest.

Answers (A), (B), and (D) are incorrect for the reasons stated above. Oscar held at death at least a $10,000 general power of appointment so at least some of the trust assets are included in his gross estate. Thus, Answer (A) is incorrect. In addition, the amount of assets deemed released each year for three years is $5,000, and not $7,000 (or the excess of 5 percent) as assumed by Answer (D).

90.   The answer to Question 89 would change because, under the new facts, Oscar did not retain an interest that would have been includible under IRC §§ 2035 through 2038 had he owned and transferred the property. Thus, the release of the power of appointment in excess of $5,000 would not cause inclusion in Oscar's gross estate under IRC § 2041(a)(2). Under the changed facts, only $10,000 of trust assets subject to the withdrawal right held at death would be included in Oscar's gross estate. IRC § 2041(a)(2).

91.   The answer to Question 90 would change because, under the additional facts, Oscar did not retain any general power of appointment at death, and did not retain any prohibited interest on release of the general power of appointment. Treasury regulation § 20.2041-3(b) indicates that if decedent may exercise the power only in the event of a contingency that has not occurred at death, such as attaining a certain age, the decedent does not possess the power at death. Here the contingency is that exercise may only occur in November. Thus, no assets would be includible under Oscar's gross estate under the facts in Question 91. Treas. Reg. § 20.2041-3(d)(3).

92.   **Answer (A) is correct.** Although Peter holds a power to pay property to himself, he holds the power jointly with Quincy, who is the grantor of the trust. IRC § 2041(b)(1)(C)(i) excepts from the definition of general powers of appointment those power exercisable only in conjunction with the grantor of the power. *See also* Treas. Reg. § 20.2041-3(c)(1). Thus, nothing will be included in Peter's gross estate.

Answers (B), (C), and (D) are incorrect. Where the power is held jointly with the grantor none of the trust assets are subject to a general power of appointment.

This rule contrasts with the other exceptions of IRC § 2041(b)(1) that provide in some instances for inclusion of a fractional portion of the trust in the power holder's gross estate.

93.   **Answer (A) is correct.** Where decedent holds a power jointly with another who has a substantial adverse interest in the trust, IRC § 2041(b)(1)(C)(ii) excepts the power from the definition of general power of appointment. Rylan's interest is adverse to Sonja's because, if principal is not paid to Rylan, it passes to Sonja. To the extent one of them receives principal under the exercise of the power (or lack of exercise of the power), the other one of them is left out. The facts specify that Sonja's interest is substantial. Treasury Regulation § 20.2041-3(c)(2) defines "substantial" adverse interest as one where its "value in relation to the total value of the property subject to the power is not insignificant." Value is determined pursuant to valuation principals specified under the IRC § 2031 Treasury Regulations. Based on this analysis, Rylan's interest is substantially adverse to Sonja's, and for that reason Rylan's jointly held power does not fall within the definition of general power of appointment. Therefore, Rylan's gross estate does not include any of the trust assets under IRC § 2041.

        Answers (B), (C), and (D) are incorrect for the reasons stated above.

94.   **Answer (C) is correct.** Tina holds a power jointly with Vicky and Wendy, none of which are the grantor of the trust. Neither Vicky's interest nor Wendy's interest in the trust is substantially adverse to Tina's because Vicky and Wendy may not exercise the power after Tina's death without the consent of Tina's daughter. Thus, Vicky's and Wendy's interests do not fall within the IRC § 2041(b)(1)(C)(ii) provision for an adverse interest where after the death of one of the joint power holders, the surviving power holder may exercise the power in her own favor. Because after application of both exceptions provided under IRC § 2041(b)(1)(C)(i) and (ii), Tina's power is still considered a general power of appointment, we must determine if IRC § 2041(b)(1)(c)(iii) applies to limit the amount of trust assets included in Tina's gross estate. Because Wendy and Vicky, after Tina's death, may continue to jointly exercise the power with Tina's daughter, the amount included in Tina's gross estate is one-third, or the portion that Tina would receive if all three joint holder's exercised the power so as to maximize the portion of trust assets passing to each of their estate. *See also* Treas. Reg. § 20.2041-3(c)(3).

        Answer (A) is incorrect because the power does not fall within any of the exceptions for jointly held powers that result in the power being excepted from the definition of jointly held power.

        Answer (B) is incorrect because the number of joint power holders at any one time is three, and not four. IRC § 2041(b)(1)(C)(iii) provides for division based on "the number of [joint power holders] (including decedent) in favor of whom such power is exercisable." For the same reason, **Answer (D) is incorrect.**

95.   **Answer (D) is correct.** IRC § 2042(1) supplies two rules of inclusion with respect to life insurance proceeds on a decedent's life. The full amount of the insurance proceeds are includible in Alena's gross estate under IRC § 2042(1), which includes proceeds receivable "by the executor." Treasury Regulation § 20.2042-1(a) interprets the Code to include proceeds receivable "by or for the benefit of the estate." For this same reason, **Answer (A) is incorrect** — "estate" falls within the meaning of "executor."

Answers (B) and (C) are also incorrect. It does not matter what, if any, consideration decedent paid for the policy. IRC § 2042 does not take consideration into account. Notably, IRC § 2043 also does not take consideration into account with respect to inclusion of life insurance proceeds under IRC § 2042. The full amount of the proceeds payable to or for the benefit of the estate are includible under IRC § 2042(1). Treas. Reg. § 20.2042-1(a)(3).

96.   The gross estate would still include the full amount of the insurance proceeds in Alena's estate, but would do so under IRC § 2042(2). IRC § 2042(2) provides the second rule of inclusion under IRC § 2042. It includes in the gross estate of decedent proceeds of life insurance on decedent's life paid to persons other than the estate or for its benefit over which decedent held "incidents of ownership" as of his or her death. An owner of a policy, such as Alena, generally holds incidents of ownership of the policy. The theory underlying IRC § 2042(2) is that if decedent holds incidents of ownership, decedent holds sufficient indicia of ownership up until death to require inclusion in the gross estate of the monies passing under the policy.

97.   **Answer (A) would be the correct answer.** IRC § 2042(1) does not apply because trustee was not obligated to pay the estate taxes owed by Alena's estate. Payment of such taxes was entirely within the trustee's discretion, and trustee was not under any legally binding obligation to pay such taxes. If the facts were changed so that the trust required the trustee to pay such taxes, then the answer would change and the "proceeds required for the payment in full (to the extent of the beneficiary's obligation)" would be includible in Alena's gross estate under Treas. Reg. § 20.2042-1(b)(1). In addition, IRC § 2042(2) does not apply because the trustee as owner of the policy held all incidents of ownership from its inception. Thus, **Answer (D) is incorrect.** As before, **Answers (B) and (C) are incorrect** because IRC § 2042 does not focus on the amount of premiums paid to determine inclusion.

98.   **Answer (A) is correct.** IRC § 2042 applies only to life insurance on decedent's life. It does not apply to life insurance owned by decedent on the life of another. For that reason, Bob's gross estate does not include any portion of the value of the policy under IRC § 2042. It may, however, include the value of the life insurance policy under a different Code section. Treas. Reg. § 20.2042-1(a)(2). In this problem, IRC § 2033 will apply to include the fair market value of the policy at the date of death as determined under the IRC § 2031 treasury regulations. Generally that amount is the terminal interpolated reserve value with some exceptions.

Answers (B), (C), and (D) are incorrect for the reasons stated above. Neither the amount paid for premiums nor the face amount of the policy give an accurate measure of the value of life insurance on the life of another. Terminal interpolated reserve value, however, is sometimes used to determine inclusion under IRC § 2033. Terminal interpolated reserve value is calculated by the life insurance policy using Form 712 and provided by the company to the taxpayer on request.

99.   **Answer (C) is the best answer.** Treasury Regulation § 20.2042-1(c)(6) provides that insurance proceeds on the life of a controlling shareholder not payable to or for the benefit of the corporation are includible in the decedent controlling shareholder's gross estate. On the flip side, if life insurance proceeds on the life of a controlling shareholder are payable to or for the benefit of the corporation, the controlling shareholder's gross estate does not directly include the amount of the life insurance proceeds. Instead, the date-of-death value of the corporation takes into account the receipt of the life insurance proceeds, and the controlling decedent's gross estate indirectly increases in value because the value of the corporate stock included in the gross estate correspondingly increases in value. The treasury regulations define "controlling shareholder" as one holding more than 50 percent of the total combined voting power of the corporation. Here, Clara held only 49 percent and, as such, her estate is not required to directly include the value of the insurance proceeds in her estate. Although the regulations provide for certain attribution rules, none of the attribution rules extend to Clara's daughter, and for that reason **Answer (B) is incorrect.** The regulations attribute to the decedent only (i) stock held by decedent's nominee or agent, (ii) a proportionate part of jointly held stock, and (iii) stock held by a grantor trust or a voting trust. Nothing in the regulations suggests that stock of a corporation in which the decedent is a minority owner causes life insurance proceeds payable to persons other than the corporation to be included in the decedent insured's gross estate when the corporation as owner holds all incidents of ownership. Thus, **Answer (C) is the best answer,** and for the same reason, **Answer (A) is an incorrect answer.** Although the date-of-death value of stock under certain circumstances will include the value of life insurance proceeds payable on decedent's death, such as where life insurance proceeds are payable to or for the benefit of the corporation, those are not the facts here. As a result, there is no double inclusion issue, and **for that reason Answer (D) is not the best answer.**

100.   **Answer (A) is the best answer.** The key inquiry under IRC § 2042(2) is whether decedent insured held legally enforceable incidents of ownership in the life insurance policy. The Supreme Court in *Commissioner v. Estate of Noel*, 380 U.S. 678 (1965), held that whether decedent possessed incidents of ownership at death "depends on a general, legal power to exercise ownership, without regard to the

owner's ability to exercise it at a particular moment." In *Noel* the decedent insured purchased flight insurance and handed the policy to his wife, indicating to her that the policy was hers. The decedent insured's plane crashed. The Supreme Court held that the policy proceeds were includible in the decedent's gross estate regardless of the practical inability of decedent to exercise the incidents of ownership. Likewise, in *United States v. Rhode Island Hospital Trust Company*, 355 F.2d 7 (1st Cir. 1966), from which the facts of this problem are derived, the court found that the legal rights to exercise incidents of ownership granted the son under the policy controlled, and not the practical ability of the son to exercise incidents of ownership. While this may not necessarily seem logical, without such a rule, neither father nor son under the facts of the problem would retain incidents of ownership in the policy. In this fashion, taxpayers could avoid taxes by engaging in such secretive behavior. For these same reasons, **Answers (B) and (C) are incorrect. Answer (D) is incorrect** because if proceeds are not payable to decedent's estate and included under IRC § 2042(1), the incidents of ownership test under IRC § 2042(2) may still include proceeds, as is the case here.

101. **Answer (C) is the best answer.** In a situation similar to the facts in this question the Service has ruled that the insurance proceeds avoid inclusion in the decedent insured's gross estate where decedent held incidents of ownership over a policy on his life transferred to the trust by someone other than decedent. Rev. Rul. 84-179, 1984-2 C.B. 195. The Service followed the holding of the court in *Estate of Skifter v. Commissioner*, 468 F.2d 699 (2d Cir. 1972), and declined to follow the contrary holding in *Terriberry v. United States*, 517 F.2d 186 (5th Cir. 1975). The ruling, however, is limited to its narrow facts. If decedent purchases a policy and transfers it to a trust of which decedent is trustee, decedent will be deemed to hold incidents of ownership. The key issue is how decedent became a fiduciary. Under the Service's ruling, Hayden's gross estate avoids inclusion of the life insurance proceeds on Hayden's death. For these same reasons, **Answers (A) and (B) are incorrect. Answer (D) is incorrect** and clearly makes no sense under these facts, as no beneficial interest in the trust sufficient to qualify for the marital deduction passes to Hayden.

102. Ingrid's gross estate includes the value of the policy proceeds because she retains an incident of ownership. Treasury Regulation § 20.2042-1(c)(2) indicates "the term 'incidents of ownership' is not limited in its meaning to ownership of the policy in the technical sense. Generally speaking, the term has reference to the right of the insured or his estate to the economic benefits of the policy. Thus, it includes the power to change the beneficiary, to surrender or cancel the policy, to assign the policy, to revoke an assignment, to pledge the policy for a loan, or to obtain from the insurer a loan against the surrender value of the policy." Here, Ingrid retained the power to cancel the policy. Retention of any incident of ownership is sufficient to cause inclusion.

103. The fact that Ingrid reserved the right to cancel the policy only with her child's consent does not change the fact that Ingrid has retained an incident of ownership. IRC § 2042(2) specifically states that it does not matter whether the incident of

ownership must be exercised "alone or in conjunction with any other person." Thus, jointly held incidents of ownership still cause inclusion in the gross estate of the decedent insured under IRC § 2042(2).

104.   **Answer (D) is correct.** If Jamie had not transferred the life insurance policy, IRC § 2042(2) would have included the policy in her gross estate. Jamie, however, transferred the life insurance policy within three years of her death. Thus, both elements of IRC § 2035(a)(2) are met. and the entire amount of the policy proceeds are included in Jamie's gross estate. **Answers (B) and (C) are incorrect** for the reasons indicated. Note, however, that if someone other than Jamie had paid the premiums, arguably based on *Estate of Silverman v. Commissioner*, 521 F.2d 574 (2d Cir. 1975), only the portion of the policy proceeds attributable to the premiums paid by the decedent insured would be includible in the gross estate. **Answer (A) is incorrect** because a decedent insured must survive for three years from the date of the transfer of a life insurance policy owned by decedent in order to achieve any estate-planning benefit from the transfer. This planning strategy, thus, only works if decedent's lives for more than three years from the date of transfer of the policy. Otherwise, IRC § 2035 steps in to include the policy proceeds in the decedent insured's estate.

105.   **Answer (A) is correct.** IRC § 2042 does not apply because the policy proceeds are not payable to or for the benefit of her estate, and because Mary never held any incidents of ownership with respect to the policy. For the same reason, IRC § 2035 will not apply to include the policy in Mary's gross estate. It applies only if decedent insured initially owned the policy and transferred it within three years of her death. **Answer (D) is incorrect** for this reason.

   Answers (B) and (C) are incorrect. In 1981, Congress amended IRC § 2035 to eliminate any argument that payment of policy premiums by the decedent insured within three years of death would cause inclusion of a portion of the policy proceeds in decedent's gross estate where, as here, the decedent insured never owned the policy. Prior to the 1981 amendment of IRC § 2035, the Fifth Circuit in *Bel v. United States*, 452 F.2d 683 (5th Cir. 1971), held that payment of premiums by decedent constituted a constructive transfer of the policy.

   This question demonstrates that the best way to achieve estate tax savings is to structure the purchase of the life insurance policy so that decedent insured never owns the policy. It is important that the application for insurance indicate the life insurance trust or, if no life insurance trust, the person to be benefited by the policy will be the owner. Note, however, that state law requires the owner to have an insurable interest in the policy.

106.   **Answer (B) is correct.** Generally, community property is deemed owned one-half by each spouse. Treasury Regulation § 20.2042-1(c)(5) provides that incidents of ownership are possessed by decedent insured as "agent" for decedent's spouse. Under the regulation, decedent insured is deemed to hold incidents of ownership to only one-half of the policy. Thus, one-half the proceeds of the life insurance policy are included in Luke's gross estate. Note that the same answer would result if

Luke instead had named his estate as beneficiary of the policy under Treas. Reg. § 20.2042-1(b)(2). **Answers (A) and (D) are incorrect** for the reasons stated. **Answer (C) is incorrect** as it is a red herring.

107. **Answer (D) is correct.** IRC § 2044 includes in the gross estate of the surviving spouse the value of property in which decedent had a qualifying income interest and for which a 2056(b)(7) QTIP election was made. (Note: IRC § 2044 also includes property for which a 2523(f) QTIP election was made for property passing from one spouse to another by gift.) The facts indicate Henry had a qualifying income interest, and also indicate a QTIP election was made. Treasury Regulation § 20.2044-1(d)(1) includes "the value of the entire interest in which the decedent had a qualifying income interest for life, *determined as of the date of the decedent's death. . . .*" (emphasis added.) Thus, Henry's gross estate includes $1 million date-of-death value. For this reason, **Answer (C) is incorrect.** This makes sense because the purpose of the QTIP election is to treat the couple as one unit for tax purposes to ensure that the survivor may benefit from the assets of both spouses during the survivor's life. Thus, the marital deduction allows only a postponement of estate tax until the survivor's death. Although Wilma's gross estate included the assets of the QTIP trust, her estate also received a 100 percent marital deduction, so in effect it paid no estate tax on the QTIP trust assets. Congress ensured that tax would be paid in the survivor's estate by enacting IRC § 2044. Thus, **Answer (A) is incorrect.** In order to ensure taxation of the assets for which a deduction was allowed in Wilma's gross estate, the full value and not the life income interest must be subject to tax in Henry's estate. For this reason, **Answer (B) is incorrect.**

108. **Answer (D) is correct.** IRC § 2207A grants to Henry's estate a right of recovery for the incremental amount of estate tax incurred by his estate due to the inclusion of the QTIP assets. The difference as to whether the right of recovery is based on the incremental additional estate tax caused or the proportionate amount of estate tax caused makes a difference when the estate faces a progressive estate tax rate for the amount subject to tax after application of the unified credit. Technically, however, the correct answer requires recovery based on the incremental increase in tax caused by inclusion of the QTIP assets. For this reason, **Answers (A) and (C) are incorrect.** The right of recovery is against the persons receiving the property from the QTIP trust. Treasury Regulation § 20.2207A-1(d) defines "persons receiving the property" as the trustee of the QTIP trust if property is still held in trust, or any person who has received a trust distribution if property has already been distributed. Thus, **Answer (B) is incorrect.** Note, that to the extent the estate does not exercise its right of recovery, the waiver may be deemed a gift and/or a below-market loan. *See* Treas. Reg. § 2207A-1(b).

109. **Answer (C) is the best answer.** The Tax Court in *Estate of Letts v. Commissioner,* 109 T.C. 290 (1997), imposed a duty of consistency. It held that if a QTIP marital

deduction has been taken in the estate of the first spouse to die, the estate of the survivor must include the QTIP trust assets under IRC § 2044, even though a technical reading of the trust indicated a QTIP election should not have been made. For this reason, **Answer (A) is incorrect.**

Answer (B) is also incorrect. A QTIP election may be deemed null and void upon request of the Service under Revenue Procedure 2001-38, 2001-2 C.B. 24. The Service will declare a QTIP election null and void when the election in the estate of the first spouse to die was not necessary to avoid an estate tax on the death of that spouse. This, however, was not the case under these facts. **Answer (D) is incorrect** as it is a red herring.

110.   **Answer (B) is correct.** IRC § 2010 provides an estate tax credit equal to $1,455,800 for estates of decedents dying in 2009. Essentially, the credit shelters from tax $3.5 million in 2009, also known as the applicable exclusion amount. Note that $3.5 million is the aggregate amount, which after taking into account lifetime and death time taxable wealth transfers made by decedent, a taxpayer may pass free of estate tax. Because Aaron died in 2009, and not 2008, the applicable exclusion amount increased from $2,000,000 to $3,500,000. In addition, the question asks for the answer to be stated in terms of a credit amount, and not the applicable exclusion amount, and for that reason, **Answers (C) and (D) are incorrect.** The $1,000,000 amount reflects the gift tax applicable exclusion amount available under IRC § 2505 in 2009, and for that reason, **Answer (A) is incorrect.**

     Historically, the amount of assets that could be sheltered by the unified credit amount has increased from $175,625 in 1976. In 1981, Congress increased the amount to $600,000, and finally, in 1997, Congress again instituted a series of increases. Prior to 1976, the Code provided for separate gift and estate tax exemptions.

111.   Betty's executor should not reduce the IRC § 2010 unified credit amount. In order to determine federal estate tax owed, the tax is computed based on the aggregate of (i) those assets included in Betty's gross estate, and (ii) the taxable gifts made by Betty after December 31, 1976. IRC § 2001(b)(1). Thus, because taxable gifts are added back into the equation, the full amount of allowable IRC § 2010 unified credit of $1,445,800 may be taken as a credit by Betty's executor. Note that Betty's gross estate may also subtract any gift taxes payable, based on the current rate schedule, so that her estate receives full credit for gift taxes previously paid. IRC § 2001(b)(2). The estate tax is calculated in this manner to ensure that all estates pay tax based on the progressive rate schedule. This was important when taxable estates faced a progressive rate schedule after application of the unified credit amount. Currently taxable estates pay tax at a 45 percent rate.

112.   **Answer (D) is correct.** Callie's gross estate is entitled to a deduction for state estate, inheritance, and succession taxes actually paid when a deduction is claimed within the specified time limits of IRC § 2058. IRC § 2058 allows a deduction for state estate taxes paid for decedent dying after 2004. Callie died in 2008, so her estate qualifies for a deduction. Because Callie's estate paid state estate taxes in the amount of $400,000, she may take a deduction for the full amount. For that reason, **Answer (C) is incorrect.** If Callie had died prior to 2005, her estate would instead have been allowed a state death tax credit, limited in amount by IRC § 2011

to $290,800. Because IRC § 2011 is repealed for estates of decedents dying after 2004, **Answers (A) and (B) are incorrect.** Prior to the repeal of IRC § 2011, many states tied the amount of state estate tax to the amount allowed by the federal government as a state death tax credit against the federal estate tax. These types of state taxes were known as "pick-up" or "soak-up" taxes designed to share federal estate tax revenue with the federal government to the maximum amount allowable, and at the same time avoid any additional tax burden to the estate. Following repeal of IRC § 2011 many states have now enacted state succession and inheritance taxes that result in an additional burden to the estates of their citizens, because at the federal level estates are allowed only a deduction and not a credit.

113. **The correct answer is (B).** The IRC § 2013 tax on prior transfers credit applies to alleviate the heavy tax burden on property passing between two persons who die within a relatively short time of each other. The estate receives a 100 percent credit if the two decedents die within two years of each other. If the initial transferor predeceases the decedent by three to four years, the estate may take 80 percent of the credit; if the transferor predeceases the decedent by five to six years, the estate may take 60 percent of the credit; if by seven to eight years, 40 percent of the credit; and if by nine to 10 years, 20 percent of the credit. If the transferor predeceases decedent by more than 10 years, the estate may not claim an IRC § 2013 credit. Thus, because Dirk died three years prior to Ed, Ed's estate receives a credit equal to 80 percent of the smaller of two limitations: (i) the amount of estate tax paid by Dirk's estate attributable to the property passed to Ed, and (ii) the amount of estate tax paid by Ed's estate attributable to the property received from Dirk. (It should be noted that to arrive at the estate tax attributable to the property passing from transferor to decedent, the Code and Treasury Regulations require certain adjustments for certain deductions taken by the estate and an adjustment for any state death taxes paid. IRC § 2013(c) and (d); Treas. Reg. §§ 20.2013-2, -3, and -4.) Based on these two limitations, the smaller is $400,000, and 80 percent of $400,000 equals $320,000. For these same reasons, **Answers (C) and (D) are incorrect. Answer (A) is incorrect** because it does not matter whether or not the decedent retains or sells the property transferred. The fact that Ed sold and reinvested the stock does not matter. It should also be noted that the term "property" for purposes of IRC § 2013 should be broadly construed and can include an interest in trust and an interest subject to a general power of appointment. IRC § 2013(e); Treas. Reg. § 20.2013-5.

114. Fred's estate will not receive an IRC § 2012 gift tax credit because the gift by Fred was made after 1976. The IRC § 2012 credit applies only to gifts made in 1976 or prior years. After 1976, Congress unified the estate tax and in doing so accounted for gift tax paid in the calculation of estate tax due under IRC § 2001. (If Fred had made the gift prior to 1976, because the gift was included in his gross estate, his estate would have received a credit for gift tax paid limited to the lesser of the amount of gift tax paid, or the proportion of estate tax attributable to the gift as adjusted for certain credits and deductions.) Because the gift was made in 2007, IRC § 2001 subtracts from tentative federal estate tax the amount of gift tax

(which would have been payable if calculated based on current rates) paid on prior taxable gifts made after 1976. IRC § 2001(b)(2). The credit is taken so rarely that the Service has deleted any reference to it on the 2008 Form 706.

115. Fred's estate may receive a credit equal to the lesser of estate tax paid to the foreign country and the proportionate amount of U.S. estate tax paid with respect to the foreign property based on the ratio of the foreign property to the gross estate. IRC § 2014. The credit may be taken only to the extent the property is situated in a foreign country, subjected to tax in that foreign country, and included in the gross estate for federal estate tax purposes. A careful practitioner would begin the analysis by first determining if a treaty between the United States and the foreign country applies. If for any reason the estate recovers the foreign tax, the executor is under a duty to report the recovery to the Service, so that the Service may redetermine estate tax owed the United States. IRC § 2016.

TOPIC 15   ANSWERS
WHAT CONSTITUTES A GIFT?

116. **Answer (D) is correct.** The gift tax is imposed for each calendar year on the transfer of any property by gift during such year by any individual who is either a citizen or a resident of the United States. *See* Treas. Reg. § 25.2501-1(a)(1). The gift tax also applies to the transfer of real and tangible personal property located in the United States at the time of the transfer. IRC § 2511(a); Treas. Reg. § 25.2511-3(a)(1). The citizenship and residency of the donee has no bearing on whether the gift tax applies. Thus, Adam, who is neither a citizen nor a resident of the United States, may gift an item of tangible personal property in his possession located in England to Bernice without U.S. gift tax implications.

> *Note:* It should be noted that Treas. Reg. § 25.0-1(a)(1) provides that some of the provisions of the regulations may be affected by the provisions of an applicable gift tax convention between the United States and other foreign countries. A gift tax convention between the United States and another country may exempt certain transfers by means of a gift from gifts otherwise subject to the gift tax under the Internal Revenue Code. An estate and gift tax convention is in force between the United States and the United Kingdom. Article 6, section (1), of the U.S.–U.K. convention addresses real property and provides real property may only be taxed in the country in which such property is situated. Thus, for example, where the real property is situated in the United States, only the United States may impose gift tax. Convention for the Avoidance of Double Taxation with Respect to Taxes on Estates of Deceased Persons and on Gifts, Oct. 19, 1978, U.S.–U.K, T.I.A.S. No. 9580 at Article 6, section (1). The convention also generally provides that except as to real property and certain types of business property, if the decedent or transferor was domiciled in either the U.S. or the U.K. at the time of the death or transfer, property held by the decedent shall not be taxable in the other State. *See* Article 5, section 1(a). Thus, with respect to tangible personal property, the outcome under the treaty is the same as the outcome under the gift tax code in that a gem held by Adam who is a citizen and resident of the U.K. will not be subject to the U.S. gift tax.

Answer (B) is incorrect. IRC § 2511(a) of the Code provides that, in the case of a nonresident who is not a citizen of the United States, the gift tax shall apply to a transfer only if the property is situated within the United States. A nonresident who is also not a citizen of the United States is generally subject to the gift tax if the property that is the subject of the gift is real estate or tangible personal property and is located in the United States at the time of the gift. § 2511(b), *see also,* Revenue Ruling 56-438, 1956-2 C.B. 604; PLR 8342106. Because the real property here is situated in the state of Wyoming within the United States, it will be subject to U.S. gift tax. As described in the above note regarding international estate and gift tax treaties, real property located in the United States may be taxed only in the country in which such property is situated. Thus, the transfer of the real property here is subject to the U.S. gift tax. **Answers (A) and (C) also are incorrect.** Gift tax is imposed for each calendar year on the transfer of property by gift during such year by any individual residing in the United States. *See* IRC § 2501(a)(1). In Answers (A) and (C), the grantor of the gift is a U.S. citizen and therefore, the gift is subject to tax. Again, it is of no consequence that the gift is made to either a resident or, as is the case in Answer (A), to a nonresident. The rule focuses on the residency of the individual giving the gift and not the residency of the individual receiving the gift.

117. **Answer (D) is correct.** Again, the gift tax applies to a transfer in trust and applies to any transfer of property wherein the donor has parted with dominion and control. Treas. Reg. § 25.2511-2(b). But if the donor of the property transferred (in trust or otherwise) reserves any power over the disposition of the property, the gift may be either wholly or partially incomplete. *Id.* A gift is wholly incomplete in every instance in which the donor reserves the power to revest beneficial title to the property in himself. Treas. Reg. § 25.2511-2(c). During the 10-year period prior to the amendment, no gift of the corpus of the trust was made. Because Grant initially reserved the power to amend or revoke the trust at any time, Grant continued to have dominion and control over the trust assets. Therefore, upon creation of the trust, Grant did not make a gift of the corpus and no income had yet accrued. As income accrued each year, Grant continued to have the ability to change the terms of the trust prior to an annual distribution. However, the relinquishment or termination of a power to change the beneficiaries of transferred property, occurring otherwise than by death of the donor, is regarded as an event that completes the gift and causes the tax to apply. Treas. Reg. § 25.2511-2(f). Upon completing each annual distribution of trust income to Leta, Grant gave up dominion and control of the income, and a taxable gift occurred at the time of each distribution. Similarly, another taxable gift occurred when Grant amended the trust to become irrevocable because Grant relinquished his ability to terminate or amend the trust in any way. At that moment, the trust held only the $1 million corpus. **Answer (B) is incorrect:** Although a gift was made by Grant when he amended the trust to become irrevocable, Answer (B) fails to address each gift of annual income that occurred upon distribution to Leta. As such, Answer (B) is not the best choice. **Answers (A) and (C) are incorrect:** Answer (A) is ruled out as no gift was made upon contribution to the trust because at the time of the contribution, Grant could revoke or amend the trust. *See* Treas. Reg. § 25.2511-2(f). Answer (C) is also incorrect because gifts of annual income and finally a gift of the corpus were in fact completed 10 years later when the trust was amended to become irrevocable.

118. **Answer (C) is correct.** The facts of this problem are similar to the facts in *Commissioner v. Wemyss*, 324 U.S. 303 (1945). Donative intent is not required in determining whether a "gift" was made for gift tax purposes. Treas. Reg.

§ 25.2511-1(g)(1). It is irrelevant whether Bob intended the transfer of the cash to be a fair value exchange for Anne's promise to marry or as a replacement for income lost from Trust Z. Rather, a gift exists where property transferred by a donor exceeds the value in money or money's worth of the consideration given in return. Treas. Reg. § 25.2512-8. Consideration, such as love and affection or a promise of marriage, is not reducible to value in money or money's worth and is disregarded as consideration. Here, the entire amount of the cash transferred by Bob is treated as a gift to Anne for gift tax purposes because promise of marriage or the promise of future love and affection by Anne is not regarded as value in money or money's worth.

> *Note:* It is interesting to distinguish among the definition of a "gift" for gift tax purposes, federal income tax purposes, and a "gift" that results in a non-probate transfer during life for state property law purposes. Whereas a promise to marry is not consideration for gift tax purposes in *Commissioner v. Wemyss*, a promise to marry was determined to be consideration where a suitor offered, among other things, stock in a corporation. *See, e.g., Farid-es-Sultaneh v. Commissioner*, 160 F.2d 812 (2nd Cir. 1947). Although the release of marital rights is not treated as consideration in money or money's worth in administering the estate and gift tax laws, the income tax laws are not construed the same way. *Id.* Further, while donor intent is not a required element for a transfer to qualify as a gift for gift tax purposes, it generally is required in order for a transfer to qualify as a valid inter vivos gift under state property law. For example, in the state of New York, in order to have a valid inter vivos gift, donor intent must exist to make a gift. *See, e.g., Gruen v. Gruen*, 496 N.E.2d 869 (N.Y. 1986).

Answers (A) and (B) are incorrect because each answer concludes that the transfer does not constitute a gift. Specifically, Answer (A) is incorrect because Anne's relinquishment of the right to income from Trust Z is not consideration in money's worth to Bob. Consideration must pass to Bob, the transferor. Bob receives nothing of value in relation to Anne's relinquishment of the right to income from the trust. Answer (B) is incorrect for reasons described above. Again, Anne's promise to marry Bob is not adequate and full consideration in money or money's worth. *See* Treas. Reg. 25.2512-8. **Answer (D) is incorrect**. Answer (D) correctly states the arm's-length standard in that the exchange would have been a gift only to the extent of the difference between the fair market value of Anne's promise to marry Bob and the amount of cash in the account. However, again, the regulations specifically provide that a promise of marriage is wholly disregarded as consideration. Treas. Reg. § 25.2512-8.

119. **Answer (B) is correct.** Application of the gift tax is not confined only to transfers that completely lack consideration. The gift tax also applies to transfers in which property is transferred by the donor for less than adequate consideration. Thus, a gift arises to the extent the value of the property transferred by the donor exceeds the value of money or other property given as consideration by the donee. Treas. Reg. § 25.2512-8. Here, Mom transferred the home, valued at $250,000, to Ally for $200,000. The difference results in a taxable gift of $50,000 from Mom to Ally.

Answers (A) and (C) are incorrect. Answers (A) and (C) are incorrect because partial consideration of $200,000 was paid by Ally to Mom. The regulations clearly allow for a transfer that qualifies as part gift and part sale. Thus, the donee's gift is reduced by the amount of consideration given. In each Answers (A) and (C), Mom is improperly determined to have made a $250,000 taxable gift. **Answer (D) is also incorrect.** For reasons explained above, the transaction cannot be treated strictly as a sale. It is important to note, however, that an exception exists in the regulations for transactions between unrelated parties. The regulations provide that the gift tax does not apply to ordinary business transactions. Treas. Reg. § 25.2511-1(g)(1); § 25.2512-8.

120. Yes, if the parties were unrelated, the answer provided in Question 119, above, would change. A sale or exchange of property in the ordinary course of business is considered under the regulations to be made for adequate consideration. Treas. Reg. § 25.2512-8. Where the parties are truly unrelated, the transaction will be treated as arm's length and free from any donative intent. *See* Id. It is in this fashion that the regulations address the bad business deal. Notwithstanding that the seller was asking $250,000, the seller accepted a counter-offer of $200,000 from the buyer. Seller may well have transferred an asset to buyer that was worth more than the offer he or she accepted. Nevertheless, the seller had no donative intent in consummating the transaction. Therefore, notwithstanding that it may have been a bad business deal, there is no gift in this transaction.

121. **Answer (B) is correct.** The issue being explored here is whether the use of property rent-free qualifies as "property" such that the value of Junior's use of the Manhattan flat qualifies as a taxable gift. IRC § 2501(a)(1) generally provides that the gift tax is imposed for each calendar year on the "transfer of property." In *Dickman v. Commissioner*, 465 U.S. 330 (1984), the Supreme Court addressed the issue of whether the gratuitous transfer of the right to use money is a "transfer of property" within the meaning of § 2501(a)(1). In holding that the right to use money interest-free is a cognizable interest in property and is a "transfer of property" for purposes of imposing the gift tax, the court noted that ". . . a parent who grants to a child the rent-free, indefinite use of commercial property having a reasonable rental value of $8,000 a month has clearly transferred a valuable property right." *Dickman v. Commissioner*, 465 U.S. 330, 336 (1984). Here, Mom has rented her flat out in the past for $10,000 per month ($120,000 per year). As such, the flat is akin to a commercial property and, consistent with the reasoning in *Dickman*, the annual rent-free use of the property by the son should be treated as a gift equal to the $120,000 of the forgone rent. **Answer (D) is incorrect.** Answer (D) takes the position that the rent-free use of Mom's flat is not a gift at all. In *Dickman*, the taxpayers argued that such intra-family gifts should not be treated as taxable gifts as a matter of policy. The Court acknowledged that parents are required to provide their minor offspring with the necessities and conveniences of life. However, the Court cautioned that tax issues arise when parents provide more than the necessities in significant quantities. The Court reasoned that while it is common that parents provide their adult children with such things as the use of cars and vacation cottages, the Court assumed that the focus of the IRS is not on

such traditional family matters and declined to address such issues. *Dickman, supra* at 341. While in theory one could argue that Junior's use of the Manhattan rental property is similar to the temporary use of a vacation condominium, it is unlikely that the Court would agree. Rather, it is more likely that the Court would treat the rent-free use of a Manhattan rental property by Junior, Mom's adult son, as a significant gift of more than the necessities and not a mere familial gift. **Answers (A) and (C) are also incorrect.** Answers (A) and (C) are incorrect because Mom has not made a gift of the Manhattan flat itself. Thus, the $2,000,000 value of the flat would not, where the flat is being leased or rented to Junior, be considered a gift.

122. As alluded to in the answer to Question 121 above, the Supreme Court has specifically held that an interest-free demand loan results in a taxable gift of the reasonable value of the use of the money lent. *Dickman, supra* at 344. Thus, Gary's $100,000 demand loan to Martin will be treated as a gift equal to the reasonable value of the use of the $100,000. Since the Court's opinion in *Dickman*, Congress enacted IRC § 7872, which applies in calculating the amount of the interest treated as a gift. Generally, in the case of any below-market loan that is either a gift or demand loan, the foregone interest must be treated as transferred from lender to borrower and retransferred from borrower to lender as interest. IRC § 7872(a)(1). The deemed transfer of interest is treated as having occurred on the last day of the calendar year. IRC § 7872(a)(2). A "below-market loan" is defined as any loan if, in the case of a demand loan, interest is payable at a rate less than the applicable federal rate (the "AFR") in effect under IRC § 1274(d) for the period compounded semiannually. IRC § 7872(e)(1)(A); 7872(f)(2)(A). Under these rules, because the demand loan from Gary to Martin has stated interest at 9 percent, which is less than the 10.45 percent AFR, it will be classified as a below-market loan. The amount of the forgone interest that will be treated as a taxable gift from Gary to Martin is equal to the excess of (i) the interest due at 10.45 percent (the AFR blended annually), over (ii) the sum of all amounts payable as interest on the loan. IRC § 7872(e)(2); Prop. Reg. § 1.7872-13(a)(1). Thus, the amount of the forgone interest is $1,450, computed as follows:

$10,450 = $100,000 × 10.45%	This calculation represents annual interest calculated on the loan at the AFR.
$1,450 = $10,450 - $9,000	This calculation represents the difference between annual interest of $10,450 as calculated above and the $9,000 (2 × $4,500) interest paid by Martin at 9% percent.

The forgone interest of $1,450 is treated under the holding in *Dickman* and the requirement under IRC § 7872(a)(1)(A) as transferred from Gary to Martin as a taxable gift. *See* Prop. Reg. § 1.7872-13(a)(2)(Example).

123. **Answer (A) is the correct answer.** Among other things, Topic 1 analyzed whether a gift was actually made. In general, the gift tax applies to any transfer of "property" wherein the donor has parted with dominion and control. Treas. Reg. § 25.2511-2(b). There are, however, instances in which an individual does not hold legal title to property but nevertheless may control property to such an extent that gift taxes are imposed when the individual exercises control over the property.

For example, the exercise of a general power of appointment is "deemed a transfer of property" by the individual possessing such power. IRC § 2514(a). A general power of appointment is any power that is exercisable in favor of the individual possessing the power. IRC § 2514(c). A general power of appointment will also exist in favor of the possessor if the power of appointment is exercisable in favor of the possessor's estate, his or her creditors, or the creditors of his or her estate.

Ally has the right to appoint any portion or the entire corpus of a trust created by her father Jim to anyone other than Betty. Except for the restriction with respect to Betty, Ally is free to appoint to anyone. Ally may appoint the trust corpus to herself, her creditors, or her estate. This results in Ally having a general power of appointment over the trust corpus. It is important to note that while Ally has a power that is exercisable, she has not in fact exercised her right. A gift will occur when Ally actually exercises her right to control the trust corpus by directing it to another person. IRC § 2514(c).

Answers (C) and (D) are incorrect. Answer (C) does not result in a general power of appointment. IRC § 2514(c)(3) contains several exceptions that apply to powers of appointment created after October 21, 1942. IRC § 2514(c)(3)(A) provides that if a power is exercisable only in conjunction with the creator of the power, then it is not considered a general power. Note that this makes sense because the creator to an extent continues to retain the right to control the disposition of the property. *See* IRC §§ 2036, 2038.

In Answer (C), Ally can exercise her power only with Jim's consent, and Jim was the creator of the trust. By retaining the power to cancel or reject any exercise of Ally's power over the trust corpus, Jim has retained a degree of control over the trust property. Further, by requiring that Ally first obtain Jim's consent, Jim has not granted Ally a general power of appointment.

The circumstances of Answer (D) also do not result in Ally possessing general power. Under IRC § 2514(c)(3)(B), if Ally's power is exercisable only in conjunction with a person having an adverse interest in the property, the power is not general. In order for this exception to apply in these circumstances, George must have an interest substantially adverse to the exercise of the power in favor of Ally. George's interest is substantially adverse to Ally's interest because George alone has the power to appoint the trust corpus to anyone, including himself, after Ally's death. Id. Here, after Ally's death George has the right to appoint the trust corpus to himself, and he would likely do so. Thus, George's interest is deemed to be substantially adverse to Ally's, and Ally does not hold a general power of appointment over the trust corpus for gift tax purposes.

It is important to note that the Tax Court has indicated a substantial adverse interest does necessarily result where a person is both a coholder of power of appointment and permissible appointee under the power. *See Estate of Towle v. Commissioner*, 54 T.C. 368 (1970); Rev. Rul. 79-63. In order for the interest of a coholder to be substantially adverse, the coholder must become the holder upon a failure to exercise the power. *See Estate of Towle v. Commissioner*, supra, at 372.

Answer (B) is also incorrect. To a certain extent, Answer (B) does result in Ally having a general power of appointment over a portion of the trust corpus. However, under these circumstances Ally does not have a general power over "all" of the trust property. IRC § 2514(c)(3)(C) contains a final exception that applies to powers of appointment created after October 21, 1942. If such circumstances exist, then the possessor will be deemed to have a general power of appointment only over an allocable share of the property determined with reference to the number of joint power holders. *See* Treas. Reg.§ 20.2041-3(c)(3).

In Answer (B), Ally and Cindy jointly have the power to appoint. Ally's power to appoint is not exercisable without the consent of Cindy, who also has the power to appoint the assets to herself, her estate, or her creditors. Under IRC § 2514(c)(3)(C), Ally is deemed to possess a general power of appointment over an allocable share of the property as between her and Cindy. Because Ally and Cindy are the only two joint holders of the power, Ally has a general power of appointment only in respect to one-half of the trust assets.

124.   In general, the answer would not change. With respect to a power of appointment created on or before October 21, 1942, the power was not considered a general power of appointment if it was exercisable only in conjunction with another person. IRC § 2514(c)(2). No distinctions were made as to the specific kind of rights or powers held by the coholder of the power. As discussed in Question 123, above, after October 21, 1942, property is not treated as subject to a general power of appointment if the power was exercisable only in conjunction with another person *and* one of the three exceptions under IRC § 2514(c)(3) were met. Because Answers (B) through (D) each meet one of the exceptions under IRC § 2514(c)(3) and because all include scenarios wherein Ally may only exercise her power in conjunction with another person, no general power of appointment would exist either before or after October 21, 1942.

The question should now arise as to what scenario would result in a difference in pre– versus post–October 21, 1942 rules? A power of appointment created today that restricts the holder's power by requiring that any appointment made by the holder be made in conjunction with another person does not automatically destroy the general nature of the power. Such restrictions are more likely to fall under classification as a general power because the additional limitations under IRC § 2514(c)(3) result in a narrower application of the rules, resulting in fewer instances where classification as a general power can be avoided.

For example, assume that Ally and Lorri are trustees of a trust under which income is to be paid to Lorri for life. Assume further that, as trustees, Ally and Lorri may designate whether corpus of the trust is to be distributed to Ally or to Ally's brother Tyler after Lorri's death. Under these circumstances, Lorri will receive trust income for life, but Lorri is not designated to receive the corpus. Thus, Lorri has no interest in the trust corpus and, therefore, no interest that is adverse to Ally's interest in the corpus. Post–October 21, 1942, because Lorri's interest is not adverse to the exercise of the power in favor of Ally, Ally continues to have a general power of appointment over the trust corpus. *See* Treas. Reg. 25.2514-(3)(b)(example (3)). However, if the trust had been created on or before October 21, 1942, solely because Ally must obtain Lorri's consent prior to making a distribution of corpus, Ally's power over the trust corpus is not treated as a general power of appointment.

125. Answer (D) is the correct answer. The issue explored in this problem is the difference in treatment between the exercise or release of a power of appointment during life versus the a power of appointment that is possessed at death. Generally, property subject to a post-1942 general power is included the holder's estate upon his or her death. IRC § 2041(a)(2). Because Martine can cause the trust assets to be distributed to her estate, her creditors, or the creditors of her estate, she possesses a general power of appointment. IRC §§ 2041(b)(1), 2514(c).

With respect to a general power of appointment created after October, 21, 1942, a release of such power is equivalent to the exercise of the power. IRC § 2514 treats a complete release of a post-1942 general power as a transfer of property for gift tax purposes. Treas. Reg. § 25.2514-1(a). Dimitri created the general power in favor of Martine in 1999, long after 1942. When Martine irrevocably gave up her interest in the trust in July of 2004, she completely released the power that she had over the trust assets. As a result of her release of the power, she will be treated as having gifted all of the trust assets to the three children.

Answer (A) is incorrect. Although Martine never exercised her power of appointment during her lifetime, she continued to possess the power until her death. For purposes of IRC § 2041(a)(2), so long as Martine possessed the power of appointment upon her death, the trust property subject to her general power is included in Martine's estate. Treas. Reg. § 20.2041-3(a). It is irrelevant that she never exercised it. *See* Treas. Reg. § 20.2041-3(b).

Answers (B) and (C) are also incorrect. While a lifetime release of a general power of appointment created in 1999 is equivalent to an actual exercise of the power, if the power is released by means of a testamentary disposition, it is included in the holder's estate as opposed to being treated as a gift. The question of whether the release of the power is gift or testamentary disposition depends on the manner in which the holder released the power of appointment. Property subject to a post-1942 general power of appointment is includible in the estate of the decedent holder of the power if the property would have been includible in the decedent holder's estate under IRC §§ 2035, 2036, 2037, or 2038. *See* Treas. Reg. § 20.2041-3(d).

In Answer (B) Martine amended the trust to provide that her sister Cindy would receive all remaining trust property upon Martine's death. However, Martine retained the right to alter, amend, or revoke the trust. IRC § 2038(a)(1) applies to revocable transfers after June 22, 1936, and generally requires a decedent's gross estate to include the value of all property that the decedent had at any time made a transfer where the enjoyment of the property was subject at the date of the decedent's death to a change via the exercise of a power to amend or revoke the transfer. Martine did transfer the remainder interest in the trust property to her sister Cindy. However, Martine retained the right, as contemplated by IRC § 2038(a)(1), to revoke Cindy's right to enjoy the property. Martine's revocable transfer does not result in a gift. Rather, it is more in the nature of a testamentary transfer whereby the trust property is required to be included in Martine's estate upon her death.

In a similar fashion, IRC § 2036 transfers with retained life estates apply to the facts presented in Answer (C). A decedent must include the value of all property to the extent that he or she transferred the property but retained for life the right to possess or enjoy the income from the property. IRC § 2036(a)(1). Here, Martine did irrevocably amend the trust to provide that her sister Cindy would receive all remaining trust property upon Martine's death. However, because Martine retained the right to receive trust income for the duration of her life, the transfer is testamentary in nature and is not treated as a gift.

126.   **Answer (C) is the correct answer.** The lapse or failure to exercise a general power of appointment or the intentional release of such a power is treated for gift tax purposes as a transfer of property by the individual possessing the power of appointment. IRC § 2514(b). Because Lisa has the power to cause the trust to distribute the accumulated income to her, she has a general power of appointment over the trust income in favor of herself. By choosing not to exercise her power or by failing to exercise her power, Lisa has allowed the power to lapse. By allowing the power to lapse, Lisa is deemed to have transferred her interest in the property, and a gift has occurred. Even though Lisa did not actually direct where the accrued trust income will go, Lisa's failure to exercise the power effectively resulted in a transfer to Randall. The deemed transfer is treated as a gift from Lisa to Randall for gift tax purposes. *See* Treas. Regs. §§ 25.2514-3(c)(4), 25.2514-3(e)(example 2). Treating the lapse as a gift for gift tax purposes makes sense in that Lisa effectively was in a better economic position prior to the release as compared to after the release.

Answer (D) is incorrect. A power to consume, invade, or appropriate income or corpus, or both, for the benefit of the possessor that is limited by an ascertainable standard relating to health, education, maintenance, or support is a non-general power of appointment. IRC § 2514(c)(1). The exercise or release of a non-general power of appointment generally is not treated as a taxable gift. *See* Treas. Reg.

§ 25.2514-3(e)(example 2). Here, Lisa has a non-general power of appointment because her ability to request a distribution is limited to an ascertainable standard. The fact that she allows the 10 years to expire without requesting a distribution does not result in a gift. The distinction between Answer (C), the correct answer, and Answer (D) is that in Answer (C) Lisa had a general power of appointment that allowed her to take for herself without any limitation. In Answer (D), Lisa is limited in her ability to control the trust property. By limiting her ability to request a distribution, the trust property here passes in full to Randall without any action or control on the part of Lisa.

It is important to note, however, that under these circumstances the release of a non-general power of appointment is not treated as a taxable gift. There are some instances in which a special power of appointment may be exercised or released and treated as a gift for gift tax purposes. *See* Treas. Reg. § 25.2514-3(e)(example 4).

Answers (A) and (B) are incorrect. Answer (A) does not result in a gift from Lisa to Randall, as Lisa retains all of her rights in the income. Answer (B) also does not result in a gift. By failing to exercise his right to appoint trust principal to Lisa, Randall has merely allowed Lisa to retain her annual income interest in the trust. Randall's power here is only a right to dispose of his remainder interest., a right that he will continue to possess regardless of the expiration of the 10-year period. *See* Treas. Reg. § 25.2514-3(e)(example 4).

127. The facts in this problem are similar to the facts in *Estate of Regester v. Commissioner*, 86 TC 1 (1984), wherein the Court held that the exercise of a non-general or special power of appointment in relation to the corpus of a trust resulted in a taxable gift of the power holder's lifetime income interest in the trust. As previously discussed, IRC § 2514 governs the imposition of the gift tax on the exercise, release, or lapse of powers of appointment. In general, a power that can be exercised for the benefit of the holder of the power is a general power of appointment. However, if an individual cannot exercise a power of appointment in his or her favor, it is a non-general power or "special" power of appointment.

Under circumstances such as those presented in this problem, an indirect gift may arise where a special power of appointment is exercised. For example, if a person has the right to trust income for life and the ability to transfer the right to the income to any other person, such a transfer results in a taxable gift. If Lisa had transferred her right to trust income during her life to another, there would have been a taxable gift. The issue arises in the context of this problem in that while Lisa does not directly transfer her income interest in the trust, her exercise of the special power over the corpus of the trust results in Taylor receiving all future income. As stated by the Court in *Regester*, "because the income from the corpus follows the corpus, the method used to transfer the income interest was to 'piggyback' it onto the property that was transferred under the [special] power of appointment." *Estate of Regester v. Commissioner*, 86 TC 1, 16 (1984). Thus, when Lisa exercises her power to specially appoint the corpus of the trust to Taylor, Lisa's right to the income interest in the corpus is also "piggybacked" or transferred to Taylor. It is the transfer of the value of the income interest by Lisa that results in a taxable gift to Taylor.

128. **Answer (C) is correct.** In general, "taxable gifts" include the total amount of gifts made during the calendar year less any deductions. IRC § 2503(a). However, the first $10,000 of present-interest gifts made by a donor to a donee during any calendar year after 1982 is excluded in determining the total amount of taxable gifts for the calendar year. IRC § 2503(b)(1). The exclusion provided applies on a per donee, per year basis. There is no limit to the number of persons that may receive an excludible gift in one calendar year from a particular donor. For example, in 1985 a donor could give $10,000 ($1 million total) each to 100 different individuals and no gift tax would be due in 1985 in relation to the transfers.

> *Note:* In the case of gifts made after 1998, the maximum amount of the exclusion is increased by a cost-of-living adjustment from time to time. *See* IRC § 2503(b)(2). Thus, for gifts made during the calendar year 2007, the first $12,000 of gifts to any person (other than gifts of future interests in property) are not included in the total amount of taxable gifts made during that calendar year.

Assuming no changes in the law and that the cost-of-living adjustment will either remain the same or increase in the annual exclusion amount in future years, IQ's plan to give each of his four children $12,000 every year for the next 40 years will result in $1,920,000 of excluded transfers for gift tax purposes. Because each annual gift of $12,000 to each of his four children ($48,000 total per year) is equal to the annual exclusion amount, none of the gifts are "taxable gifts." Under Answer C, most of the $2,000,000 of excess cash in IQ's bank account can be transferred to IQ's children free of any transfer taxes. The annual exclusion will apply in each succeeding year.

Answers (A) and (B) are incorrect. While Answers (A) and (B) each succeed in gifting the full $2,000,000, each plan proposes to gift substantial amounts annually in excess of the exclusion provided by IRC § 2503(b). The amount of the gift that exceeds the annual exclusion allowed is treated as a "taxable gift." Because IQ has used up his lifetime gift tax credit and has no allowable deductions, IQ will be liable for gift taxes calculated at the rates provided in IRC § 2001(c). *See* IRC § 2502(a). Answer (A) results in the highest current tax liability in that only $10,000 of each $500,000 gift will be excluded. The remaining $490,000 (a total of $1,960,000) of each gift currently will be subject to tax at the marginal rates provided in § 2001(c).

Answer (D) is also incorrect. By bequeathing the whole $2,000,000 all at death, IQ has failed to take advantage of benefits provided by the gift tax annual exclusion. As compared with Answer (C), IQ has lost his ability to take advantage of the annual per- person gift tax exclusion. Instead, the estate tax will apply to the whole transfer. Assuming that the $2,000,000 will appreciate at a rate in excess of the inflation rate over the next 40 years, it is likely that a substantially larger amount of taxes will be due at IQ's death.

129. **Answer (A) is correct.** The annual exclusion from gross gifts provided by IRC § 2503(b) applies only to present-interest gifts. IRC § 2503(b)(1). A transfer (or portion thereof) that constitutes a future interest may not be excluded in determining the total amount of taxable gifts made during a calendar period. A "future interest" includes, for example, reversions, remainders, and other interests that may be used, possessed, or enjoyed only by the recipient at some future point in time. Treas. Reg. § 25.2503-3(a). Under Answer (A), each of the four children has an equal right to the trust principal when the youngest of the children reaches the age of 35. Because the children cannot enjoy their interest in the trust principal until a later date, the annual exclusion will not apply to the children's future interest in the principal. The present value of the children's remainder interest in the principal will be treated as a taxable gift in the current year.

On the other hand, an unrestricted right to immediate possession or enjoyment of property or income from the property is treated as a present interest to which the annual exclusion applies. Treas. Reg. § 25.2503-3(b). For example, the value of an interest in a life estate or an interest in property for a term certain qualifies as an excludible present interest. Here the trustee is required to distribute all net income equally to each of the four children on an annual basis until the youngest reaches the age of 35. The mandatory payment of net income allows each of the children to benefit immediately from the property for a period of years. Because each of the four children immediately benefits from mandatory distributions of income, the value of the children's interests are excludible present interests. An annual exclusion is allowable, but the amount of the exclusion is limited to the value of the term interest. At this point, it is sufficient to conclude that each term of years has some positive value that is less than $10,000. To the extent the value of the present interests are each less than the annual exclusion, their value is completely excluded under IRC § 2503(b).

Answers (B) and (D) are incorrect. Unlike Answer (A), the trustee in Answers (B) and (D) is not required to distribute income on an annual basis equally to the four children. While in Answer (B) the trustee is required to distribute the income, the trustee may distribute in her discretion as she deems advisable. The result is that the trustee may choose not to distribute to any one particular child, and the amount of income any one of the four beneficiaries will receive remains wholly within the trustee's discretion. Such an interest is a future interest and its value cannot readily or presently be ascertained. *See* Treas. Reg. § 25.2503-3(c). Similarly, in Answer (D), the trustee has the right to make discretionary distributions but is limited to distributing income and principal only for purposes of maintenance, health, or support during their lives as necessary. Again, under this distribution provision, there is no guaranty that any of the beneficiaries will receive any income in a given year and the interest fails to qualify as a present interest. With respect to Answer (B), the remainder to IQ's brother upon IQ's death is a future interest. Similarly, in Answer (D) the remainder equally to the 12 children when the youngest of the children reaches 35 years of age is also a future interest. Neither future interest qualifies for the annual exclusion.

Answer (C) is incorrect. Answer (C) completely fails as a present interest for the same reason the remainder interests fail in Answers (B) and (D). Even though the result in Answer (C) is to execute a larger number of $10,000 transfers among the 12 children, all of the income and principal are retained until the youngest reaches age 35. Therefore, none of the 12 transfers in Answer (C) qualifies as present interest, and none of the transfers is subject to the annual exclusion.

130. Yes, under these new circumstances **Answer (C) would become the best answer**. Now, there is an unrestricted right to immediate possession or enjoyment of annual income from the property. This makes the value of the annual income interest a present interest to which the annual exclusion applies. The payment of net income allows each of the children to benefit immediately from the property for a specific term of years. In Answer (C), IQ is providing for his eight nieces and nephews and his four children, and the annual contribution of $120,000 qualifies for 12 annual exclusions. Again, it is sufficient to conclude that each of the 12 income interests has a positive value that is less than $10,000. Answers (A) and (B) anticipate contributions of only $40,000 annually ($10,000 annually for each of IQ's four children). Thus, Answers (A) and (B) result in only four annual exclusion gifts. Answer (D) continues to fail to qualify for annual exclusion because there is no present interest in relation to the gifts in Answer (D).

131. **Answer (A) is the correct answer.** The question asks which of the alternative answers will best effectuate IQ's tandem goals of maximizing the annual exclusion while at the same time limiting or preventing the children from accessing trust income and principal prior to reaching the age of 40. By its terms, the trust provisions in Answer (A) limit access of the beneficiaries in accordance with IQ's wishes by requiring trustee to make distributions of net income and principal under a restrictive ascertainable standard (e.g., maintenance, education, support, or health). Consistent with IQ's wishes, the trustee may distribute the remaining income and principal only when the beneficiary attains the age of 40. However, it must be acknowledged that the children under Answer (A) each have the ability to withdraw amounts contributed within the 15-day notice period. As discussed more fully below, it is unlikely that such withdrawals will occur.

An important issue in this problem is whether the full amount of the $120,000 contribution to the trust qualifies as present interest gifts for purposes of the annual exclusion as allowed under IRC § 2503(b). The Tax Court addressed this issue under similar facts in the *Estate of Cristofani v. Commissioner*, 97 T.C. 74 (1991). In *Cristofani*, taxpayer decedent had two adult children and five minor grandchildren. Taxpayer's estate argued that the right of the decedent's grandchildren to withdraw an amount equal to the annual exclusion within a 15-day period after contribution constitutes a present-interest gift in property qualifying for the full amount of the annual exclusion. The Commissioner argued that the annual exclusions should be disallowed on the grounds that the gifts to the minors were not gifts of present interests in property. Specifically, the Commissioner disallowed the annual exclusions for the minor beneficiaries on the ground that the minors' powers alone, without any likelihood that the minors would actually receive property from the trust if the powers of withdrawal remained unexercised, were not gifts of present interests in property.

In holding that the minor grandchildren's right to withdraw represents a present interest for purposes of IRC § 2503(b), the Tax Court relied heavily on the holding *Crummey v. Commissioner*, T.C. Memo. 1966-144, aff'd in part and rev'd in part, 397 F.2d 82 (9th Cir. 1968). In *Crummey*, the Ninth Circuit Court of Appeals focused on the legal right of the minor beneficiaries to demand payment from the trustee. The Ninth Circuit indicated that the only requirement to find a present interest is that the trustee could not legally have resisted the minor beneficiary's demand for payment from the trustee. The Court rejected a test based upon the likelihood that an actual demand would be made. Thus, the ability of an individual to demand an amount equal to the annual exclusion from the trustee results in an unrestricted right to the immediate possession or enjoyment of property or the income from property is a present interest in property. Under the provisions of the trust in Answer (A), IQ contributes $10,000 per year per donee and he will be allowed to exclude all contributions (total of $120,000) from gross gifts under IRC § 2503(b).

Answer (B) is incorrect. Answer (B) is incorrect because the trustee has the power to deny a beneficiary's request for annual withdrawal. By authorizing the trustee to deny a request for withdrawal, the beneficiaries have lost their legal right to elect to presently enjoy and possess the contributed property as required by the reasoning of both courts in *Crummey* and *Cristofani*. The inability to presently possess the contributed property causes the contribution to be treated as a future interest not qualified for the annual exclusion.

Answers (C) and (D) are also incorrect. IRC § 2503(c) generally provides that all or any part of a transfer for the benefit of a minor under the age of 21 will be considered a gift of a present interest if three conditions are met. First, both the property and income from the property may be expended by or for the benefit of the donee before he or she reaches 21 years of age. Treas. Reg. § 25.2503-4(a). Second, any remaining portion of the property and its income not disposed under the first condition must pass to the donee when he or she reaches 21 years of age. Id. Finally, if a donee dies prior to reaching 21 years of age, any portion of the property and its income not disposed under the first condition must be payable either to the donee's estate or as the donee appointed under a general power of appointment. Id. Where a trust contains provisions that satisfy each of the three conditions, contributions to the trust qualify for annual exclusion. Moreover, the three conditions will remain satisfied even though a trustee is given discretion in determining the amount and purpose for which trust expenditures are to be made. Treas. Reg. § 25.2503-4(b)(1).

The trust provisions in Answers (C) and (D) each satisfy the three requirements qualifying contributions to the trusts for the annual exclusion. Further, the trust provisions in Answers (C) and (D) providing that the trustee may distribute net income and principal to the beneficiary for maintenance, education, health, or support during the life of the beneficiary will not prevent the annual contributions from satisfying the three IRC§ 2503(c) conditions. *See, e.g.,* Rev. Rul. 67-270, 1967-2 CB 349. However, with respect to Answer (C), the trust provisions require the trustee to distribute trust principal and accrued income when the beneficiary attains 21 years of age. Similarly, in Answer (D), the trust beneficiary may elect to receive any and all trust income and principal upon attaining the age of 21. Both of these provisions are designed to satisfy the requirement that all the trust property including any remaining income must pass to the donee when he or she attains the age of 21. But neither provision satisfies IQ's preference that his children, nieces, and nephews not receive any of the trust corpus until they reach the age of 40.

132.   The Ninth Circuit's holding in *Crummey* and the Tax Court's holding in *Cristofani* authorize an annual exclusion where the minor beneficiaries have a legal right to demand a trust distribution. Indeed, the legal right may be exercised by one or more of the children, and the children may take possession of the amount of the contribution. IQ should be advised that there is no way to stop the child from exercising his or her right. Of course, IQ is not obligated to make a contribution to the trust in the future. However, it is important to note that the court in *Cristofani* determined under similar facts that there was no agreement or understanding between decedent, the trustees, and the beneficiaries that the grandchildren would not exercise their right of withdrawal following a contribution to the trust. IQ should be warned that he cannot have a separate understanding in which his children are not allowed to exercise their right of withdrawal. Such an understanding would prevent the contribution from being a present interest qualified for the annual exclusion.

However, in the absence of any agreement, if one or more of the children exercise their right of withdrawal, IQ is not prevented from deciding that he will not make any more contributions to the trust. In the event that the beneficiaries continue to exercise their right to withdraw during the 15-day period, IQ may wish to consider a, IRC § 2503(c) trust for a minor. In general, as explained in Question 131 above, a trustee distributing net income and principal to the minor beneficiary for maintenance, education, health, or support during the life of the beneficiary will not prevent the annual contributions from satisfying the three IRC § 2503(c) conditions. Thus, there can be trustee oversight and management, and an outright gift need not be made in order to qualify the gift as a present interest.

133.   **Answer (A) is the correct answer.** For purposes of the gift tax, any contribution to a qualified tuition program on behalf of an individual is treated as a completed present-interest gift. IRC § 529(c)(2). In general, a "qualified tuition program" includes any state program under which a person may purchase credits that entitle the beneficiary to waive payment of qualified higher education expenses. *See* IRC § 529(b). Such expenses include tuition, fees, books, supplies, and equipment required to attend or enroll in an eligible education institution. IRC § 529(e)(3). With certain restrictions, costs in relation to room and board are also included as qualified expenses. *See* IRC § 529(e)(3)(B). Virtually every state college or

university is an eligible education institution. *See* IRC § 529(e)(5).

In Answer (A), with respect to the $50,000 contributed by IQ this year to the 12 separate IRC § 529–qualified tuition programs, no gift tax is due. As here, if the aggregate contribution made by IQ exceeds the annual gift exclusion amount for the year, IQ may make an election to treat the gift as being made ratably of the succeeding five-year period. Thus, given the proper election, IQ is allowed to make a $50,000 contribution to each of the 12 qualified tuition programs and, for gift tax purposes, it will be treated as if IQ had made $10,000 annual contributions to each of the tuition programs for each of the next five years. While no specific limitation is placed upon the amount of the contribution, the Code disqualifies a tuition program unless it implements safeguards against contributions in excess of the amount necessary to cover beneficiary's qualified higher education expenses. IRC § 529(c)(2)(B). Further, by making a gift of $50,000 in the first year ($600,000 total), IQ will avoid inclusion of any appreciation on that amount that would have occurred during the five years in his estate. From an income tax perspective, IQ may also avoid paying income tax on any of the investment income that may result from holding the excess funds.

Answers (B) and (C) are incorrect. Answer (B) is very close to Answer (C). Because IQ will have used his annual exclusion amounts with respect to gifts made to the 529 plans, any gifts to the *Crummey* trusts will be subject to gift tax.

Answer (D) is also incorrect. Answer (D) fails to take advantage of IQ's ability to make $600,000 of gifts in year 1 and, thus, avoid tax on any appreciation that would have been associated with the additional amount of gift in Answer (A).

134.   **Answer (B) is the correct answer.** Any amount of tuition *paid to an educational organization* "on behalf of an individual" is excluded from treatment as a gift. IRC § 2503(e). Under the rule, the payment must be made to an educational organization that maintains a regular faculty and curriculum and normally has a regularly enrolled student body in a particular place. Treas. Reg. § 25.2503-6(b). The amount of the exclusion for tuition expenses is unlimited. Answer (B) is correct because it is the only answer wherein IQ makes a direct payment to Harvard.

Answers (A), (C), and (D) are incorrect. Contribution to a trust, as proposed in Answers (A) and (C), that contains provisions requiring the use of the funds for tuition results in a completed gift for federal gift tax purposes. Treas. Reg. § 25.2503-6(c)(example 2). The same result occurs where the payment is directly to the student as is the case in Answer (D). The transfer must be a direct transfer to the educational organization. IQ's failure to pay Harvard directly disqualifies the transfer from the unlimited exclusion from gross gifts. In each of these answers, since IQ otherwise uses his full annual exclusion from year to year, the full amount of the transfer will result in a taxable gift for which IQ must file a gift tax return and pay gift tax.

Answer (A) results in the worst gift tax outcome because IQ appears to be attempting to exclude the $16,000 for room and board in addition to the $34,000 transferred to the trust for tuition. There is no unlimited exclusion available for amounts paid for books, supplies, dormitory fees, board, or other similar expenses that are not direct tuition costs. Answer (A) results in a $50,000 taxable gift to each child.

135.   First, one should indicate to Paul that any amount that he pays directly to a medical care provider who treats Paul would qualify for exclusion from gross gifts under IRC § 2503(e). IQ is free to assist Paul with his medical expenses in an unlimited amount. However, in order to exclude any amount, Paul must pay the medical provider directly in order to qualify for the unlimited exclusion. One should also apprise IQ that the $50,000 check that he made out to Paul (instead of directly to his medical provider) earlier in the year would not qualify for the unlimited exclusion for medical expenses. If IQ has made no other gifts to Paul during the year, then IQ may take advantage of the IRC § 2503(b) annual exclusion in relation to a portion of the $50,000 earlier transfer to Paul.

136. **Answer (A) is the correct answer.** Gift tax is imposed on the transfer of any property by gift during such year by any individual who is either a citizen or a resident of the United States. *See* Treas. Reg. § 25.2501(a)(1). The gift tax will apply to gifts of cash made by David, who is a citizen of the United States, to his children. However, Antonia is neither a citizen nor a resident. Therefore, in general, the gift tax will not apply to gifts made by Antonia to the children. The issue then becomes whether a gift made by David and Antonia can qualify for split gift treatment under IRC § 2513. Under IRC § 2513, a gift made by one spouse to any person other than his spouse is considered to be made one-half by him and one-half by his spouse. However, the general rule is only applicable if at the time of the gift each spouse is either a citizen or a resident of the United States. If either spouse was a nonresident and not a citizen of the United States during any portion of the year, the consent is not effective. Treas. Reg. § 25.2513-1(b)(2). Antonia is neither a citizen nor a resident of the United States, and this prevents the couple from making a valid consent to split gifts. Lack of valid consent by both spouses results in the failure to qualify for split-gifts treatment and results in David making 10 separate $100,000 gifts (a total of $1,000,000) to his children.

Answers (B), (C), and (D) are each incorrect. Answer (B) is incorrect because it underreports the amount of gifts required to be reported by David. Further, Answer (B) treats Antonia as having to report one-half of David's gifts to the children as taxable gifts made by her. As explained above, Antonia's consent is ineffective. Answers (C) and (D) are incorrect because each choice under-reports the amount of gifts being made by David.

137. **Answer (B) is the correct answer.** Antonia is now a resident of the United States. IRC § 2513(a) requires that at the time of the gift, each spouse must be either a citizen or a resident. Antonia's residency in the United States allows her to join the consent required by IRC § 2513(a)(2) to allow the gift made by David to be considered as made one-half by him and one-half by Antonia. Each of the 10 gifts of $100,000 will be treated as two gifts of $50,000 to each child made by David and Antonia.

Answers (A), (C), and (D) are each incorrect. Answer (A) does not acknowledge the application of IRC § 2513(a), which specifically allows for split gifts under the circumstances. Answers (C) and (D) are incorrect because each choice underreports the gifts made by both David and Antonia for reasons described above.

138. **Answer (B) is the correct answer.** Again, both David and Antonia reside in the

United States, so they meet the residency requirements. However, the question that appears to arise here is whether the failure to file a second consent upon making the gifts in December disqualifies the gifts from attracting split-gift treatment. It does not. A gift made by one spouse is considered as made one-half by him and one-half by his spouse only if both spouses have signified their consent to splitting all gifts made by either during the calendar year while married to each other. IRC § 2513(a). The regulations further provide that the election to split gifts will apply to gifts made during a "particular calendar period." Thus, only one election is required per year, and it applies to all gifts made.

Because both David and Antonia appropriately consented to split gifts in the manner prescribed by Treas. Reg. § 25.2513 in relation to the January gifts, the 10 December gifts of $100,000 are each considered to be split gifts made one-half ($50,000) by David and one-half ($50,000) by Antonia. In addition, the 10 gifts made in January attract the same split-gift treatment. Thus, a total of $2,000,000 of gifts were made by the couple in 2006, which resulted in a total of $1,000,000 of gifts made by David and $1,000,000 of gifts made by Antonia.

Answers (A), (C), and (D) are incorrect. Answer (A) is incorrect in that it attributes all the gifts to David and no gifts to Antonia. Answer (C) incorrectly contemplates that a consent must be filed for each gift. However, as explained above, once a valid election is made, it applies to all gifts made during the calendar year. Answer (D) is wrong because it simply ignores any of the gifts regardless of whether they were split.

139.   **Answer (B) is the correct answer.** A gift made by one spouse to a person other than his spouse generally is treated as a split gift. Such gift splitting is only allowed between "spouses." The statute clarifies the use of the term "spouse" by providing that "an individual shall be considered as the spouse of another individual only if he is married to such individual at the time of the gift and does not remarry during the remainder of the calendar year." IRC § 2513(a)(1). For the purpose of Treasury Regulation § 25.2513-1(a), two people are considered to be married if they have not actually divorced at the time of the gift and do not remarry during the remainder of the year. *See* TAM 6407139610A (July 13, 1964). If the consenting spouses were not married to each other during a portion of the calendar year, the consent is not effective with respect to any gifts made during that portion of the year. Treas. Reg. § 25.2513-1(b)(1).

Under the rule, David and Antonia are allowed to treat the 10 January gifts of $100,000 as made one-half ($50,000) by David and one-half ($50,000) by Antonia. Thus, David and Antonia are each treated as having made $500,000 of gifts in January. However, because David and Antonia were not married in December when the second gifts of $100,000 were made by David to each of the 10 children, the couple may not treat the December gifts as split gifts. David will be treated as having made the full $1,000,000 (10 times $100,000) of gifts in December, and David will have made a total of $1,500,000 ($500,000 in January plus $1,000,000 in December) of gifts in 2006. Antonia will be treated as having made only $500,000 of gifts (10 times $50,000) in January of 2006.

Answers (A), (C), and (D) are incorrect. Answer (A) is incorrect because it fails to accord split-gift treatment to the January gift wherein David and Antonia were married. Answers (C) and (D) are incorrect for similar reasons in that Antonia is not attributed any gifts in 2006.

140. **Answer (B) is the correct answer.** As discussed in Question 138, the couple each has appropriately consented to splitting gifts and, therefore, each gift to each child is split. In addition, however, the fact pattern now reflects the availability of both annual exclusions and an unused gift tax applicable exclusion amount for David and Antonia. The question seeks for the student to determine the amount of "taxable gifts" made by David and Antonia. The term "taxable gifts" means the total amount of gifts made during the taxable year less certain deductions that are not relevant here. IRC § 2503(a). With respect to gifts made to any person by the donor during the calendar year, the first $12,000 of the gift to such person is excluded from the total amount of gifts made during the year. IRC § 2503(b). Stated otherwise, David and Antonia each may exclude $12,000 from the total amount of gifts in relation to each child. This results in each of the 10 children receiving a gift of $88,000 from each spouse. The $88,000 can be arrived at by adding two gifts of $50,000 made by each parent to each child less $12,000 (one annual exclusion per child for the 2006 tax year) for a total of $88,000 ($50,000 plus $50,000 less $12,000) from each parent. Therefore, David and Antonia each made taxable gifts of $880,000 in 2006 (10 × $88,000).

Answer (D) is incorrect: Answer (D) takes the position that there are not taxable gifts made by either Antonia or David in the 2006 tax year. The availability (or not) of the $1,000,000 gift tax applicable exclusion amount is not relevant to the determination of the amount of "taxable gifts" pursuant to IRC § 2503. While it is true that the applicable exclusion amount may translate into a credit that may fully offset an ultimate gift tax liability and that David and Antonia may not be liable for any gift tax in 2006, they must still file a gift tax return in which they report their respective gifts made to their children. It would, however, be incorrect to say that they made "no taxable gifts" in 2006.

Answers (A) and (C) are also incorrect. Answer (A) is incorrect because it does not take the IRC § 2503(b) annual exclusion into account for either David or Antonia. Conversely, Answer (C) doubles up on the annual exclusion, which results each of them underreporting taxable gifts.

141. **Answers:**

(a) The purpose of this problem is to explore the gift tax benefits of the use of each spouse's $1,000,000 gift tax exclusion and annual exclusions. David and Antonia, having made no gifts prior to 2006, each have $1,000,000 of gift tax exclusion available. Also, as previously explained, David and Antonia are each allowed to gift $12,000 per person per year, which will be excluded under IRC § 2503(b). Each spouse is allowed to exclude $120,000, representing 10 annual exclusions of $12,000 per child in 2006.

The calculation is as follows:

	David	Antonia	Total
Gross split gifts for the current year:			
January 2006 $1,000,000 (10 gifts at $100,000 per child)	$500,000	$500,000	$1,000,000
December 2006 $2,000,000 (10 gifts at $200,000 per child):	1,000,000	1,000,000	2,000,000
Equals: Total gifts before annual exclusions:	1,500,000	1,500,000	3,000,000
Less: 10 IRC § 2503(b) annual exclusions per spouse:	(120,000)	(120,000)	(240,000)
Equals: Total taxable gifts for 2006:	1,380,000	1,380,000	2,760,000
Tentative tax on aggregate taxable gifts at § 2001(c) rates:	504,200	504,200	1,008,400
Less: Applicable Gift Tax Credit:	(345,800)	(345,800)	(691,600)
Equals: Gift tax for current year:	158,400	158,400	316,800

As reflected in the above calculation, David may transfer a total of $3,000,000 in 2006, which results in a total gift tax liability for 2006 of $316,800. Although most of the above calculation is self-explanatory, it should be noted that the tentative tax of $504,200 per spouse on aggregate taxable gifts of $1,380,000 per spouse was arrived at using the graduated rates provided in IRC § 2001(c)(1). As directed by the table rates, the first $1,250,000 results in a tentative tax of $448,300, and the remaining $130,000 ($1,380,000 - $1,250,000) is taxed at 43 percent resulting in additional tentative tax of $55,900. Adding the $448,300 and the $55,900 produces the aggregate tax on taxable gifts of 504,200. This amount of tax is reduced dollar for dollar by the $345,000 gift tax credit. For detailed discussion of how the rates work, see Topic 1 under the Estate Tax section of the materials.

The splitting of gifts equally between David and Antonia has therefore resulted in both David and Antonia utilizing each of their $1,000,000 gift tax exemption equivalents and $12,000 annual per child exclusions. Finally, it is important to note that under IRC § 2513(d), because the couple filed consents to split gifts in 2006, they are jointly and severally liable to pay the $316,800 gift tax due.

(b) Unlike the circumstances in Question (a) above, no consents were filed and, therefore, no gift splitting is allowed. Now, David is treated as having gifted the full $3,000,000 to the 10 children ($300,000 each), and Antonia is not treated as having made any gifts in 2006.

The calculation of gift tax liability is as follows:

Gross gifts for the current year:	
January 2006 $1,000,000 (10 gifts at $100,000 per child)	$1,000,000
December 2006 $2,000,000 (10 gifts at $200,000 per child):	2,000,000
Equals: Total gifts before annual exclusions:	3,000,000
Less: 10 IRC § 2503(b) annual exclusions per spouse:	(120,000)
Equals: Total taxable gifts for 2006:	2,880,000
Tentative tax on aggregate taxable gifts at § 2001(c) rates:	1,185,600
Less: Applicable Gift Tax Credit:	(345,800)
Equals: Gift tax for current year:	831,000

Again, in the above calculation, the graduated rates provided under IRC § 2001(c) were used to arrive at the tentative tax on aggregate gifts. In 2006, the maximum tax rate was phased down to 46 percent. The first $2,000,000 of total taxable gifts results in a tentative tax of $780,800. The remaining $880,000 ($2,880,000 - $2,000,000) results in an additional $404,800 ($880,000 × 46%) of gift tax for a total gift tax liability of 1,190,600 ($780,800 + $404,800) of tax.

As reflected in the above calculation, David has again transferred a total of $3,000,000 in 2006 to his children. However, without gift splitting, David may not utilize Antonia's $1,000,000 gift tax exemption or Antonia's $12,000-per-child annual exclusion in 2006. The transfers result in a total gift tax liability for 2006 of $831,000. Comparing the $316,800 liability that arises with gift splitting to the $831,000 gift tax liability where gift splitting is not consented to, the couple will be able to reduce gift tax liability by $514,200 if they file consents. It should again be pointed out that where gift splitting is not consented to, IRC § 2513(d) will not apply and Antonia will not be jointly or severally liable to pay the $831,000 gift tax incurred by David.

142. **Answer (C) is the correct answer.** IRC § 2512 governs the valuation of property for gift tax purposes. The regulations under IRC § 2512 closely mirror (but are not as complete as) the regulations under IRC § 2031, which governs property valuation for estate tax purposes. The basic valuation principles of IRC § 2031 apply equally for both gift and estate tax purposes. The gift tax regulations provide that the amount of a gift of property is the value of the item of property on the date of the gift. Treas. Reg. § 25.2512-1. *See also* Treas. Reg. § 20.2031-1(b). The value is defined as "the price at which such property would change hands between a willing buyer and a willing seller, neither being under any compulsion to buy or to sell, and both having reasonable knowledge of relevant facts." Treas. Reg. § 25.2512-1. In applying this standard, price is not determined by reference to a forced sale or a market in which such a piece of property would not commonly be sold. Id. Rather, fair market value is the price at which a comparable item would be sold at retail. Id.

The retail price or "value" of an automobile is equal to the price for which an auto of same description, make, model, age, and condition could be purchased by a member of the general public from a retail seller. Treas. Reg. § 25.2512-1. The price is not determined by the amount that a dealer in used autos might pay for the same auto. Id. Answer (C) provides the best comparator value because several retail sellers are attempting to sell similar cars in the same geographical area for $25,000. Given that the price is determined by reference to the retail market, the value for gift tax purposes should be set at $25,000, the retail price in the location where Benny made the gift to Joseph.

Answer (B) is incorrect. Answer (B) sets the value at $18,000 or the price at which a local auto dealer would purchase the car. This price would be more akin to a wholesale price that a dealer in property might pay for inventory. As noted, the regulations distinguish between the price at which something might be purchased versus the price for which the property would be sold. Valuation is based specifically on the price at which a similar item is sold at retail and not the wholesale purchase price. Thus, although a donor might prefer to value something at the lower price a dealer in such property might offer, the lower price is not "value" contemplated by the statute for gift tax purposes.

Answers (A) and (D) are also incorrect. Answer (A) presents only the original cost that Uncle Benny paid for the car. That may once have been the retail value but, after 40 years, the retail value of the Mustang has fluctuated immensely. Of course, $2,500 is not the value of the car today. Answer (D) does not represent the value at which a 1964 ½ Mustang could be purchased by a member of the general public. Note that if such an offer could affect value, then an opportunity would arise in every valuation event to support an artificially low value based upon possibly spurious offers.

143. Joseph's basis in the Mustang is $2,500, the same as the basis of the Mustang in Uncle Benny's hands immediately prior to the gift. Pursuant to IRC § 1015(a), the basis of property acquired by gift is the same as it would be in the hands of the donor. As pointed out above, Uncle Benny paid $2,500 for the Mustang, and that becomes Joseph's transfer basis. The purpose of this question is to point out that in a simple gift, where no consideration is paid by the donee, there is no relationship between the basis of a gift and the value of such gift.

144. Where consideration is provided by the donee, the exchange is classified as a transfer that is in part a gift and in part a sale. Consideration paid by the donee affects the value of the gift given and can affect the basis that the donee ultimately retains in the property.

Uncle Benny and Joseph are related, and Benny's obvious intent to give a gift operates to take the exchange out of the definition of a transfer in the ordinary course of business. *See* Treas. Reg. § 25.2512-8. Because the transfer was not free from donative intent, the payment of $7,000 for the car cannot be considered its value. Inasmuch as the $25,000 value of the Mustang exceeds $7,000 given by Joseph in consideration for receiving the car, there is a gift of $18,000. Id. The $18,000 represents the excess of the $25,000 value of the car over the $7,000 of consideration given therefore.

With respect to Joseph's basis in the Mustang, Treasury Regulation § 1.1015-4 applies to determine the transferee's basis. Where a transfer of property is part gift and part sale, the basis of the property in the hands of the transferee is the greater of either the consideration paid or the transferor's basis in the property at the time of the gift. Treas. Reg. § 1.1015-4(a)(1). The basis is further increased by any gift taxes paid as a result of the transfer. *See* IRC § 1015(d). Thus, Joseph's basis in the Mustang is $7,000, the consideration he paid to Uncle Benny. Note that the $7,000 is far in excess of Uncle Benny's $2,500 basis in the auto. There is no adjustment for gift taxes paid, as the problem assumes this issue away.

145. **Answer (B) is the correct answer.** This question and Question 146, following, inquire as to the basis to be used for purposes of determining any gain or loss. Although this is essentially an income tax issue, these basis questions indirectly also relate to value of the Mustang at the time of the gift. We determined in Question 143, above, that where the basis is less than the fair market value at the time of the gift, the general rule of IRC § 1015 requires that Joseph take Benny's basis as his basis in the Mustang. If we were to apply the same rule here, Joseph would take the Mustang with a $30,000 basis.

However, IRC § 1015(a) contains an exception whereby if the donor's basis is greater than the fair market value before the date of the gift, then *for purposes of determining loss* (emphasis in original), the donee must use the fair market value of the Mustang as his basis. IRC § 1015(a). Here, on the date of the gift, the fair market value of the car is $25,000, but Benny's original cost basis is equal to $30,000. The exception in IRC § 1015(a) applies here because Benny's basis exceeds the fair market value of the auto at the time of the gift to Joseph and because Joseph has sold the Mustang for a price less than the date-of-gift value. Inherently, the Mustang was a loss asset in Benny's hands. By forcing the donee to use the date of gift value as basis for calculating loss on the sale of the property, the Code prevents the donor from transferring tax losses from the donor to the donee. If, instead of gifting the Mustang to Joseph, Benny simply sold the Mustang for its $25,000 fair market value, Benny would realize a loss of $5,000 ($30,000 basis less $25,000 amount realized) and Benny could indeed recognize the $5,000 loss on his annual income tax return.

However, as indicated, Benny gifts the Mustang to Joseph, who sells it for $3,000. While, Joseph would prefer to apply the IRC § 1015(a) general rule and use Uncle Benny's transfer basis of $30,000 to report as large a loss as possible, his loss is calculated by instead applying the exception. The exception requires Joseph to use the lower fair market value of $25,000 as his basis for purposes of determining his loss. Using the $3,000 as the amount realized on the sale of the Mustang and the $25,000 basis, Joseph realizes a loss of $22,000 ($3,000 amount realized less $25,000 basis). In this fashion, the Code prevents Benny from transferring any losses that were realized prior to the date of the gift to Joseph.

It is interesting to note from a planning perspective that a donor considering giving a gift may wish to avoid giving away assets that have bases in excess of fair market value. Rather, it may be prudent for such loss assets to be sold on the market, thereby resulting in losses that the donor may use on his or her own personal tax return. Indeed, the donor may then give the post-sale proceeds to the donee and be in a better position than if the assets were gifted and the donee sold the asset for a loss.

Answer (A) is incorrect. As mentioned above, Joseph would prefer to use Benny's basis of $30,000 as his transfer basis. However, the exception in IRC § 1015(a) prevents Benny from transferring the losses realized prior to the gift to Joseph. Indeed, if taxpayers were allowed to use the higher transfer basis, then taxpayers such as Benny could benefit by trafficking in losses. Under certain circumstances, taxpayers might be inclined to transfer loss assets to individuals in higher tax brackets. The exception in IRC § 1015(a) thwarts this type of activity by requiring Joseph to use the lower fair market value of the Mustang on the date of the gift as his basis for purposes of calculating losses.

Answers (C) and (D) are also incorrect. Answer (C) represents the amount of loss that is recognized when Joseph sells the Mustang for $3,000. The question asks for the Joseph's basis for purposes of calculating gain or loss. Answer (D) attributes insufficient basis in the car to Joseph, which is inconsistent with any applicable rule.

146. Yes, the answer would change. **Answer (A) would now be correct.** As indicated in Question 145, the fair market value of the auto at the time of the gift was $25,000, and Benny's original cost basis was $30,000. The exception in IRC § 1015(a) applies when basis is in excess of fair market value at the time of the gift and the property is later sold at a loss. Under such circumstances, the rule would continue to apply

only if Joseph sold the Mustang for a loss. Since Joseph sold the Mustang for $35,000, the Mustang is a gain asset in Joseph's hands and the exception is no longer applicable. Instead, the general rule of IRC § 1015(a) applies to require Joseph to use $30,000, Benny's original cost basis, as his transfer basis. Joseph now realizes a gain of $5,000 ($35,000 amount realized less $30,000 transfer basis).

Note that by allowing taxpayers to use a basis equal to the transfer basis (as opposed to the fair market value) on the date of the gift where the donee sells the gift at a gain, the Code prevents recognition of excess gain upon sale of the property. It would not make logical sense for the Code to require the donee use the lesser fair market value at the time of the gift. If such were the case, the Code result would effectively be to negate basis that the donee was appropriately credited with upon purchase.

147.   **Answer (D) is the correct answer.** For gift tax purposes, the value of a share of stock is the fair market value of the share on the date of the gift. Treas. Reg. § 25.2512-2(a). If the stock shares that are the subject of the gift are traded on a stock exchange or in an over-the-counter market, the mean between the highest and lowest quoted selling prices on the date of the gift is deemed to be the fair market value of such share of stock. Treas. Reg. § 25.2512-2(b). The regulation's use of the word "mean" between the highest selling price and the lowest selling price on the date of gift is an average that is equal to the arithmetic mean or the amount obtained by adding the highest selling price to the lowest selling price and dividing by two.

On July 10, the day of the gift, ABC Corporation stock sold at a high of $10.25 and a low of $8.75. The mean selling price and the value of one share of ABC Corporation is $9.50, derived by adding the highest selling price of $10.25 to $8.75, the lowest selling price to obtain $19.00, and then dividing $19.00 by two to arrive at the mean of $9.50 per share. The per-share value is then multiplied by 2,000, the number of shares that Uncle Benny gave to Katie on July 10, to arrive at $19,000, the total deemed value of the gift.

Answers (A), (B), and (C) are incorrect. Answer (A) reflects the correct mean value between the high and the low on July 10, but the $9.50 answer does not reflect the full value of the gift from Uncle Benny to Katie, which is 2,000 times that amount. Answers (B) and (C) simply fail to reflect the correct full value.

148.   **Answer (C) is the correct answer.** The goal of the regulations remains the same in that the value of a share of stock is the fair market value of the share on the date of the gift. Treas. Reg. § 25.2512-2(a). However, if there were no sales of shares in the gifted stock on the date of the gift, then the regulations require the donor to determine the value of the shares with reference to sales that occurred on dates "within a reasonable period both before and after the date of the gift. . . ," Treas. Reg. § 25.2512-2(b). Thus, the fair market value is determined by calculating the "weighted average of the means between the highest and lowest sales on the nearest date before and the nearest date after the gift." Id.

No sales took place on Tuesday, July 10. Rather, sales of ABC stock on the nearest date before July 10 took place on Monday, July 9. On Monday, July 9, the lowest recorded selling price was $11.50 and the highest recorded selling price was $14.75. Again, the "mean" is the amount obtained by adding the $14.75, the highest selling price, to $11.50, the lowest selling price, obtaining $26.25, and then dividing by two to arrive at $13.125. With respect to the nearest date after the gift, sales of ABC Stock took place on Friday, July 13, when the mean was $10.00 [($7.00 + 13.00) / 2]. Having determined the means between the highest and lowest sales on the nearest date before and the nearest date after the gift, we must now determine the weighted average of the two means. The weighted average is determined "inversely by the respective number of trading days between the selling dates and the date of the gift." Treas. Reg. § 25.2512-2(b). The following formula for determining the weighted average is derived from examples given in Treasury Regulation § 25.2512-2(b)(3):

$$\frac{[(\text{first mean} \times \text{trading days before gift}) + (\text{second mean} \times \text{trading days after gift})]}{(\text{total number of trading days before and after date of gift})}$$

In the current problem the "first mean" is $13.125, or the mean on Monday, July 9, the nearest date before the gift. The "second mean" is $10.00, or the mean on Friday, July 13, the nearest date after the gift. The first mean was one trading day before the date of the gift and the second mean was three trading days after the date of the gift. Thus, there were a total of four trading days before and after date of gift. The formula can again be given as follows after inserting the values from the current problem:

$$\frac{[(\$13.125 \times 1) + (\$10.00 \times 3)]}{(4)}$$

The above equation arithmetically equals $10.78, and this amount represents the deemed value of one share of ABC Corporation stock given as a gift on July 10. In order to arrive at the final answer, the $10.78 must be multiplied by 2,000, the number of shares given by Uncle Benny to Katie on July 10, to arrive at $21,562.50 as the full value of the gift.

Answers (A), (B), and (D) are incorrect. Answer (A) reflects the correct mean value between the high and the low on July 10 from the prior problem, but where there were no sales on July 10 under these facts. Answer (B) reflects the weighted average between the high and the low on July 9 and July 13, but the $10.78 does not reflect the full value of the gift from Uncle Benny to Katie, which is 2,000 times that amount. Answer (D) reflects the correct mean value between the high and the low on both dates but is inaccurate because it is not the weighted average and is further not multiplied by the number of shares gifted.

149. **Answer (B) is the correct answer.** A gift of property is valued as of the date of the transfer. *See* IRC § 2512(a). Again, the fair market value of the transferred property is the price at which the property would change hands between a willing buyer and willing seller, neither being under a compulsion to buy or to sell and both having reasonable knowledge of relevant facts. *See United States v. Cartwright*, 411 U.S. 546 (1973); Treas. Reg. § 25.2512-1. It is assumed within this basic standard that the hypothetical willing buyer and seller will seek to maximize

economic advantage to the benefit of both. *See Estate of Jones v. Commissioner*, 116 T.C. 121, 130 (2001); *Estate of Davis v. Commissioner*, 110 T.C. 530, 535 (1998). Guidance on the specific process of determining a fair market value between a hypothetical buyer and seller is done in different ways. As was seen in the prior problem, the regulations specifically address the manner in which stock values are arrived at. *See* Treas. Reg. § 25.2512-2. The regulations also specifically address, among other things, valuation of cash on hand, notes, annuities, insurance contracts, business interests, and household effects. *See* Treas. Regs. §§ 25.2512-2 through 25.2512-6. With respect to certain assets such as certain types of securities, the rules are specific.

However, the estate and gift tax regulations provide only general guidance on the manner in which certain property interests are valued. For example, valuations of business interests and personal effects are to be done with reference to all relevant facts and circumstances. *See* Treas. Regs. §§ 25.2512-3; 20.2031-3; 20.2031-6. In order to gather and analyze all the relevant facts and circumstances, taxpayers often rely on the opinions of an expert or qualified appraiser to substantiate the fair market value of many types of gifted property. *See, e.g., Estate of Jones v. Commissioner*, 116 T.C. 121 (2001)(valuation of partnership interests). In general, courts and the IRS will evaluate the opinions of the experts and appraisers based upon their professional qualifications. *See Estate of Jones v. Commissioner*, 116 T.C. 121, 131 (2001); *Estate of Davis v. Commissioner*, 110 T.C. 530, 536 (1998). It is important to note that neither the courts nor the IRS are bound by an opinion provided by an expert. *See Estate of Jones v. Commissioner*, 116 T.C. 121, 131 (2001).

With respect to valuing Uncle Benny's southern California beach home, there is only general and no specific guidance in the regulations. Certainly the value of the home will require Uncle Benny to report the fair market value of the home on a gift tax return. Therefore, Uncle Benny is required to determine the value at which the property would change hands between a willing buyer and willing seller. Without experience of his own, Uncle Benny is best advised to substantiate the value that he reports on the gift tax return by relying on the opinion of an expert appraiser. Because a qualified expert appraiser is most likely to arrive at a reasonable determination of the value of the home, Uncle Benny should report $1,200,000 as the value of the gift. Of course, the value of the home as determined by the appraiser can always be challenged by the IRS.

Answer (C) is incorrect. The assessed value of Uncle Benny's home as reflected on the county tax rolls does not necessarily reflect fair market value as is required by the estate and gift tax Code and Regulations. Indeed, the gift tax regulations specifically indicate that the value of property shall not be reported at the value at which it is assessed for local tax purposes unless that value accurately represents the fair market value of the property on the date of the gift. Treas. Reg. § 25.2512-1. It is clear in this case that $900,000 is substantially less than the appraiser's estimate of fair market value and that the value for property tax purposes is not representative of the fair market value of the house.

Answers (A) and (D) are also incorrect. As previously indicated, Benny's cost basis of $700,000 as indicated in Answer (A) is not relevant in determining the fair market value of the home. And, again, Benny's belief that the home is actually worth $1,000,000 is not sufficient to support a valuation of the home at that amount. The regulations are clear that a taxpayer must take all facts and circumstances into consideration in determining the value of the home. Benny's isolated belief that the home has a certain value ignores the objective facts that appear to support a higher value of $1,200,000 as determined by the appraiser.

Actuarial Concepts

150. **Answer (B) is the correct answer.** Benny's goal is to give a life estate in the Colorado home to his brother Brett with a remainder interest equally to Joseph and Katie. Benny's immediate issue is which actuarial table is the correct one to use. Benny's overriding issue is to value the gifts, which we will address in the next several questions. There are actually three gifts here. One gift is the life estate, and there are two gifts, one to Katie and one to Joseph, associated with the remainder.

The fair market value of a life estate or remainder is equal to the present value of the interest. Treas. Reg. § 25.2512-5(a). Determination of the present value of gifts given after April 30, 1999, is governed by Treasury Regulation § 25.2512-5(d). In general, the fair market value of a specific interest in a life estate or remainder is obtained by reference to the appropriate interest rate and a standard actuarial factor. Treas. Reg. § 25.2512-5(d).

In this question we are concerned only with which table the appropriate standard actuarial factor comes from. IRS Publication 1457, Book Aleph, contains actuarial values for remainder factors for one life, two lives, and terms certain. Book Aleph includes actuarial factors for an interest for the life of one individual in Table S. Further, Table S applies only where property is gifted after April 30, 1999. Treas. Reg. § 20.2031-7(d). Because Benny gave the Colorado home to Brett "for life" as of July 15, 2007, Benny must refer to Table S, which provides the factor for determining the value of a remainder interest.

While not necessarily intuitive, Benny has given 100 percent of the home away, but he has given it away in parts. It is important to note that the value of the remainder interest in the home is based upon the expected duration of Brett's "single" life. The shorter the life interest holder's expected lifespan is, the sooner the remainder interest holders, here Joseph and Katie, will take the home. In general, the sooner they are expected to get the home, the more the remainder value of the home is worth in Joseph and Katie's hands. Because Brett's life is the measuring life for determining the remainder factor, reference to Table S will allow Benny to obtain the appropriate single-life remainder factor that, as expanded upon in the following questions, will allow him to calculate both the value of Brett's life estate and the value of Joseph and Katie's remainder interests.

As a final note and from a practical standpoint, Table S is also provided to a limited extent in the regulations under Treasury Regulation § 20.2031-7. Students can sometimes become frustrated with edited versions of the Code and Regulations that sometimes do not contain all of the available actuarial tables. Reference to

Book Aleph is common in practice.

Answers (A), (B), and (D) are also incorrect. For reasons explained above, the remaining answers are not correct. Table B contains factors for determining the value of a remainder interest after a term of years' interest in the property has expired. Answer (B), suggesting Table R(2), Two Life Last-to-Die Factors, applies when a life estate is measured by two lives and the value sought to be calculated is a remainder interest after the second life holder dies. This table might have been used in this problem if, hypothetically, Benny had given the home to Brett and his wife and it was to be passed to Katie and Joseph upon the death of either Brett or his wife, whichever was the last to die. Finally, Table K applies to valuation of annuities. Neither the life interest held by Brett nor the remainder interests held by Joseph and Katie qualify as annuities. In general, an annuity is a contract whereby one party is guaranteed to receive an amount of money on a regular interval (e.g., monthly or annual) for a defined period of time.

151. **Answer (A) is the correct answer.** Now that you have assisted Benny in identifying the appropriate actuarial table, it becomes apparent that in order to use Table S to identify the specific standard valuation factor, Benny needs to know Brett's age and the applicable federal rate ("AFR") of interest that applies. *See* Treas. Reg. § 20.2031-7(d). Brett's age is obtained from Benny; as the problem tells you, he is 52 years old.

Obtaining the appropriate AFR is a little more technical. Use of Table S to determine the fair market value of the gifted property requires reference to IRC § 7520 interest rates for the month in which the gift occurs and the appropriate actuarial tables. Treas. Reg. § 25.2512-5(d)(2)(iii). The value of any interest for life or remainder interest must be determined by using an interest rate (rounded to the nearest two-tenths of 1 percent) equal to 120 percent of the annual federal midterm rate in effect for the month in which the valuation date falls. IRC § 7520(a)(2); Treas. Reg. § 1.7520-1(b).

Each month the Secretary of the Treasury is directed to determine the federal short-term, mid-term, and long-term rates that apply for the following calendar month. IRC § 1274(d). The IRS publishes revenue rulings near the end of each month, and each revenue ruling has tables that contain the applicable federal rates for the following month for purposes of IRC § 1274(d). As a practical matter, the rates can be found on the Internet in many places. Historically, the IRS has published the rulings at http://www.irs.gov/

Benny's gift of the home was made on July 15, 2007. Therefore, in order to determine the appropriate rate, Rev. Rul. 2007-44 must be referenced and 120 percent of the mid-term AFR rate for July 2007 must be cross-referenced. The relevant portion of the ruling appears as follows:

	Annual	Semiannual	Quarterly	Monthly
		Mid-term		
AFR	4.95%	4.89%	4.86%	4.84%
110% AFR	5.45%	5.38%	5.34%	5.32%
120% AFR	5.96%	5.87%	5.83%	5.80%

	Annual	Semiannual Mid-term	Quarterly	Monthly
130% AFR	6.46%	6.36%	6.31%	6.28%
150% AFR	7.47%	7.34%	7.27%	7.23%
175% AFR	8.74%	8.56%	8.47%	8.41%

For purposes of valuing Joseph and Katie's remainder interests after Brett's life estate, the appropriate AFR rate is 5.96 percent.

Answers (B), (C), and (D) are also incorrect. For reasons already explained, the values reflected in Answers (B) through (D) are incorrect. Answer (B) is incorrect because 6.20 percent is 120 percent of the annual AFR rate for long-term instruments (as opposed to mid-term rates). Answer (C), 4.95 percent, reflects the mid-term rate but without adjustment for the 120 percent requirement. Finally, Answer (D) at 4.97 percent is the unadjusted short-term rate. All the wrong options represent common errors made after obtaining the correct revenue ruling.

152. **Answer (D) is the correct answer.** We are now asked to calculate the value of Brett's life interest in Benny's Colorado home. We have determined that Table S is the appropriate actuarial table to use. We have also identified the appropriate AFR rate for use in Table S to be 5.96 percent, and we know Brett is 52 years of age as indicated in the problem. The Code and Regulations are specific in requiring that 120 percent of the annual mid-term rate rounded to the nearest two-tenths of 1 percent. Rounding 5.96 percent to the nearest two-tenths of 1 percent requires us to round up, producing a result of 6 percent. Cross-referencing 6 percent with 52 years of age on Table S, we arrive at a single-life remainder factor of 0.25584. Multiplying the remainder factor of 0.25584 by $2,000,000, the stated fair market value of Benny's Colorado home, results in Joseph and Katie's remainder interest value of $511,680.

It is important to note that Joseph and Katie's remainder interest is proportional to Brett's life interest. By gifting a life interest in the home to Brett and a remainder interest to Joseph and Katie, Benny has gifted the full value of the home away. Brett's life interest is equal in value to the full $2,000,000 value of the home reduced by Joseph and Katie's combined remainder interest valued at $511,680. Thus, Brett's life interest is worth $1,488,320.

Alternatively, one can arrive at the same answer by first deriving Brett's life interest factor from Joseph and Katie's Table S single-life remainder interest factor. Mathematically, one minus the remainder factor of 0.25584 results in Brett's life interest factor of 0.74416. Multiplying Brett's life interest factor by $2,000,000 results in $1,488,320.

Answers (A), (B), and (C) are also incorrect. Answer (A) is incorrect, as it represents the full value of the home. Brett's interest is only a partial interest for life. In general, a remainder interest must have some positive value. Answer (B) reflects one-half of the value of Katie and Joseph's combined remainder interest. Finally, Answer (C) reflects the value of Joseph and Katie's combined remainder interests.

153. **Answer (B) is the correct answer.** As indicated in the answer to Question 152, the appropriate single-life remainder factor is 0.25584. Application of this factor results in a determination that the present value of Joseph and Katie's remainder interest in the home as being worth $511,680. Since Joseph and Katie each have an equal interest in the home after Brett's death, their individual interests equal one-half of the full remainder value or $255,840.

   Answers (A), (C), and (D) are also incorrect. Again, Answer (A) is incorrect, as it represents the full value of the home. Answer (C) reflects the full value of Katie and Joseph's combined remainder interest. Finally, Answer (C) reflects the value of Joseph and Katie's combined remainder interests.

154. **Answer (C) is the correct answer.** The issue here is how to determine the value of Brett's term interest in the home. Whereas previously we referred to Table S to identify the specific single-life remainder factor, we now must refer to Table B. Again, reference to Publication 1457, Book Aleph, or reference to Treas. Reg. § 20.2031-7(d)(6) would provide access to Table B. Table B contains term certain remainder factors that apply to gifts made after April 30, 1999. In general, Table B is used in a manner similar to Table S. However, with respect to a term interest, Table B requires the donor taxpayer to cross-reference the number of years that the interest in the gifted property lasts with the appropriate AFR rate for the month in which the gift is made. The AFR rate is same rate that was used in the preceding problems for remainder interests. Thus, the AFR rate is the published rate for the month in which the gift was given.

   Benny gifted use of the home to Brett for a term of 10 years. As determined above, the applicable AFR rate is obtained from Rev. Rul. 2007-44. The relevant rate is 120 percent of the mid-term AFR rate for July 2007, which is stated as 5.96 percent. Rounding up to the nearest two-tenths of 1 percent, we arrive at 6 percent and cross-reference this rate with the 10-year length of the term, to obtain a term certain remainder factor of .558395. The $2,000,000 value of the home is multiplied by the 0.558395 remainder factor to arrive at $1,116,790. This dollar amount represents the present value of Katie's remainder interest in the home. Again, the call of the question targets the value of Brett's term interest. Therefore, since the value of the term interest plus the remainder interest equals $2,000,000, the full value of the home, we must subtract the value of Katie's remainder interest from the full value. Subtracting $1,116,790 from $2,000,000 we arrive at $883,210, the present value of Benny's gift to Brett of the 10-year term interest.

   Similar to the discussion above in relation to valuation of a life interest, the value of Brett's life interest may be obtained by first determining the term certain factor. Subtracting 0.558395 from one, we arrive at 0.441605 as a term certain factor. Then, multiplying $2,000,000, the value of the home, by the 0.441605 term certain factor, we arrive at $883,210, the present value of Benny's gift to Brett.

   Answers (A), (B), and (D) are incorrect for the reasons stated above.

Valuation Premiums and Discounts

155. **Answer (B) is the correct answer.** In Uncle Benny's hands each share of UB Corporation has a fair market value of $10.00 ($10,000,000 total value divided by 1,000,000, the total number of outstanding shares). If, for example, Uncle Benny were to sell all 1,000,000 shares to a single buyer for $10,000,000, each share would have a value of $10.00. This is true because the 1,000,000 shares represent all of the value of the assets of the corporation.

However, the valuation of shares of stock in a closely held company must take into account all relevant facts and circumstances of the particular corporation at issue. *See Northern Trust Co. v. Commissioner*, 87 T.C. 349, 384 (1986); Treas. Reg. § 20.2031-2(f). One relevant fact in valuing corporate shares is the number of shares given. Shares of stock of a corporation that represent a minority interest are normally worth less than a proportionate share of the value of the assets of the corporation. *See Estate of Bright v. United States*, 658 F.2d 999 (5th Cir. 1981). The reduction in value associated with a minority of shares is referred to as a minority discount. The minority discount applies because, among other things, the holder of a minority interest has no control over corporate policy, is not capable of authorizing a corporate dividend, and cannot compel liquidation or other corporate actions that require the a vote of the shareholders. *See Harwood v. Commissioner*, 82 T.C. 239, 267 (1984), affd. 786 F.2d 1174 (9th Cir. 1986); *Estate of Andrews v. Commissioner*, 79 T.C. 938, 953 (1982).

Benny initially owned 100 percent of the company, and each share of stock in Benny's hands had a $10.00 value. Upon receipt of the 150,000 shares from Benny, Katie became merely a minority shareholder. A minority shareholder does not have sufficient voting rights to cause the corporation to take any action. Unlike Uncle Benny, Katie lacks any control over corporate actions. Having only a minority interest, Katie cannot direct the board of directors to resolve to pay dividends or compel the corporation to take any action requiring a vote of the shareholders. Without such rights, Katie's shares have little value.

Answer (C) is incorrect. A control premium operates to increase the per-share value of stock where the amount of stock gifted represents a controlling interest in the corporation. The amount of stock ownership in a particular corporation that represents a "controlling interest" can vary from corporation to corporation. For example, in a simple setting where a majority vote is all that is required under the corporation's articles of incorporation for corporate action to be ratified, a greater than 50 percent share interest would represent "control" of the company. Where a super majority vote is required to induce corporate action, a greater than 50 percent interest may be required to maintain control. Benny has only given Katie a 1.5 percent interest in UB Corporation. Under these circumstances, Katie does not have a controlling interest, and no control premium adjustment would be required.

Answers (A) and (D) are incorrect. A blockage discount, also sometimes referred to as an absorption discount, generally applies, for example, where an owner of stock traded on a public market owns such a large proportion of a corporation's stock that selling all or a substantial portion of the block of stock would likely operate to depress the stock price on the public exchanges. A blockage discount would not apply to a 1.5 percent interest in a privately held corporation. **Answer (D) is incorrect** as it is a red herring.

156. **Answer (C) is the correct answer.** When determining the value of closely held stock, a discount is allowed in order to reflect lack of marketability. A lack-of-marketability discount is applied under the theory that there is no recognized market for closely held stock. *See, e.g., Mandelbaum v. Commissioner,* TC Memo 1995-255. The Tax Court has summarized the factors that impact a marketability discount as follows: (1) financial statement analysis, (2) dividend policy, (3) outlook of the company, (4) management of the company, (5) control factor in the shares to be purchased, (6) company redemption policy, (7) restriction on transfer, (8) holding period of the stock, and (9) costs of a public offering. *See Estate of Jelke v. Comm'r,* T.C. Memo 2005-131; *Mandelbaum v. Comm'r,* T.C. Memo 1995-255.

While an extensive analysis of each of the factors elucidated in *Mandelbaum* is beyond the scope of this answer, a weighing of the list of factors assists courts in establishing the amount, if any, of a marketability discount. For example, the availability of regular financial statements reviewed by a qualified certified public accountant (CPA) firm showing strong financial performance from year to year would lean in favor of increased marketability of the stock and, therefore, reduced marketability discount. *See Mandelbaum v. Comm'r,* supra. Similarly, the outlook of the company, including its history, its rank in the industry, and its economic forecast, are also relevant factors for determining the stock's marketability or value. If, for example, a company is not the leader in its industry, an increased marketability discount may be appropriate. Id. Restrictions on transfer also impact the marketability of stock. If a shareholders' agreement restricts a shareholder's ability to freely transfer stock in the corporation, such restrictions may warrant a decrease in value and, therefore, an increased marketability discount. Id. Further, an interest in closely held stock is less marketable if an investor must hold it for a long period of time in order to profit. Id. Thus, market risk tends to increase (and marketability tends to decrease) the lengthier the holding period becomes. Id.

Here, Katie's shares are subject to an enforceable shareholder's agreement. The shareholder's agreement restricts Katie's ability to sell the shares to a third party under certain circumstances. Such a restriction makes Katie's shares less marketable, and these facts support an increased marketability discount.

Answers (A), (B), and (D) are incorrect. For reasons already explained, Answers (A) and (B) are incorrect. Answer (D) refers to a capital gains discount, which generally applies in valuing a corporation's stock where the corporation holds assets that are appreciated and are subject to built-in capital gains. When a corporation holds appreciated assets, sale of the assets will result in taxable capital gains. Prior to sale of the assets, the entity will accrue a deferred tax liability associated with the built-in (but as yet unrealized) capital gains. In *Estate of Davis,* 110 TC 530 (1998), the Tax Court held that in determining the fair market value of closely held corporate stock, built-in capital gains discounts are appropriate under certain circumstances. Id. at 547. There is no indication in the fact pattern that UB Corporation holds a material amount of appreciated assets. Under these circumstances, it would not be appropriate to apply a capital gains discount.

157. **Answer (B) is the correct answer.** Where more than one discount (or premium) applies to an equity interest, the discounts apply in seriatim. If a 20 percent minority discount is first applied to the undiscounted value of a minority interest in stock (100 percent), this will leave 80 percent of the value subject next to a 20 percent marketability discount. Applying a 20 percent marketability discount to 80 percent of the remaining value results in a 64 percent (20 percent of 80 percent results in an additional 16 percent reduction from the remaining 80% percent). *See, e.g., Estate of Frank v. Commissioner*, T.C. Memo 1995-132 (Tax Court first applied a 30 percent lack of marketability discount and next applied a 20 percent minority interest discount to arrive at a 56 percent overall discount).

Katie's 150,000 shares has an undiscounted value of $1,500,000 (150,000 shares times $10 per share). Applying first the 20 percent minority discount to the $1,500,000 results in a reduction in value to 1,200,000 ($1,500,000 × 20% = $300,000; $1,500,000 - $300,000 = $1,200,000). Next, applying the 20 percent marketability discount to the remaining $1,200,000 value of the stock results in a value of $960,000 ($1,200,000 × 20% = $240,000; $1,200,000 - $240,000 = $960,000).

Answers (A), (C), and (D) are incorrect. Answer (A) represents the undiscounted value ($1,500,000) of Katie's 150,000 shares of UB Corporation. Answer (C) incorrectly applies a cumulative 40 percent discount rather than a sequential application of two 20 percent discounts. Answer (D) has little if any relevance to the fact pattern.

158. Yes, in valuing Uncle Benny's gift of an additional 1,500,000 shares, no discount will apply, and a premium (as opposed to the discounts previously discussed above) may instead apply. Under the arm's-length standard, a willing buyer will logically pay more for a block of shares that results in the purchaser acquiring a majority or controlling interest. In general, federal tax law has isolated control as a separate element for purposes of determining the fair market value of corporate stock. *Philip Morris, Inc. v. Commissioner*, 96 T.C. 606, 628 (1991). In *Philip Morris*, the Tax Court indicated payment of a premium for control is based on the notion that the per-share value of a controlling interest is higher than one would pay per share for a minority interest. Id. at 629.

The Tax Court has indicated that a discount will not apply in situations where a minority block of stock has "swing vote characteristics." *Estate of Magnin v. Commissioner*, T.C. Memo 2001-31. A "swing vote premium" may be assigned to the value of a minority block of shares that if sold may result in another shareholder gaining control. In *Estate of Winkler v. Commissioner*, T.C. Memo 1989-231, three shareholders held stock interests of 50 percent, 40 percent, and 10 percent. The issue addressed was whether a minority discount applied for estate tax purposes of valuing the 10 percent interest. The Tax Court determined that because a third hypothetical buyer would be able to combine with one of the two remaining shareholders to either effect or block control of the company, the 10 percent interest possessed "swing vote characteristics." As such, an unrelated willing buyer may be willing to pay a premium for a 10 percent block of voting stock.

Here, Katie owns 45 percent of the shares prior to receiving an additional gift from Uncle Benny. An additional 15 percent block of UB stock would result in Katie holding a majority interest in UB Corporation. After the gift, Uncle Benny would own a minority of shares of UB Corporation. Similar to the outcome in the *Estate of Winkler*, a willing buyer would likely pay a premium for the additional 15 percent of the shares due to the fact that such shares would represent a swing vote. Thus, rather than a discount for a minority interest, the Service will likely assert that a valuation premium should be assigned.

159. **Answers (A) and (B) are both correct answers.** Historically, family limited partnerships (FLPs) have been used by taxpayers to accomplish a number of business, estate tax, and gift tax goals. Prior to the advent of the limited liability company (LLC), FLPs were purportedly formed by many taxpayers for, among other things: consolidation of financial interests with a goal of improving investment opportunities while minimizing their risks through diversification; centralized management of assets; orderly succession of the family assets; allowing family members to become equity holders through gifting of FLP (or LLC) interests; and assuring long-term business continuity by restricting sales of FLP interests outside of the family.

Limited partnerships generally provide the flexibility to allow these goals to be accomplished. Importantly, unless an election is made otherwise, a limited partnership is treated as a partnership for federal income tax purposes. *See* Treas. Reg. § 301.7701-3(a). A partnership is generally not subject to income tax on items of income, gain, loss, or deduction. Rather, partnerships are treated as "pass-through" entities in which the individual partners are subject to income tax. Tax is imposed on each partner's ratable share of the partnership tax items passed through to each partner. A taxpayer may contribute assets to a limited partnership in return for general partner units, limited partner units, or both. Under state law, a general partner is authorized to manage assets held by the limited partnership. Limited partners are not allowed to participate in management decisions. In this fashion, a taxpayer who is also a general partner in a limited partnership can maintain control over the assets he or she contributed. Limited partners remain liable only for the amount contributed to a limited partnership whereas general partners remain individually liable. In order to shield the general partner's personal assets from liabilities arising from the LLC, a taxpayer general partner may form a wholly or partially owned corporation to act as the general partner of the limited partnership. After formation of a limited partnership and pursuant to the terms of the partnership agreement, a taxpayer may choose to gift general or limited partner units (or both) to various family members (or unrelated third parties), thereby taking advantage of various valuation discounts. See the previous topic for a detailed discussion of the types of discounts and how they may apply.

With the advent of the LLC in the 1980s and its increasing popularity as an accepted business entity, LLCs are also used for the same general purposes as FLPs. As in a corporation, all the equity holders of an LLC are shielded from individual liability. However, like a general or limited partnership, LLCs are also treated as partnerships for federal income tax purposes. There is no managing general partner in an LLC. Rather, LLCs are managed either by one or more members who are appointed by the other members (manager-managed) or managed by all the members in unison (member-managed). In order to retain control of assets contributed to a family limited liability company (FLLC), a taxpayer may initially appoint himself or herself as the sole manager. As a manager, a taxpayer who creates an LLC may maintain control over assets contributed to the LLC.

Answers (C) and (D) are both incorrect. A general partnership consists of a group of general partners who are each individually liable for partnership liabilities. Additionally, each general partner in general partnership may participate in managing the entity. Uncle Benny's goals of retaining control of the contributed assets and obtaining a liability shield are not furthered by creation of a general partnership. While a Subchapter C corporation (C corporation) may have some of the attributes that Uncle Benny seeks, a C corporation is subject to income tax in its own separate right. Because a C corporation and its shareholders are each subject to tax on the earnings of the corporation, it is not the most efficient entity to implement for Benny.

160.   **Answer (B) is correct.** In the last decade, the IRS has more aggressively challenged valuation discounts attributed to gifts of interests in FLPs. The IRS has proceeded under a number of theories with some success and some failure. Among other things, the IRS has argued: an indirect gift occurs upon formation of an FLP; the taxpayer improperly retained an interest under IRC § 2036(a); and the formation of an FLP, contribution of assets, and gifting of units constitutes a tax-motivated transaction. Under the facts of Answer (A), Benny is likely to be determined to have given an indirect gift of the assets contributed to the LP to Katie and Joseph. A transfer to a partnership for less than full and adequate consideration may represent an indirect gift of the contributed assets to the other partners. *See Shepard v. Commissioner*, 115 TC 376, 389 (2000), aff'd, 283 F.3d 1258, (11th Cir. 2002). In *Shepard*, the taxpayer contributed land and stocks to a limited partnership. 115 TC 376, 377 (2000). Taxpayer's two children each received a 25 percent interest in the partnership upon taxpayer's initial contribution. The taxpayer took the position that the transfers of partnership interests represented two separate gifts and that these gifts should each be subject to minority and marketability discounts. Id. at 384. The Commissioner argued that the discounts were inappropriate because the taxpayer gave his sons gifts of the contributed assets rather than an interest in the partnership. Id. Further, it was argued that the taxpayer completed the two gifts prior to the formation of the partnership. Id. The Tax Court agreed with the Commissioner, holding that the transfers were indirect gifts to the sons of a ratable share of the assets contributed and that no valuation discounts applied. Id. at 389.

The facts in Answer (A) are similar to the facts in the *Shepard* case. Benny contributes his assets to the LP today with the LP issuing 90 percent of the limited partner units to Uncle Benny, and Katie and Joseph each receive a 5 percent capital interest. Like the children in the *Shepard* case, Benny's contributions of assets are allocated to Katie and Joseph's partnership capital accounts. Katie and Joseph contributed no assets. Thus, Benny's contribution is likely to be treated as an indirect gift of a ratable share of the contributed assets. It is important to note, however, that the *Shepard* Court made it clear that not every capital contribution to a partnership will result in a gift to the other partners. Id. at 389. This is especially true where the contributing partner's capital account reflects the full amount of his or her contribution. Thereafter, the contributing partner may gift an interest to other persons. Id.

In Answer (C), Benny is initially credited with 100 percent of his contribution. However, questions have also arisen regarding the proximity of a gift of limited partnership units in relation to the formation of the limited partnership. In *Senda v. Commissioner*, TC Memo 2004-160, aff'd., 433 F.3d 1044 (8th Cir. 2006), the taxpayer was unable to prove that the contribution had been made before a gift of limited partnership units. The taxpayer made an initial contribution to the partnership and then on the same day made a gift of LP units to his children. The Eighth Circuit Court of Appeals affirmed the Tax Court's finding that the taxpayer failed to prove that the contribution was made prior to the gifts of the partnership interests. 433 F.3d 1044, 1047 (8th Cir. 2006). The Court of Appeals then went on to indicate that the taxpayer overlooked the ultimate finding of the tax court, stating that "[a]t best, the transactions were integrated (as asserted by respondent) and, in effect, simultaneous." Id. at 1048. The Court of Appeals further noted that even if the taxpayer's contribution would have first been credited to his capital account, this extra step would not have had an impact on the determination that the transaction was integrated. The Court then implicated the step transaction doctrine by stating that "formally distinct steps are considered as an integrated whole, rather than in isolation, so federal tax liability is based on a realistic view of the entire transaction." Id. at 1049. Under the reasoning in *Senda*, the formation of the partnership by Benny could be viewed as a single transaction in which the assets contributed to the LP are treated as indirectly transferred to Katie and Joseph rather than a contribution by Benny followed by a separate gift of 5 percent of the LP units to each Katie and Joseph.

Thus, in Answer (C), Benny's contemporaneous gift of 5 percent of the limited partnership units may not survive scrutiny under the *Senda* reasoning. However, under the facts of Answer (B), Benny, Katie, and Joseph each contribute property to the newly formed LLC. Their respective capital accounts are credited with the full value of the assets that each contributed. Further, a substantial period of time passes before Benny gifts additional interests of the LP to Katie and Joseph. The reasoning in *Senda* is not likely to apply to the facts in Answer (B).

Answers (A), (C), and (D) are all incorrect answers. For reasons explained above, Answers (A) and (C) are incorrect. Answer (D) would not likely be challenged by the IRS for reasons explained above. However, Answer (D) does not effectuate Benny's desire to begin gifting.

161. Yes, the answer to Question 160 would change. If Benny contributed 100 percent of his assets as opposed to only half of his assets, none of the answer options would likely survive challenge by the Commissioner. Gross estate includes the value of all property to the extent that a decedent has at any time made a transfer under which he or she has retained possession or enjoyment of the property. IRC § 2036(a)(1).

For purposes of section 2036(a), enjoyment of property is retained if there is an express or implied agreement at the time of the transfer that the transferor will enjoy present economic benefits of the property. *See Estate of Reichardt v. Commissioner*, 114 T.C. 144, 151 (2000).

In *Reichardt*, the decedent taxpayer failed to limit his enjoyment of property transferred to a partnership. The Tax Court found that notwithstanding that taxpayer transferred actual legal title of property to the partnership, the taxpayer's relationship to the assets was the same both before and after the assets were contributed. Id. at 153. Therefore, the value of the assets held by the partnership were included in the taxpayer's gross estate at fair market value. Id. As support for its conclusion, the Tax Court found, among other things, that the taxpayer-decedent commingled partnership funds with personal funds, depositing some partnership income in his personal account. Taxpayer also used the partnership's checking account as his personal account and resided in a residence held by the partnership without paying rent to the partnership. Id. *See also Estate of Harper v. Commissioner*, TC Memo 2002-121 (decedent-taxpayer commingled partnership assets with personal assets and made distributions to himself that were not proportionate to his interest in the partnership); *Estate of Schauerhamer v. Commissioner*, TC Memo 1997-242 (decedent commingled partnership funds with personal funds).

By contributing 100 percent of his assets to the partnership, Benny would have no personal assets or income to live off. In order to subsist, Benny would have to take distributions from the partnership. In order to avoid comingling of funds and using partnership funds for personal purposes, taxpayers should avoid contributing most or all of their assets to a family limited partnership (or LLC). Further, regular non–pro rata distributions from the partnership to a decedent taxpayer are also indicative of personal use of partnership assets.

162. **Answer (A) is correct.** Answer (A) is correct because Benny is always free to sell his interest in the partnership. Sale of his interest will result in Benny receiving fair market value in cash in exchange for his units. Of course, a sale of his interest will also result in reducing or eliminating Benny's interest in the LP. Sale of an LP interest does not result in an improper use of LP funds for personal reasons, nor does it result in any improper commingling of LP assets with personal assets. From a practice perspective, it should be noted that family limited partnership agreements often contain provisions restricting transfer of interest in the LP. Restrictions on transfer generally result in valuation discounts for lack of marketability. Commonly, the terms of a family limited partnership agreement will limit transfer of units to certain permitted classes of individuals, which, for example, may only include other family members. Here, Benny has transferred his interest in the FLP to Katie or Joseph (or both). Typically, such a sale would be in compliance with the provisions of an FLP agreement. Another possibility that was not given in the answer options would be for the FLP to redeem some or all of Benny's interest in the FLP. Such a redemption would result in the FLP distributing cash in exchange for the units held by Benny.

Answer (B) is incorrect. The facts under Answer (B) would likely result in Benny improperly retaining an interest under IRC § 2036(a), causing the assets contributed to the LP to be included in his estate at fair market value. In *Strangi v. Commissioner*, 417 F.3d 468 (5th Cir. 2005), the Fifth Circuit Court of appeals held that "possession or enjoyment" under IRC § 2036(a) will be found where assets contributed to a family limited partnership remain available to pay expenses and debts incurred by the taxpayer-decedent both before and after the taxpayer-decedent's death. Id. at 478. Upon contribution, taxpayer-decedent began receiving monthly payments from the FLP to cover his rent and other living expenses. After taxpayer's death, the FLP formed by the taxpayer-decedent distributed substantial amounts of money to pay for funeral expenses, estate administration expenses, specific bequests, and personal debts that taxpayer had incurred. The court found that the distributions were strong evidence that taxpayer and his children had an implicit understanding by which taxpayer would continue to use his assets as needed, and therefore retain "possession or enjoyment" within the meaning of IRC § 2036(a)(1). Id. The court also noted that, upon formation of the FLP, taxpayer did not retain assets sufficient to meet his own living expenses and expenses that would have been expected upon his death. Id. If as suggested under Answer (B), Benny, as general manager, begins making distributions to himself, he risks a successful challenge that he retained an interest in the limited partnership assets.

Answers (C) and (D) are incorrect. For reasons explained above, the partnership's payment of Benny's debt would be considered an improper retained interest under IRC § 2036(a). Answer (D) may solve part of Benny's problems, but Benny's creditors in bankruptcy will likely levy on Benny's partnership units. Often, as a practical matter, this will result in the trustee in bankruptcy becoming an assignee of the partnership units. It would be better for Benny to attempt first to sell his interest in the partnership and settle his debts.

163.   This question is designed to elicit a discussion of the possible IRS attacks under the Code. In short, the facts are an example of the wrong manner in which to form a family limited partnership. As discussed previously, Benny should avoid contribution of substantially all of his assets, leaving nothing for him to subsist upon after creation of the entity. By contributing all of his assets, Benny risks an assertion by the IRS that he inappropriately retained an interest in the contributed assets under IRC § 2036(a)(1). Further, the fact that Katie and Joseph immediately received a 5 percent interest in the capital of the partnership could result in a holding similar to the holding in *Senda v. Commissioner* where gift and the contribution were determined to be simultaneous and that the two transfers were "integrated." Indeed, the facts presented here are worse than the facts in *Senda v. Commissioner*. See discussion in Question 160 above.

The facts of this problem raise additional issues in relation to § 2036(a). In *Strangi v. Commissioner*, also discussed in Question 162 above, the taxpayer contended that, even if an interest was retained in assets contributed to a family limited partnership as contemplated under IRC § 2036(a)(1), the value of the assets contributed should nonetheless be excluded from the taxable estate, based on the "bona fide sale" exception contained in IRC § 2036(a)(1). 417 F.3d 468, 480 (5th Cir.

2005). IRC § 2036(a)(1) provides an exception for any transfer of property that is a "bona fide sale for an adequate and full consideration in money or money's worth." Id. In order for the exception to apply, there must be (1) a bona fide sale and (2) adequate and full consideration. Id. Indicating that the requirement of adequate and full consideration requirement was fulfilled, the Court focused on whether the transfer was a "bona fide sale." In an effort to support a bona fide sale, the taxpayer forwarded several non-tax reasons for transferring the assets to the partnership. Id. Among other things, the taxpayer argued that the partnership was formed to create a joint investment vehicle for the partners and to permit centralized active management of assets owned by the taxpayer. Id. In rejecting the taxpayer's arguments, the court reasoned that while a relatively small contribution of a minority partner is not, by itself, sufficient grounds for finding that a contribution of assets is not bona fide, where the partnership never actually makes any investments, the existence of minimal minority contributions may be insufficient to overcome taxpayer's assertion that a joint investment purpose existed. Id. at 481.

With respect to active management of the taxpayer's assets, the court reasoned that because 70 percent of the transfer consisted of various brokerage accounts, which were not and would not be actively managed by the partnership, no actual management by the partnership ever took place. Like the taxpayer in *Strangi*, it would appear that Benny predominantly owns securities held in brokerage accounts that upon contribution will not result in the partnership meaningfully managing the securities. Also, Katie and Joseph did not contribute any assets to the partnership. They merely acquired an interest upon formation. Therefore, it is not likely that Benny's goal of pooling resources or consolidating the ownership of his assets will be accomplished. It is more likely that a court will agree with an assertion by the Commissioner that there was not a bona fide sale for adequate consideration. It is also more likely that the court will not accept these as non-tax reasons as a foundation for forming the partnership and less likely that the court would find that Benny's transfer of assets to the partnership lacked a substantial non-tax purpose. Given the IRS's current predisposition to challenge valuation discounts assigned to gifts of FLP interests, Benny should be cautious to form the limited partnership within the bounds of the numerous recent court decisions.

164. **Answer (D) is the correct answer.** The issue being explored here is whether a transfer was effectuated and, if so, whether the transfer was complete enough to incur gift tax. At the heart of these issues is the question of whether a trust was created for the benefit of Barry. If so, a taxable gift was effectuated. The gift tax is not applicable to a mere transfer of bare legal title. §Treas. Reg. 25.2511-1(g). Thus, for example, the gift tax does not apply to a transfer of bare legal title in property to a trustee. Id. In order for a gift to occur, there must be a transfer of a beneficial interest in the property. Id. A trustee who holds legal title to property but who has no beneficial interest in the same will not incur gift tax upon distribution of the property from the trust. Instead, the grantor of the trust will be liable for gift tax when he or she has parted with dominion and control of the property. Generally, the grantor will have departed with dominion and control either when the assets are irrevocably contributed to the trust or, if the trust is revocable, when a distribution of assets takes place.

The creation of certain types of bank accounts may result in the formation of a trust if the creator of the account intends that a trust be formed. For example, a "totten" trust can be created when a settlor deposits money in a bank account for the benefit of another. *See, e.g., Green v. Green*, 559 A.2d 1047 (R.I. 1989). However, a gift requires a transfer of property to the recipient. The validity of a trust does not require actual delivery of property to the beneficiary. In the bank account setting, the property is money that is delivered or deposited into a bank account. As discussed above, a simple deposit or transfer of the money does not amount to a gift unless there is also intent to create a trust for the benefit of another individual. The settlor's intent to transfer a beneficial interest in the money is paramount to the creation of a trust in the form of a bank account or otherwise. Id. at 1050. Intent to create a trust must be shown by an act or declaration made during the settlor's lifetime. Id.

Here, Dad creates a joint bank account for himself and names Barry as a cosignatory of the account. Upon deposit of funds into the account, there has been no delivery of a beneficial interest in the property (here money) to Barry and, therefore, no gift at the time of the deposit. If Dad retains the right to withdraw amounts from the account without Barry's consent, then Dad can regain control of all the account funds without Barry's consent. *See* Treas. Reg. § 25.2511-2(c). However, in Answer (D), Dad indicates that if Barry gets into financial trouble he is welcome to withdraw some of the money for himself. Dad's assertion here indicates clear intent to transfer the funds for the benefit of Barry. The gift occurs when Barry actually withdraws some of money and pays off his sports car. When Barry draws upon the account for his own benefit, delivery has taken place. With both intent to transfer a beneficial interest and delivery, Dad has completed a gift to Barry at the time of and to the extent Barry withdraws amounts without any obligation to account for the proceeds to Dad. *See* Treas. Reg. § 25.2511-1(h)(example 4).

> *Note:* Determination of the donee's rights under local law is important to the determination of gift tax consequences associated with the transfer. As discussed above, where a donor retains the ability to revoke, amend, or modify the rights of the donee, there is no completion of the gift and no gift tax is incurred. This outcome is consistent with Section 6-211 of the Uniform Probate Code (the "UPC"). Section 6-211(c) of the UPC takes the position that a donee or beneficiary in an account having a payable-on-death ("POD") designation has no right to sums on deposit during the lifetime of any party to the account. Under UPC § 6-211(c), it is presumed that a person who deposits funds in an account normally does not intend to make an irrevocable gift of the deposited funds. *See* Official Comment to § 6-211(c). The presumption can be overcome where there is a showing that a gift was intended.

Answers (A), (B), and (C) are all incorrect. In each of the remaining answers, unlike Answer (D), Barry is either not authorized to take any of the money for himself or is authorized to take some of the money but does not actually take any. In Answer (C), Dad has indicated intent to transfer a beneficial interest by authorizing Barry to withdraw funds. However, no deliver has occurred because Barry never actually withdraws. He simply continues to pay his father's medical bills.

In Answer (B), Dad has delivered the money, but he has only delivered bare legal title. By indicating that from that point in time forward, he wanted Barry to use the money only to pay his medical bills, the requisite intent to make a gift is lacking on Dad's part. The fact that Barry thereafter takes the money and purchases a new boat does not reflect a gift. Rather, Barry has taken the money without authorization.

Finally, in Answer (A), Dad stuffed some money into his bed mattress and authorized Barry to use the money if necessary to pay Dad's medical bills. By taking some of the money to pay one of Dad's hospital bills, Barry has not received any amounts. Under these circumstances, delivery does not exist, and no gift has been made from Dad to Barry. However, Dad's remark to Barry indicating that whatever money is left when I die is yours would indicate intent to give some as yet undetermined amount. However, in order for a gift to exist, the donor must depart with dominion and control. Dad continues to reserve the right to use of the funds in his mattress while he continues to live. Again, no gift would result under these facts.

165.   Answer (C) is the correct answer. The facts in this problem are similar to the facts presented in example 5 of Treas. Reg. § 25.2511-1(h) and Rev. Rul. 78-362. Chuck purchases the home with his own funds and has title conveyed to himself and Rhonda as joint tenants with rights of survivorship. Under applicable law, if

Chuck purchases the home with his own funds, has title conveyed to him and Rhonda as joint tenants with rights of survivorship and either Chuck or Rhonda may individually sever his or her joint interest, Chuck is deemed to have made a gift to Rhonda. Treas. Reg. § 25.2511-1(h)(example 5). Because either party may sever their interest, Chuck is deemed to have made a gift to Rhonda of an equal share of the home. *See* Treas. Reg. § 25.2511-1(h); Rev. Rul. 78-362.

The amount of the gift that Chuck is deemed to have given to Rhonda must be determined. Treasury Regulation § 25.2512-8 provides that a transfer is taxable as a gift to the extent that the value of the property transferred exceeds the consideration in money or money's worth received by the transferor. Chuck and Rhonda owned equal interests in the home. Since Chuck contributed the $60,000 for the down payment and received no consideration from Rhonda, Chuck made a taxable gift of a one-half interest in the house to Rhonda when the property was placed into joint ownership. *See* Rev. Rul. 78-362. Thus, Chuck made a gift of $30,000 or one-half of the net value of the property ($300,000 less mortgage of $240,000) placed in the joint tenancy.

The second issue that arises is in relation to Chuck's payment of the mortgage from month to month. In general, a mortgage debt on mortgaged property is regarded as an obligation of the owner of the property. Id. Payment of the mortgage debt by someone else is treated the same as a cash transfer to the owner of the property. Because the mortgage expenses were obligations of both Chuck and Rhonda in equal shares, Chuck's monthly payments of the mortgage were gifts to Rhonda each time the payments were made. Thus, Chuck made gifts to Rhonda of $2,000 each time he made a monthly mortgage payment. For the year, Chuck made an additional $24,000 (12 times $2,000) gift to Rhonda. Combined with the $30,000 gift in relation to the down payment, Chuck has made a $54,000 ($30,000 plus $24,000) gift to Rhonda for the year.

Answers (A), (B), and (D) are all incorrect. Answer (A) contemplates a gift of one-half the value of the home. It remains to be seen whether over time Chuck will continue to make the mortgage payments. If Chuck continued to make the mortgage payments, the full amount of all of the annual gifts would be $150,000. However, the gift for the first year would not include payments in following years. Answer (B) is incorrect because it does not factor in the gifts related to the mortgage payments during the year. Answer (D) is incorrect because it overlooks the fact of any gift at all from Chuck to Rhonda.

166.   No, the answer will be the same. As discussed at length above, state law plays an important role in determining whether the creation of either type of tenancy results in an absolute right to take possession. Creation of either a joint tenancy or a tenancy in common may result in a taxable gift so long as the tenancy gives each owner the absolute right to take possession of an allocable or proportional share of the property. Where one party owns the property out right and later puts the property into a joint tenancy or tenancy in common with another person, the transfer is treated as a complete gift if the transfer is irrevocable under local law. Where the transfer is revocable, then a gift has not yet occurred. In Question 165, because local law allowed a tenant to sever his or her interest, an irrevocable

transfer occurred. When Chuck made the down payment and again when Chuck made each mortgage payment, each payment became irrevocable and, therefore, each transfer became a completed gift.

167. Answer (C) is still the correct answer. The rules as discussed above continue to apply in the sense that Chuck was still making gross gifts to his wife Rhonda when he made the down payment and is doing so each time he makes a mortgage payment. With respect to determination of the gross amount of the gift, the analysis is the same as in Question 165. However, IRC § 2523(a) applies such that where a donor gifts property to his or her spouse, there shall be a deduction in computing taxable gifts equal to the value of such property given. Thus, a deduction would be allowed in an amount equal to the gift. Due to the equal and offsetting marital deduction provided by IRC § 2523(a), there would be no gift tax liability in relation to Chuck's gift to Rhonda. Note that Answer (D) is inaccurate because it asserts that there is "no gift" rather than "no tax." By gifting a one-half joint interest in the home to Rhonda, as his spouse, Chuck will obtain a marital deduction equal to $30,000 or one-half the value of the down payment. Each time Chuck makes a mortgage payment, he will be making a gift of $2,000 to Rhonda and an equal and corresponding marital deduction will be allowed.

Moreover, IRC § 2523(d), applying specifically to inter-spousal gifting of joint interests, indicates that if one spouse gifts property to the other spouse as sole joint tenant, the donor spouse's interest in the property as a survivor, or allocable share if severance occurs, is not to be considered a retained interest. This rule provides an exception to the terminable interest rule and serves to avoid disqualification of the marital deduction. In general, a gift of terminable interest property does not qualify for the marital deduction. IRC § 2523(b)(1). Here, each gift to Rhonda will qualify for the marital deduction notwithstanding that the Chuck will retain a survivorship interest.

IRC § 2053: Expenses

168. **Answer (C) is the correct answer.** The issue here revolves around what impact state law has on the ability of a taxpayer to take an estate tax deduction. A deduction for estate tax purposes is allowed for funeral expenses, administrative expenses, claims against the estate, and certain unpaid mortgages that "are allowable by the laws of the jurisdiction under which the estate is being administered." IRC § 2053(a). If applicable state law "allows" a deduction for a given expense, then such expense is authorized as a deduction for federal estate tax purposes. The narrow question here is whether the $1,000 expense incurred by the executor is an allowable expense under state law. In *Commissioner v. Estate of Bosch*, the Supreme Court indicated that a federal court faced with interpreting state law in order to determine whether a deduction was allowed for federal estate tax purposes is required to give "proper regard" to state trial court decisions. 387 U.S. 456, 465 (1967). The underlying substantive rule involved is based on state law, and the state's highest court is the best authority on its own law. Id. If there has not been a decision by the highest state court, then federal authorities must attempt to determine what the highest court would find to be the state law after giving "proper regard" to lower state court rulings. Id. Federal courts will, in effect, sit as a state court where the availability of a deduction for federal estate tax purposes is dependent upon state law. Id. Under the facts of Answer (C), the state's highest appellate court ruled that the decedent could be buried in the cement-encased truck. Under *Estate of Bosch*, a federal court would be bound by the state court's decision that local law "allowed" the $1,000 deduction. Therefore, the cost of burying the decedent in his truck encased in cement is deductible.

Answers (A), (B), and (D) are incorrect. For reasons explained above, Answers (A), (B), and (D) are incorrect.

169. Again, funeral expenses are allowed as deductions from gross estate to the extent that they are actually expended and properly allowable by the law of the local jurisdiction. Treas. Reg. § 20.2053-2. The cost of the burial in the Ferrari is arguably deductible in full as a funeral expense in that state law appears to permit or "allow" the expense. However, for federal purposes, the regulations appear to additionally limit deductions to "reasonable" expenditures for a tombstone, monument, or mausoleum, or for a burial lot. This nonexclusive list of deductions would also include expenses incurred for a casket or burial receptacle.

On the one hand, because the estate actually paid for the Ferrari and because state law appears to allow such expenditure, the cost of the Ferrari is arguably deductible for federal estate tax purposes. On the other hand, the regulations and case law appear to limit deductions under a standard of reasonableness. Under *Davenport v. Commissioner*, the Tax Court indicated that the federal regulations suggest a standard of reasonableness in examining the amount of funeral expenditures. TC Memo 2006-215. For federal estate tax purposes, funeral deductions appear to be limited under a standard of reasonableness even though such deductions may be allowed under local law. Thus, the $367,887 of burial expenses incurred by the executor must be reasonable. Notwithstanding that the burial expenses may have been allowed under state law, if the cost of burying the decedent in the new Ferrari is determined to be unreasonable for federal tax purposes, it is likely that the Commissioner would challenge the cost of the burial as being unreasonable.

170.   **Answer (B) is the correct answer.** None of the reception expenses are deductible. In *Davenport v. Commissioner*, the Tax Court addressed similar facts and held that the reception expenses at issue were not deductible from gross estate as a funeral expense. TC Memo 2006-215. The Court found that the record was insufficient to establish the expense was connected with decedent's funeral. Id. Because the purpose of the reception was to recognize and thank third parties for their support during decedent's life, the Court distinguished the expenses from funeral expenses, which traditionally are in connection with a funeral in eulogizing and lying to rest the deceased. Id. In addition to being nondeductible for the reasons stated in *Davenport*, the reception expenses at issue in this problem are only approximated expenses. Only expenses that are actually paid are deductible. Treas. Reg. § 20.2053-2(a). In general, no deduction is allowed where the basis of the deduction is a vague or uncertain estimate. Treas. Reg. § 20.2053-1(b)(3). Here, the $4,000 deduction is merely an uncertain approximation and, therefore, is not deductible.

     Answer (A) is incorrect. For reasons explained above, Answer (A) is incorrect.

     Answers (C) and (D) are also incorrect. Answers (C) and (D) attempt to distinguish between expenses that are estimated versus those actually determined by substantiation. An otherwise allowable expense may be deducted even though its exact amount is not known at the time of the filing of the estate tax return. Treas. Reg. § 20.2053-1(b)(3). However, the amount of the deduction must be ascertainable with reasonable certainty, and the expense must actually be paid at some point. Id. And, as indicated above, no deduction may be taken upon the basis of a vague or uncertain estimate. Id. Regardless of whether the amount was actually determined or substantiated, the reception expenses are not deductible because they were not sufficiently connected with decedent's funeral.

171.   In this problem, the executor attempts to maximize the value of the estate by minimizing or avoiding the decrease in value associated with flooding the market with the paintings. In doing so, the executor incurs interim storage and commission expenses. Note that the executor had several options. She could have sold the paintings at the risk of realizing fewer proceeds in the short term. She could have sold the paintings as indicated in the facts of the problem over time. Or, she could

simply have distributed the paintings to the various beneficiaries and allowed them to sell the paintings. In the last option, there is a risk that the beneficiaries would nevertheless contemporaneously sell the paintings, thereby causing a drop in the price. In the first two scenarios, the executor would incur substantial commissions, whereas in the last option the beneficiaries would pay the commission.

The executor here goes with the second option, retaining the paintings in the estate, incurring commission expenses over time. Amounts deductible from gross estate as "administration expenses" are limited to expenses "actually and necessarily, incurred in the administration of the decedent's estate." Treas. Reg. § 20.2053-3(a). Such expenses include the costs associated with distribution of property to the persons entitled to it. Id. *See also* Treas. Regs. §§ 20.2053-3(a), -3(d). Miscellaneous administration expenses also include brokerage fees such as commissions if, likewise, the sale is "necessary" to pay administrative expenses. Treas. Reg. § 20.2053-3(d)(2). Since under the facts of the problem, the commission expenses were "actually incurred" and the expenses were "properly allowable under state law," the narrow issue becomes whether the commission expenses were "necessary" within the meaning of the regulations. However, there is a divergence of opinion in the courts as to whether expenses need only be "allowable" under applicable state law or whether an expense must be both "allowable" under state law and "necessary" under the federal treasury regulations in order for the expense to be deductible for federal estate tax purposes.

In the Seventh Circuit, an administrative expense may be deducted for federal tax purposes if local law allows the expense. *See Ballance v. U.S.*, 347 F.2d 419, 423 (7th Cir. 1965) (the definition of "administration expenses" in the Regulations including only such expenses as are necessary does not override the statutory provisions authorizing a deduction for administration expenses allowed by local state law under which the estate is being administered). Whereas the Second Circuit in *Estate of Smith v. Commissioner* agreed with the Tax Court's determination that although state law allowed certain commissions incurred by an estate in the sale of art, such expenses were not "necessary" to preserve the estate or to effect distribution of the art. 510 F.2d 479, 482–483 (2nd Cir. 1975). Thus, under the holding of *Estate of Smith*, federal courts may reexamine a lower state court's allowance of administration expenses "to determine whether they were in fact necessary to carry out the administration of the estate or merely prudent or advisable in preserving the interests of the beneficiaries." Id. at 483. Under facts similar to the problem, the Second Circuit Court of Appeals in *Estate of Smith* held that the expenses were not deductible. Thus, the executor's decision to hold the paintings and incur the expenses was not necessary to preserve the estate. Rather, under the *Ballance* and *Estate of Smith* decisions, the estate could not deduct the storage or commission expenses.

172. **Answer (D) is the correct answer.** Property taxes are deductible from gross estate to the extent that such tax liabilities are claims against the estate. Treas. Reg. § 20.2053-6(a). In order to be deductible, property taxes must be accrued prior to decedent's death, and such accrued taxes must be an enforceable obligation as of the time of decedent's death. Treas. Reg. § 20.2053-6(b). Whether property

taxes have accrued depends upon their status under state law, and deductible taxes include both matured as well as unmatured obligations. *See* Treas. Reg. § 20.2053-4. *See also Pardee v. Commissioner*, 49 T.C. 140, 151 (1967). Because the taxes for the first half of the year as described in Answer (D) are all due and payable as of the time of decedent's death, they are deductible by decedent's estate.

Answer (A) is incorrect. Income taxes are deductible only if the taxes are on income that is includible in decedent's gross income for the period *prior to* his or her death. Treas. Reg. § 20.2053-6(f). Tax on income received *after* decedent's death is not deductible. Id. In Answer (A), the income taxes are due on income received during the whole year rather than just the portion of the year in which decedent was alive.

Answer (B) is incorrect. Property taxes are not deductible unless the taxes accrued prior to the decedent's death. Treas. Reg. § 20.2053-6(b). In Answer (B), the property taxes related to the whole year as opposed to accruing prior to decedent's death.

Answer (C) is also incorrect. For reasons explained above, Answer (C) is also incorrect.

173. **Answer (D) is the correct answer,** Under current regulations, liabilities arising out of torts are deductible. Treas. Reg. § 20.2053-4. Generally, the decision of a local court as to the amount of a claim under state law will be accepted. Treas. Reg. § 20.2053-1(b)(2). Thus, if the question before the court is whether a certain claim should be allowed, a court decree in favor of that claim will ordinarily be accepted as establishing the validity and amount of the claim. Id. *See also Estate of Nilson v. Commissioner*, T.C. Memo 1972-141. In Answer (D), judgment was entered by a state court. Therefore, the $500,000 judgment is a deductible claim.

Answers (A), (B), and (C) are incorrect. In general, no deduction is allowed if the basis for the deduction is a vague or uncertain estimate. Treas. Reg. § 20.2053-1(b)(3). If the amount of the liability is not ascertainable, no deduction will be allowed. In Answers (A) and (B), offers of settlement existed but no acceptance of the offer (or counter-offer) took place. Without acceptance of the settlement offer, there is no guaranty that any settlement will take place upon which a deduction could be supported. In Answer (C), the amount of legal fees due are estimated and not yet ascertainable. No deduction is allowed if the amount of the expense is vague or uncertain. Id. Here, because the amount of legal fees is merely an approximation, no amount of deduction can be determined.

Note: On April 20, 2007, regulations were proposed that, if finally adopted, will govern the treatment of expense deductions for estate tax purposes. *See* Prop. Reg. § 20.2053-1 (Reg. 143316-03, April 20, 2007). Among other things, the proposed regulations specifically address claims related to settlements indicating that an executor may rely on a settlement to establish the amount deductible if several conditions are satisfied. The conditions required are: (1) the settlement resolves a bona fide issue in an active and genuine contest; (2) the settlement is the product of arm's length negotiations by parties having adverse interests with respect to the claim; and (3) the settlement is within the range of reasonable outcomes under applicable state law. Prop. Reg. § 20.2053-1(b)(3). Under the proposed regulations, no deduction is authorized for amounts paid in settlement of an unenforceable claim. It would appear that the Service seeks to scrutinize claims by related parties that do not appear to be at arm's length inasmuch as there is a risk under these circumstances that taxpayers may attempt to disguise a bequest to look like a deductible claim.

174. **Answer (B) is the correct answer.** Here, a controversial issue arises in relation to whether post death events are to be considered in determining the amount or "value" of an estate tax deduction. Wife had a reasonably long life expectancy as of the date of decedent's death. Due to the projected length of Wife's life, the actuarial value of her life estate in decedent's assets was correspondingly high. However, she unexpectedly died very soon after decedent and before she received any income payments. For deduction purposes, what value should be assigned to Wife's and Charity's respective claims?

In *McMorris v. Commissioner*, decedent's estate took a deduction for federal income taxes due as of the date of decedent's death. 243 F.3d 1254 (10th Cir. 2001). The IRS contested the amount that decedent reported as basis and gain in the stock, arguing that decedent's basis in the stock was lower than reported and that decedent owed tax on substantially higher gains. However, the decedent's estate was successful in proving that the decedent's basis in the stock was higher than originally reported by the decedent. As such, decedent's original sale of the stock resulted in a loss instead of gain and a refund (as opposed to a liability) arose. Notwithstanding that decedent's estate was due a refund, the decedent's estate sought to deduct the tax liabilities associated with the sale of stock that were thought to have existed as of the date of decedent's death.

The Commissioner argued that because there ended up being no tax due in relation to the stock (and indeed a refund), decedent's estate was no longer entitled to the deduction. Decedent's estate argued that post-death events are not considered in determining the amount of an estate tax deduction because the original income tax liabilities related to valid and enforceable claims against the estate at the time of decedent's death. The Tenth Circuit Court of Appeals agreed with decedent's estate finding that post-death events are not to be considered in valuing a deduction taken on an estate tax return several years before. The facts of the problem closely mirror the facts in the *McMorris* case, and the outcome of *McMorris* is most accurately reflected in Answer (B). Thus, Wife's claim against Testator's estate should be valued at $900,000 for deduction purposes.

Answers (A), (C), and (D) are incorrect. While substantial guidance is available for determining the value of an asset for purposes of determining gross estate, IRC § 2053(a) is not specific as to the manner in which to value a claim. There is some disagreement among courts with respect to the extent that post-death events are taken into consideration when valuing such claims. In *Ithaca Trust v. Commissioner*, 279 U.S. 151 (1929), the Supreme Court held that the value of a charitable remainder interest for charitable deduction purposes must be determined as of date of death. Consistent with the holding in *Ithaca Trust*, a number of courts, such as the one ruling on the *McMorris* case, discussed supra, have held that post-death events may not be considered in determining the value of a claim against an estate. On the other hand, in *Jacobs v. Commissioner*, the Eighth Circuit distinguished *Ithaca Trust*, stating that ". . . the claims which Congress intended to be deducted were actual claims, not theoretical ones." 34 F.2d 233 (8th Cir. 1929). Under the *Jacobs* line of reasoning, only claims determined to be valid and actually paid as of the date of death may be deducted. Id. at 235. Thus, in some circuits, under the *Jacobs* line of reasoning, the amount deductible under IRC § 2053(a)(3) is the actual amount paid by the estate in satisfaction of the claim, and post-death events may impact the "value" of a deduction for estate tax purposes.

> *Note:* On April 20, 2007, regulations were proposed that, if finally adopted, will govern the treatment of expense deductions for estate tax purposes. *See* Prop. Reg. § 20.2053-1 (Reg. 143316-03, April 20, 2007). Among other things, the proposed regulations specifically address claims related the deduction of taxes and post-death adjustments to tax liabilities. Subsection (g) of the newly proposed regulation provides that post-death adjustments that either increase or reduce a decedent's pre-death tax liability affect the amount of the deduction for purposes of IRC § 2053(a)(3). Id. For example, if after decedent's death the IRS asserts a deficiency of $100,000 and, pursuant to a bona fide defense against the deficiency, the tax liability is reduced from $100,000 to $90,000, then the estate may deduct $90,000. Under the proposed regulation, a post-death increase in the initially determined deficiency will correspondingly increase the deduction related to the tax liability under IRC § 2053. *See* Prop. Reg. 20.2053-6(g)(example 1). Similarly, it would appear that a post-death reduction in tax liability will reduce the deduction under IRC § 2053(a)(3). *See* Prop. Reg. 20.2053-6(g)(example 2). Obviously, adoption of the proposed regulations in their current form would likely impact the outcome of this problem.

175. **Answer (C) is the correct answer.** In order for the amount of the mortgage to be deductible, the decedent's estate must be liable for the amount of the mortgage (e.g., the mortgage must be a recourse mortgage for which the estate is liable), and the full value of the property subject to the mortgage must be included in decedent's gross estate. IRC § 2053(a)(3), see also Treas. Reg. § 20.2053-7. Under this rule, decedent must include $500,000, the undiminished value of the home, in order to qualify for a deduction of the outstanding recourse mortgage of $300,000 from gross estate.

Answers (A), (B), and (D) are incorrect. For reasons discussed above, Answers (A) and (D) are incorrect. While Answer (B) appears to result in the same tax outcome, it is inappropriate to net the mortgage against the outstanding value where the mortgage is in the nature of a recourse debt.

176. Yes, the answer to Question 175 would change. If the mortgage is nonrecourse and the decedent's estate is not liable for the mortgage, only the value of the estate's equity (fair market value of the property less the mortgage) is included in gross

estate. Treas. Reg. § 20.5053-7. Under these circumstances, as indicated in Answer (B), no deduction is allowed. Rather, decedent must include in gross estate $200,000, the net equity that decedent had in the home as of the date of death.

177. **Answer (B) is the correct answer.** This question focuses on whether the claims described in the several answer options were engaged in with good faith and accompanied by adequate consideration. In general, a claim for deduction arising out of indebtedness must be founded on a promise or agreement that is bona fide and supported by adequate consideration in money or money's worth. IRC § 2053(c)(1)(A). Where a claim is not supported by an exchange for monetary value made in good faith, no deduction will incur. Claims based on exchanges between family members are more carefully scrutinized by the Service and the courts.

In *Estate of Flandrau v. Commissioner*, taxpayer gifted cash her children and their spouses during life. 994 F.2d 91 (2nd Cir. 1993). The children then lent the money back to the taxpayer. In return for the purported loans, the children received non–interest-bearing unsecured promissory notes from taxpayer. Upon taxpayer's death, her estate deducted the children's claims represented by the outstanding promissory notes. In affirming the judgment of the Tax Court that the claim was neither bona fide nor supported by adequate consideration, the Second Circuit Court of Appeals looked at the substance of the transaction and found that the children never expected that the money they transferred to decedent would be repaid. Id. at 93.

In Answer (B), Daughter engages in an apparent loan of $100,000 to Father. Father gives his promissory note of $100,000 in exchange for $50,000 of land from Daughter. The transaction results in Daughter having a purported claim against father's estate in the amount of $100,000. However, consistent with the Court's reasoning in *Flandrau*, $50,000 of the loan from Father to Daughter is not supported by consideration and is not deductible. The remaining $50,000 of the loan is supported by consideration and is a deductible claim against the estate, and Answer (B) results in a deduction of $50,000 for estate tax purposes.

Answer (A) is incorrect. Answer (A) is incorrect because decedent received nothing at all in return for the promissory note and, therefore, no claim or deduction is allowed.

Answer (C) is incorrect. In Answer (C), decedent made a note to his fiancée in which he promised to pay her $50,000 in return for her promise to marry him. In general, consideration in the form of love and affection or a promise of marriage is not reducible to value in money or money's worth. Here, the entire amount of decedent's promise to pay his fiancée is supported only by the fiancée's promise of marriage, future love, and affection, and is not regarded as value in money or money's worth. *See, e.g., Commissioner v. Wemyss*, 324 U.S. 303 (1945). See also further discussion regarding the gift and income tax perspectives in Topic 1 of the gift tax section.

Answer (D) is incorrect. In Answer (D), decedent co-signed a promissory note that his daughter made to a third party for $100,000. Rev. Rul. 84-42 provides that where the decedent is a guarantor on a loan, the amount deductible as an administrative expense is limited to the amount the estate actually pays on the debt or for which the estate is held liable. *See also Commissioner v. Wragg*, 141 F.2d 638, 640 (1st Cir. 1944). To the extent that a decedent's estate is not actually held liable for the amount of the indebtedness, no deduction is allowed as a claim against the estate. Id. In Answer (D), because Daughter continued to make payments to the third party consistent with the terms of the note, there is no indication that decedent's estate will actually be liable for the debt or actually make a payment on the debt. Therefore, no deduction is allowed.

> *Note:* On April 20, 2007, regulations were proposed that, if finally adopted, will govern the treatment of deductions for claims against and estate. *See* Prop. Reg. § 20.2053-1 (Reg. 143316-03, April 20, 2007). Among other things, the proposed regulations specifically address claims by family members and provide that family relationships create the potential for collusion in asserting invalid or exaggerated claims in order to reduce a decedent's taxable estate. Prop. Reg. § 20.2053-4(b)(4). The proposed regulations create a rebuttable presumption that claims by a family member of the decedent are not bona fide and therefore are not deductible. Id. Adoption of these proposed regulations in their current form would at a minimum create a presumption that the claim asserted in Answer (A) is not bona fide or deductible.

IRC § 2054: Losses

178.   **Answer (A) is the correct answer.** A deduction is allowed for a loss resulting from a fire or other casualty that is incurred during the settlement of an estate. IRC § 2054. A deduction is not allowed if the loss is compensated for by insurance. In Answer (A), decedent's home valued at $250,000 was a complete loss when it burned down. Since the loss was incurred during the settlement of decedent's estate and was not compensated for by insurance, decedent's estate is entitled to a $250,000 casualty loss deduction under IRC § 2054.

Answer (B) is incorrect. Here, the loss occurred after the settlement of decedent's estate. If a loss occurs after an asset is distributed to a beneficiary, the loss may not be deducted by the estate. Treas. Reg. § 20.2054-1. Decedent's brother may be able to take advantage of the casualty loss deduction allowed under IRC § 165 on his federal income tax return.

Answer (C) is incorrect. In Answer (C), the loss arises from a fire that occurred prior to decedent's death. Again, because IRC § 2054 allows deductions only for losses incurred during the settlement of an estate, no deduction is allowed to the estate under these circumstances. Similar to the analysis in Answer (B) above, decedent may be able to take advantage of the loss deduction allowed under IRC § 165 on his final income tax return.

Answer (D) is incorrect. As discussed above, an IRC § 2054 deduction is not allowed if the loss is compensated for by insurance. In Answer (D), the loss from the fire was completely compensated for by insurance proceeds and therefore no deduction is allowed.

179. **Answer (B) is the correct answer.** This question investigates the meaning of the words "casualty" and "theft" as used in IRC § 2054 and the regulations thereunder. Neither term is defined in IRC § 2054 or the regulations thereunder. Answer (B) contains a scenario wherein decedent's stock was stolen by a stockbroker during the settlement of the estate and, therefore, will support a deduction from a loss arising from theft by decedent's estate.

Answers (A) and (D) are incorrect. While it may appear that decedent's home has lost value or that decedent's stock holdings have gone down in value due to an event that occurred after decedent's death and during the settlement of decedent's estate, no "casualty" loss has occurred directly with respect to either the home or the stock. In *Leewitz v. United States*, 110 Ct. Cl. 645 (Ct. Cl. 1948), the decedent's estate contended that it was entitled to a casualty loss deduction due to the decrease in the value of stock the decedent's estate held in several corporations that suffered losses in World War II. The corporations had operations in Belgium and France, and each of the corporations held assets that were either destroyed or sequestered by the German army. In holding that no deduction was allowed and that no casualty loss occurred, the Court reasoned that while evidence showed a reduction in value of the stock, there was no proof that the stock itself became worthless by means of a casualty. Id. at 655. Under the reasoning applied by the *Leewitz* Court, the types of losses described in Answers (A) and (D) reflect unrealized losses due to reductions in value that resulted from market forces. At the point in time that the home or the stocks are sold by the estate, the estate may be able to substantiate a loss deduction under the provisions of the Code for income tax purposes. Another avenue that the decedent's estate may benefit from is the alternative valuation date election provided for under IRC § 2032.

Answer (C) is also incorrect. Under the facts of Answer (C), a theft occurred when the broker took the stock from the decedent's account. However, as previously discussed, the loss must be incurred during the settlement of the estate. Here, the loss occurs prior to decedent's death.

180. **Answer (B) is the correct answer.** While neither IRC § 2054 nor the regulations thereunder describe how the loss is calculated, if the property is not completely destroyed, loss is determined by figuring the decrease in fair market value of the damaged property as a result of the casualty event. Here, the value of the home prior to the storm was $250,000, and the value of the home after the storm was $150,000. As such, the decrease in value was $100,000 ($250,000 - $150,000). It is at least worth noting that the original basis of $100,000 is not relevant. When decedent passed away, her estate received a step up in the basis of the home to its fair market value of $250,000. Thus, the decrease in value to $100,000 due to storm damage again resulted in an actual loss of $100,000.

Answers (A), (C), and (D) are incorrect. For reasons explained above, Answers (A), (C), and (D) are incorrect.

181. Yes, the loss would be reduced from $100,000 to $25,000. If a loss is partially compensated for by insurance, the excess of the amount of the loss over the insurance proceeds received is deductible. In this case, the loss of $100,000 exceeds the $75,000 of insurance proceeds by $25,000. Thus, the deductible loss is only $25,000.

IRC § 2055: Charitable Transfers

182. **Answer (B) is the correct answer.** The issue that arises in this problem is whether the person or organization that receives the bequest is a qualified recipient. A charitable contribution deduction from gross estate is allowed for all bequests, legacies, devises, or transfers to certain qualified recipients. IRC § 2055(a). In general, qualified recipients include governmental entities such as the United States, any state, any political subdivision of a state, or the District of Columbia. Id. Additionally, any religious, charitable, scientific, literary, or education organization will qualify as a recipient. Id. A contribution to a state university such as the University of Wyoming would be deductible as a charitable contribution.

Answer (A) is incorrect. While a contribution to the Roman Catholic Church may be deductible as a charitable contribution to a church, a contribution to an individual priest for his own use would not be a contribution for religious purposes.

Answers (C) and (D) are also incorrect. Answers (C) and (D) result in contributions to organizations or trusts that are formed to either participate in a political campaign or that attempts to influence legislation. An estate may not deduct a bequest to an organization (or trust) if the organization does not meet the requirements outlined under IRC § 501(c)(3). IRC § 2055(a)(3). IRC § 501(c)(3) disqualifies organizations that attempt to influence legislation, participate in, or intervene in any political campaign on behalf of (or in opposition to) any candidate for public office. IRC § 2055(a)(3), see also *Buder v. United States*, 7 F.3d 1382, 1385 (8th Cir. 1993). Thus, neither a lobbying group nor the Democratic National Committee would not qualify as an exempt organization under IRC § 501(c)(3) and would not qualify for an estate tax charitable deduction under IRC § 2055(a).

183. **Answer (D) is the correct answer.** In general, a direct transfer to a qualified charity will be deductible for estate tax purposes. However, a failure on the part of a decedent to name a specific qualified recipient may result in a denial of a charitable bequest. In Answer (D), the executor of decedent's estate receives the amounts in trust to give to one of three qualified charities. The executor has a duty to distribute the bequest for purposes that are exclusively charitable within the meaning of IRC § 2055(a). Although the executor is not a qualified person, the $35,000 passing to the United Way is eligible for a federal estate tax charitable deduction. *See* Rev. Rul. 69-285. It is noteworthy to point out that in certain states, local law may have an adverse impact on this analysis. *See* Rev. Rul. 71-441, 1971-2 C.B. 335. However, the facts of the question specifically negate the impact of state law.

Answers (A) and (B) are incorrect. In Answers (A) and (B), the bequest is not made to a charity. Rather, the bequest is made to an executor who is not a qualified charity or decedent's widow who must consent. Thus, the bequest is conditional upon some third party giving consent. The regulations provide that unless the possibility of the condition occurring is highly remote, no deduction will be allowed where the charitable transfer is dependent upon some condition precedent. Treas. Reg. § 20.2055-2(b)(1). In *Delaney v. Gardner*, 204 F.2d 855 (1953), the decedent bequeathed cash amounts to a decedent's executors, ". . . not subject to any trust, but in the hope that they will dispose of it at their absolute discretion and according to their own judgment, but giving due weight to any memoranda I may leave or any oral expressions by me to them made during my life." Id. at 856. The executors made distributions to charities on the list provided in the memorandum. The Court disallowed a charitable deduction because the executors had discretion to withhold part or the entire bequest from the several charities. Id. at 859–860. Answer (A) mirrors the facts of *Delaney v. Gardner*. Similarly, in Answer (B), because the wife has discretion to prevent the charities from receiving the bequest, no charitable deduction is allowed. *See also First Trust Co. of St. Paul v. Reynolds*, 137 F.2d 518 (8th Cir. 1943). Thus, under the facts of Answers (A) and (B), either a trustee or a wife has discretion to prevent the bequest from going to a qualified charity.

Answer (C) is also incorrect. Answer (C) is incorrect because although it may be laudable that the decedent bequeathed money to an indigent person, Byron T. Watson as a private individual is not a qualified recipient.

184. **Answer (B) is the correct answer.** The issue in this problem is whether a disclaimer that results in a transfer to a charity will affect the estate's ability to obtain a charitable deduction. As was seen in the previous problem, under certain circumstances where a contingency must occur in order for a charitable bequest to occur, the estate may not be authorized to take the deduction under IRC § 2055. However, for decedents dying after 1976, if a charitable transfer results from either a qualified disclaimer or termination, the estate tax charitable deduction generally is allowed. Treas. Reg. § 20.2055-2(c). Answer (B) contemplates a situation whereby the decedent's son disclaimed property that the decedent had bequeathed to him. Because the son executed a qualified disclaimer, the property passed to the residuary, which thereafter was transferred to a qualified charitable recipient. Regardless of the fact that the transfer was contingent upon the disclaimer, the estate will be able to deduct the value of the bequest that the son disclaimed.

Answers (A) and (C) are incorrect. In Answers (A) and (C) there is no qualified disclaimer. In order for there to be a qualified disclaimer under IRC § 2055(a), there must be a complete termination of the power to consume, invade, or appropriate property for the benefit of an individual before such power has been exercised and before the filing of the estate tax return. IRC § 2055(a). In Answers (A) and (C), the daughter does not completely terminate her life income interest in the assets. Rather, she attempts to give only a portion of her interest to the Red Cross. Under the circumstances set forth in Answer (A), no amount is actually remitted to the Red Cross unless income from the assets exceeds $1,000,000 in a given year. In Answer (C), the daughter gives up the income only for the foreseeable future.

Answer (D) is also incorrect. In general, receipt of consideration for a disclaimer will prevent the disclaimer from being qualified under the rules. In PLR 7809043, a beneficiary proposed to disclaim an interest in a trust in exchange for a lump sum payment. The Service found that the proposed disclaimer did not constitute an unqualified refusal by the beneficiary. Instead the Service reasoned that the beneficiary would merely be engaging in a sale or exchange as opposed to a charitable contribution. *See* PLR 7809043. Although in Answer (D) the daughter disclaims all of her interest in the residual assets, it appears that she has received consideration in form of a job offer from the Red Cross. Like the beneficiary in the PLR, the daughter's disclaimer is likely to be disqualified for charitable deduction purposes.

185. **Answer (A) is the correct answer.** What is the correct amount of the charitable deduction allowed where the charitable bequest is in-kind? IRC § 2055(a) indicates that an estate tax charitable deduction is allowed in "the amount" of all qualified bequests and transfers. The Regulations clarify that a deduction is allowed for the "value" of property included in gross estate at the time of death that is transferred to a qualified recipient. Treas. Reg. § 20.2055-1(a). So long as the sculpture was included in the decedent's gross estate, the date-of-death value of the property transferred to a qualified recipient may be deducted. In this case, the date-of-death value is $2,000,000 and, therefore, the deduction amount is also $2,000,000, consistent with Answer (A).

     Answers (B), (C), and (D) are incorrect. For reasons explained above, the remaining answers are all incorrect.

186. Yes, the answer to Question 185, above, would change if an IRC § 2032 election was made. If an alternative valuation election is made under IRC § 2032 to value the assets of an estate six months after the date of death, then for purposes of the IRC § 2055 charitable deduction, an adjustment must be made for any difference between the date-of-death value and the value as of the date six months after the date of decedent's death. IRC § 2032(b). In this instance, the value of the sculpture decreased from $2,000,000 to $1,500,000, thereby reducing the amount of the deduction available by $500,000. As is displayed in the facts of this question, in addition to reducing the value of assets *included* in a decedent's estate, an IRC § 2032 election to report the value of gross estate six months after the date of death will cause a corresponding decrease in the IRC § 2055 charitable deduction.

187. **Answer (A) is the correct answer.** Here, IRC § 2522(a), pertaining to gift tax charitable deductions, is implicated rather than IRC § 2055, related to the estate tax. However the two rules operate similarly under the circumstances of the problem. A charitable deduction is allowed in computing total taxable gifts for a calendar year for gifts made to qualified recipients. The definition of a "qualified recipient" for gift tax purposes is essentially the same as the definition for estate tax purposes under IRC § 2055. Thus, because the National Museum of Art is an IRC § 501(c)(3) organization, it is a qualified recipient under IRC § 2522. For gift tax purposes, the amount of the deduction is set at the fair market value of the property on the date that it was transferred to the charity. IRC § 2522. Consistent with Answer (A), a gift tax deduction of $2,000,000 is allowed.

Answers (B), (C), and (D) are incorrect. For reasons explained above, the remaining answers are all incorrect.

188. No, the answer to Question 187 above would remain the same. With several exceptions not relevant here, a nonresident individual who is not a citizen of the United States is treated the same as a citizen who is a resident. IRC § 2522(b), see also Treas. Reg. § 25.2522(b)-1. It is also worth noting that if we assumed instead that Rose, a nonresident noncitizen, had passed away and had made a charitable bequest of the sculpture, an estate tax charitable deduction would be allowed in lieu of the gift tax deduction. Again, the rules pertaining to charitable deductions are not meaningfully different as between the gift tax and the estate tax.

189. **Answer (A) is the correct answer.** The various scenarios provided in the answer options require an analysis of transfers that have both private and charitable purposes. For decedents passing away after December 31, 1969, where property passes in part to a charity and in part to a private noncharitable party, no estate tax charitable deduction is allowed for the value of the portion of the interest that passes to the charity. IRC § 2055(e)(2). Under the facts of Answer (A), the decedent retained a present interest in the income from the property while leaving a remainder interest to the charity. During decedent's life a split interest in the property may have existed. However, by retaining a life interest in the rental property, the full value of the property is included in decedent's gross estate. *See* IRC § 2036. Thus, the decedent did not make a split-interest transfer as contemplated by IRC § 2055(e)(2). The bequest of the post-death interest in the rental property to a qualified charity will result in a IRC § 2055 charitable deduction.

Answers (B) and (C) are incorrect. Unlike the transfer described in Answer (A), the transfers in Answers (B) and (C) are split-interest bequests. In Answer (B), decedent's brother will receive a life estate in the rental property and the remainder will pass to a charity. As discussed above, no charitable deduction is allowed for the charitable portion of a split-interest gift. Therefore, decedent's bequest of the remainder interest in the rental property to the charity will not result in a charitable deduction. IRC § 2055(e)(2). Similarly, in Answer (C), the decedent's estate may not deduct the value of the bequest passing to the charity because the bequest is contingent upon decedent's brother surviving him. If decedent's brother survives decedent, then the charity will never receive a bequest.

Answer (D) is also incorrect. Because under the terms of the decedent's will no property will pass from decedent to a charity, no charitable deduction will be allowed.

Note: Although this question asks whether a charitable deduction would exist for the decedent's *estate* tax purposes, it is also relevant to ask whether a charitable deduction exists for *gift* tax purposes under the circumstances presented in Answer (A). Section 2522(c)(2) of the gift tax provisions provides a similar rule to that found in the estate tax sections of the Code. In general, where a split-interest gift is made after December 31, 1969, no deduction is allowed for the charitable portion of the gift unless specific conditions not present here are met. Thus, no gift tax deduction would have been available on creation of the trust.

IRC § 2056: Marital Deduction

190. **Answer (A) is the correct answer.** A decedent's estate may take a marital deduction under IRC § 2056 only if the decedent was either a U.S. citizen or a U.S. resident (or both). In general, the U.S. estate tax will not apply to one who is neither a U.S. citizen nor resident. Additionally, with certain exceptions, no marital deduction is allowed unless the decedent's spouse is a U.S. citizen. IRC § 2056(d). It is not sufficient that the surviving spouse be merely a U.S. resident. In Answer (A), the decedent is a resident of the United States and therefore is subject to the estate tax. *See* IRC § 2001(a). Further, in Answer (A), the surviving spouse is a citizen of the United States. It is not relevant that she is at the time of the bequest a resident of United Kingdom.

Answers (B), (C), and (D) are incorrect. In Answers (B) and (C), the surviving spouse is not a citizen of the United States and, therefore, no deduction is allowed pursuant to IRC § 2056(d). In Answer (D), although the surviving spouse is a citizen and resident of the United States, the decedent was neither a citizen nor a resident of the United States. *See* Treas. Reg. § 20.0-1(b).

> *Note:* Treas. Reg. § 20.0-1(a) provides that some of the provisions of the regulations may be affected by the provisions of an applicable death tax convention between the United States and other foreign countries. A death tax convention between the United States and another country may exempt certain transfers by means of a bequest. An estate and gift tax convention in force between the United States and the United Kingdom may impact the outcome of this answer.

191. No, as discussed in the previous problem, a marital deduction is not allowed because the surviving spouse is not a citizen of the United States. Rather, the surviving spouse is both a citizen and resident of France. IRC § 2056(d). However, the general rule of disallowance based upon noncitizenship of the surviving spouse does not apply to property that passes to a surviving spouse in a "qualified domestic trust." IRC § 2056(d)(2). Such trusts are often referred to as QDOT trusts and are governed by the provisions of IRC § 2056A. In order to qualify as a QDOT, the trust instrument must require that at least one trustee be either a U.S. citizen or domestic corporation. The trust instrument must also provide that no distributions (other than income) may be made unless the trustee has the right to withhold taxes from the distribution. With certain exceptions beyond the scope of this discussion, a tax is imposed upon any distributions made from the trust prior to the surviving spouse's death and upon the value of the property remaining in the trust on the date of the surviving spouse's death. *See* IRC § 2056A(b). Thus, amounts that are contributed to a QDOT do not completely escape U.S. taxation. It is important to note that if the Code allowed the estate of a deceased U.S. resident to benefit from a marital deduction in relation to assets distributed to a noncitizen surviving spouse, the assets received by the spouse may escape U.S. estate taxes.

192. **Answer (B) is the correct answer.** A deduction from gross estate is authorized in an amount equal to the value of property that "passes" from a decedent to his or her surviving spouse, and the value of the property is included in the decedent's estate. IRC § 2056(a). Under IRC § 2056(a) there are three basic requirements. There must be (1) a "surviving spouse" to which, (2) the property "passes," and (3) the property must be included in decedent's estate. Id. In order to qualify as a surviving spouse, the transferee must survive the decedent and the decedent must be married to the transferee at the time of death. *See* Rev. Rul. 79-354. If at the time of death the decedent was not married to the transferee, no marital deduction is allowed with respect to transferred property. Id. Under the circumstances set forth in Answer (B), the decedent's ex-spouse received a substantial amount of decedent's estate under his will, and his surviving spouse received nothing. Because the ex-spouse was not married to decedent at the time of his death, she does not qualify as a "spouse" for purposes of the statute and, therefore, no marital deduction is allowed.

Answer (A) is incorrect. In Answer (A), the property passes directly to the decedent's surviving spouse. Pursuant to IRC § 2056(c)(2), property is considered as "passing" to a surviving spouse if the property interest is inherited from the decedent. Because the surviving spouse directly inherited the assets, a marital deduction is allowed.

Answer (C) is also incorrect. Again the issue revolves around the definition of "passing," but in Answer (C) the assets are subject to the surviving spouse's elective share. "Passing," as used in the statute, includes, among other things, a dower interest or statutory interest in lieu of dower. IRC § 2056(c)(3). Because the surviving spouse's interest is an elective share more in the nature of a dower interest or a forced share, the transfer qualifies for the marital deduction.

Answer (D) is also incorrect. Despite the fact that the trust was created during decedent's life and that decedent was not married to his surviving spouse when the trust was created, the property transferred still qualifies for the marital deduction. In Rev. Rul. 79-354, the IRS ruled that a marital deduction is allowed with respect to money transferred when decedent was not married to the transferee at the time of the transfer but was married to transferee at the time of his death. Consistent with Rev. Rul. 79-354, a marital deduction should be allowed under the facts presented in Answer (D).

193. **Answer (C) is the correct answer.** Which one of the various real property interests described in the four answer options result in the property passing to his surviving spouse within the meaning of IRC § 2056(a)? Not only is it important to analyze which one qualifies for a marital deduction but also why any of the forms of property interests in the various answer options fail to "pass" to the surviving spouse. A decedent's interest held as a tenancy in common or as community property is governed by the decedent's will provisions. Such forms of property ownership do not operate as will substitutes. However, real property held in a joint tenancy with a right of survivorship causes property to pass outside the will and results in the survivor, here the decedent's spouse, vesting in full ownership of the property upon decedent's death. Specifically, IRC § 2056(c)(5) indicates that where

at the time of decedent's death property is held in joint tenancy with a right of survivorship, the property is considered to have passed to the surviving joint tenant for purposes of the marital deduction provisions. At decedent's death, his wife is the surviving joint tenant, and the decedent's interest in the property passes directly to his surviving spouse outside the will. In this respect, the transfer qualifies for the marital deduction.

Answers (A) and (B) are incorrect. For reasons explained above, the form of ownership in these two answers does not result in property passing to the surviving spouse.

Answer (D) is also incorrect. In Answer (D), the property does not pass to the surviving spouse. Even though the property is held in joint tenancy, the surviving joint tenant is the decedent's daughter and not his spouse. No marital deduction will arise in relation to a transfer to the daughter.

194.   **Answer (C) is the correct answer.** In addition to requiring the property to "pass" to the surviving spouse, IRC § 2056(a) requires that the property be included in the decedent's estate to support a marital deduction. Because the property interest that is received by the surviving spouse here is insurance proceeds on the life of the decedent, the proceeds will have "passed" from decedent to the surviving spouse regardless of the fact that the insurance company was the source of the proceeds. *See* IRC § 2056(c)(7). However, regardless of the fact that the proceeds may have been transferred from the insurance company to the surviving spouse, no marital deduction is allowed because the proceeds are not included in the decedent's estate. Decedent's wife owned the policy, and decedent possessed no incidents of ownership in the insurance policy. *See* IRC § 2042(2). In the absence of any incidents of ownership on the part of the decedent, the policy proceeds are not included in decedent's gross estate and no marital deduction is allowed.

Answer (A) is incorrect. Although the result in Answer (C) is the same as that in Answer (A) (spouse received the proceeds of a life insurance policy on decedent's life), because decedent owned the policy, he held incidents of ownership of the policy as contemplated under § 2042. *See* IRC § 2042(2). By holding incidents of ownership on the policy, the policy proceeds must be included in decedent's gross estate. Id. Additionally, under IRC § 2056(c)(7), the insurance proceeds are treated as having passed to decedent's surviving spouse where she is the designated beneficiary of the policy and the proceeds are receivable by her. Because the policy proceeds passed to surviving spouse and are included in decedent's estate under IRC § 2042, a marital deduction is allowed to the decedent's estate.

Answers (B) and (D) are also incorrect. In Answers (B) and (D) the decedent had either a limited or general power to appoint property upon his death. Where the decedent has a general power of appointment, the property subject to the power is included in the decedent's estate if the decedent fails to exercise the power. *See* Treas. Reg. § 20.2041-3(a). Similarly, a non-general power is included in the decedent's estate if the power is exercised by will. *See* Treas. Reg. § 20.2041-3(e)(1)(i). By exercising the special power via his will, the property is included in his estate under IRC § 2041, and the property passes to his surviving spouse under

IRC § 2056(c)(6).

195. No, the surviving spouse may not waive the application of the marital deduction. Section 2056(a) provides that taxable estate "shall" be determined by deducting an amount equal to the value of property that qualifies for the marital deduction. To the extent that assets that are included in decedent's gross estate are passed to surviving spouse, a mandatory marital deduction applies. However, it is important to note that under the circumstances provided in the problem, surviving spouse may effectuate a valid disclaimer under IRC §§ 2046 and 2518 that will cause the assets to pass through the residuary of the decedent's will. For example, if surviving spouse disclaims $1,500,000 of assets specifically bequeathed to her, such assets will pass to the daughter. This will result in a total of $2,000,000 of assets that will neither pass to the surviving spouse nor reduce decedent's estate through the marital deduction. The $2,000,000 passing to the daughter will be sheltered by the decedent's estate tax exemption equivalent.

196. **Answer (D) is the correct answer.** Property interests that pass from the decedent must fall into two categories, those with respect to which the marital deduction is authorized and those that do not. Treas. Reg. § 20.2056(a)-2(a). Deductible interests include all interests that are not categorized by the regulations as "nondeductible interests." The regulations identify four interests that are nondeductible when they pass to the surviving spouse: (1) interests that are not included in the decedent's gross estate, (2) interests that are otherwise deductible as administrative expenses under IRC § 2053, (3) interests that are otherwise deductible as IRC § 2054 losses, and (4) interests that are classified as "terminable interests." The interest described in Answer (D) does not fall into any of the four categories of nondeductible interests. An elective share is not deductible under IRC § 2053 or § 2054. As discussed more fully in the next section of questions and answers, an elective share is an interest that is included in decedent's gross estate, and an elective share is not a terminable interest. A spouse's interest in dower or other statutory interest in lieu of dower is property that passes from the decedent to surviving spouse and qualifies as a marital deduction. Further, if property is assigned or surrendered to a surviving spouse pursuant to a settlement in recognition of the surviving spouse's enforceable rights in the decedent's estate, it will qualify as marital deduction.

Answers (A) and (B) are incorrect. The circumstances in Answers (A) and (B) do not qualify for a marital deduction because the administrative expenses are deductible under IRC § 2053.

Answer (C) is also incorrect. The circumstances of Answer (C) represent a sale or exchange. The purchase of the cemetery lot by the executor is also an administrative claim.

Marital Deduction, Terminable Interest

197. **Answer (D) is the correct answer.** In addition to previously discussed nondeductible interests, no marital deduction is allowed with respect to a "terminable interest" in property. IRC § 2056(b). A terminable interest is an interest that will terminate or fail upon lapse of time or on the occurrence or failure to occur of some contingency. Id. In general, a life estate or term of years is a terminable interest. A life estate fails when the surviving spouse dies and a term of years fails upon lapse of time. However, in Answer (D), the interest described is merely a contractual obligation that is discharged upon satisfaction of the terms of the note. See Treas. Reg. § 20.2056(b). Notwithstanding that payments on the note will terminate, obligations such as notes or bonds do not fall under the definition of a terminable interest.

Answers (A) and (B) are incorrect. For reasons explained above, Answers (A) and (B) are incorrect.

Answer (C) is also incorrect. Answer (C) is incorrect because surviving spouse's ability to take under the will is conditioned upon her survival beyond the life of decedent's daughter. A condition such as this causes the wife's interest to fail if she predeceases the daughter, and results in the surviving spouse's interest being terminable.

198. **Answer (B) is the correct answer.** Unlike the prior question, this question seeks to determine which circumstance qualifies as a terminable interest. Once again, analyzing why the other three answers are wrong is just as instructive as determining the correct answer. In addition to life estates and terms of years as discussed previously, a "terminable interest" also includes annuities, patents, and copyrights. Thus, by devising a patent to his surviving spouse, the decedent has devised an interest that will fail upon a lapse of time and, therefore, will qualify as a terminable interest.

Answers (A), (C), and (D) are incorrect. In Answer (A), the wife receives an interest in the remainder of the real property. The remainder interest will neither terminate nor fail upon lapse of time. Instead, the wife has the ability to transfer or sell her remainder interest. The surviving spouse's interest is a partial interest that is not terminable. Answer (C) is not a terminable interest for similar reasons. Because the interest received by the spouse is a vested interest in a trust that will not terminate or fail upon lapse of time, nor is there any condition placed upon her ability to recover her interest, the devise is not a terminable interest. Finally, and again, the circumstances in Answer (D) also do not describe a terminable interest. When the decedent passes away, the $1,000,000 will pass without any condition or limitation. The fact that the wife had to survive the decedent is requisite for any marital deduction and has little to do with whether the interest itself is terminable.

199. **Answer (C) is the correct answer.** Note that the problem here asks you whether the interest bequeathed to the surviving spouse is deductible rather than just asking whether the interest is classified as a terminable interest. In general, annuities are classified as terminable interests. See Treas. Reg. § 20.2056(b)-1(b). However, notwithstanding that an interest received by the surviving spouse is classified as a terminable interest, it may be deducted if it passes to a surviving spouse only and no other person obtains an interest in the same property. Treas. Reg. § 20.2056(b)-1(c). If property interest passes to the surviving spouse and an

interest in the same property also passes to a third party for less than full consideration, a marital deduction is not allowed. *Id.* In Answer (C), all of the decedent's interest in the annuity passes to his surviving spouse, and no part passes to any other party. So, while the wife's interest in the annuity is a terminable interest, no other interest in the annuity goes to another person, and no other person may enjoy any part of the annuity payments passing to the surviving spouse. *See* Treas. Reg. § 20.2056(b)-1(g)(example 3).

Answers (A) and (D) are incorrect. In Answers (A) and (D), a third party has an interest in the same property that the decedent has bequeathed to the surviving spouse. In Answer (A), the remaining value of the annuity goes to decedent's daughter, and in Answer (D), the remainder goes to the decedent's heirs. *Id.*

Answer (B) is also incorrect. Answer (B) is incorrect because no marital deduction is allowed where decedent leaves amounts to his surviving spouse with directions to his executor to convert such amounts into a terminable interest. *See* Treas. Reg. § 20.2056(b)-1(f). Since the executor is directed to use the amounts bequeathed to the surviving spouse to acquire an annuity for surviving spouse, the bequest is a nondeductible terminable interest. *Id.*

200. **Answer (C) is the correct answer.** The circumstances in Answer (C) satisfy most of the requirements for a marital deduction but fail to specify that an appropriate election to treat the property as qualified terminable interest property under IRC § 2056(b)(7)(B)(i)(III) was made. As is clear by now, the interest that passes to the surviving spouse must be a deductible interest. Because decedent devised property in trust to his wife for life, remainder to his son, decedent has devised a terminable interest to his surviving spouse that will lapse or fail when she passes away. A devise of such an interest generally will not qualify for the marital deduction. However, the regulations provide several exceptions wherein a devise of terminable interest property may qualify for deduction. *See* Treas. Reg. § 20.2056(b)-1(d). Where part of the property passed from the decedent to another person (in addition to his surviving spouse), the full value of the property interest transferred is treated as if it had passed to the surviving spouse and is deductible if it is "qualified terminable interest property." Treas. Reg. § 20.2056(b)-7(a). Qualified terminable interest property is defined as property that passes from the decedent, in which the spouse has a qualifying income interest for life and an appropriate election is made. IRC § 2056(b)(7)(B). The surviving spouse's interest here is a qualifying income interest because she is entitled to all income from the property annually for life, and no other person has power to appoint any part of the property. *See* IRC § 2056(b)(7)(B)(ii). However, there is no indication that an appropriate election was made under IRC § 2056(b)(7)(B)(i)(III). Without the election, the interest is not qualified, and no deduction will be allowed.

Answer (A) is incorrect. Here, the devise goes to the surviving spouse subject to the condition that she does not die with the decedent in a common disaster, making her interest an apparent disallowed terminable interest. A condition that deprives the surviving spouse of the property interest when there is a death in a common disaster or where there is a condition that surviving spouse survive by at least six months are exceptional circumstances under which a marital deduction is allowed.

Treas. Reg. § 20.2056(b)-3(a).

Answer (B) is also incorrect. IRC § 2056(b)(5) allows a marital deduction here because the decedent devises a life estate with a general power of appointment in the surviving spouse. This rule applies so long as the surviving spouse is entitled to annual (or more frequent) payments of all income from the property for her life and she alone receives a general power of appointment over the property. Note that by giving the surviving spouse a general power of appointment, the decedent has effectively given the surviving spouse the right to exercise her power and take the assets for herself.

Answer (D) is also incorrect. Again, in order to be a "nondeductible" terminable interest for marital deduction purposes, another person must have an interest in the same property that passes to the surviving spouse. However, where the third party must pay full consideration to the surviving spouse, a marital deduction is allowed. Treas. Reg. § 20.2056(b)-1(c)(1).

201. **Answer (A) is the correct answer.** There are a number of goals that testators may have in relation to making a QTIP election. It is true that a testator may want to prevent his surviving spouse from controlling his assets after his death, but it is not necessarily true if he loves his spouse that he would want to prevent her from benefiting from the assets after his death. Indeed, to be effective, a QTIP election requires that the surviving spouse benefit by receiving all of the income from the assets at least annually for the rest of his or her life. Therefore, it is unlikely that the decedent could or would devise property via a QTIP trust in an effort to prevent the surviving spouse from benefiting from the property. Rather, it is more likely that decedent would like his surviving spouse to benefit from at least the income from the assets.

Answers (B), (C), and (D) are incorrect. Where the decedent has a daughter that is his genetic child and surviving spouse has a child from another marriage, a testator may desire to control the remainder of the assets in an effort to assure that his own child will share in the assets. Answers (B), (C), and (D) outline real concerns that a testator may have under the facts of the question. A testator is likely to be concerned about the possibility that the surviving spouse may: favor her own son versus decedent's daughter, waste the assets if she is given more than an income interest, or remarry with testator's assets going to a future husband under state intestate succession statutes. Indeed, the surviving spouse could also devise any assets she received from decedent to any future husband that she may have. All of these possibilities are likely to enter into the decedent's decision process in determining how his estate should be distributed.

202. No, while under the newly stated facts there might be less reason for decedent to be concerned about his surviving spouse favoring the son over the daughter, the remaining reasons for creating a QTIP will likely continue to enter into the decedent's decision-making process. Thus, decedent is likely to consider the possibility that the surviving spouse may favor one child over the other, may waste

assets if they are given to her outright, or may remarry in the future, causing assets from decedent's estate to go to a future husband. Any or all of these concerns may induce a testator to make a marital bequest that includes a QTIP election.

203. **Answer (D) is the correct answer.** An income interest in a trust will not fail to constitute a qualifying income interest for life because the trustee has the power to distribute principal to the surviving spouse. Treas. Reg. § 20.2056(b)-7(d)(6). There is no limitation on the amount of access that a surviving spouse may have over the principal or corpus of the property held in the QTIP trust. It is important to note that the purpose of the QTIP rules is to assure that the surviving spouse has, at a minimum, the right to income annually for life without the possibility that either income or principal will be diverted to another person's use. To give the surviving spouse more access to principal does not violate the policy behind the QTIP rules.

Answers (A), (B), and (C) are incorrect. None of the first three answers describes the most access to trust property that may be allowed to a surviving spouse. Answer (A) simply is not accurate in that all income must be paid annually to the surviving spouse, and while Answers (B) and (C) offer two possible distribution schemes that are allowed under the rules, they fall short of the maximum access that is allowed.

204. **Answer (B) is the correct answer.** Under the QTIP rules, the decedent may exclude the surviving spouse from receiving any of the terminable interest property. In effect, decedent may give the wife an interest that terminates upon her death, and decedent may further direct where the property goes after the death of the surviving spouse. Such is not necessarily the case with a bequest that arises under IRC § 2056(b)(5) wherein a life estate plus a general power of appointment is given to the surviving spouse. By giving the surviving spouse a general power of appointment, she may exercise her power to give the property to anyone at any time, thereby frustrating the decedent's wishes regarding who he wanted the property to go to.

Answers (A), (C), and (D) are incorrect. For reasons already explained, these answers are incorrect. Although it may be worth pointing out one difference. Under § 2056(b)(5) and § 2056(b)(7), the first spouse to die can give an income interest to the surviving spouse and identify one or more persons who will take the remainder. However, under the former section, the surviving spouse may thereafter change the remainder person by exercising his or her power of appointment.

GENERATION-SKIPPING TRANSFER TAX BASICS

Basic Concepts

205.   **Answer (B) is the correct answer.** A transfer from Hank to his son's daughter constitutes a transfer to a skip person, which is subject to the generation-skipping transfer (GST) tax. In order for a generation-skipping transfer to occur, there must be one of three types of transfers: (1) a direct skip, (2) a taxable termination, or (3) a taxable distribution. IRC § 2611. In each of the three types of transfers, there must be a transfer from a donor to a "skip person" either directly or to or from a trust. IRC § 2612(a). A skip person includes a natural person assigned to a generation that is at least two generations below the generation assignment of the transferor. IRC § 2613(a)(1).

While it may be obvious in this case that Miley is two family generations below Hank, reference must be made to the definitional sections of the generation-skipping transfer rules to support this conclusion. Generation assignments are made pursuant to two separate rules, including one for lineal descendants and another that serves as a catch-all for everyone who is not a lineal descendant. But that raises the question of what constitutes lineage. More narrowly, whose lineage is used to determine whether a recipient is appropriately related to the donor/transferor for purposes of the generation assignment rules? To be classified as a skip person, a transferee must be separated by two generations or more from a transferor. Family generation assignments are made by comparing (1) the number of generations between the grandparent and the transferor, with (2) the number of generations between the grandparent and the recipient. Here, a diagram is useful:

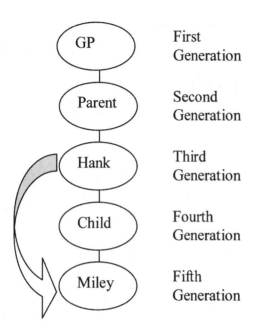

First Generation

Second Generation

Third Generation

Fourth Generation

Fifth Generation

Because Miley is a lineal descendant of Hank's grandparent (GP), family generation assignments must be made and compared. The comparison between generations is statutorily determined by comparing (1) the number of generations between Miley (e.g., fifth generation) and Hank's grandparent (GP) (e.g., first generation), which is three generations, with (2) the number of generations between the GP (e.g. first generation) and Hank (e.g., third generation), which is one generation of separation. Thus, comparing three generations to one generation, it is seen that there are two generations of difference.

Because there are two generations between Hank and Miley, Miley is a skip person under the rules. While the question does not inquire further, the next step would be to determine whether the transfer qualifies as a direct skip, taxable termination, or taxable distribution. These topics are explored more fully below.

Answers (A) and (C) are incorrect. Again, generation assignments are made by comparing the number of generations between the transferor's grandparent and the transferee with the number of generations between the grandparent and the transferor. With respect to the transfers to Hank's mother and grandfather, there is no possible comparison that will end up in more than one generation of difference. Note that all generational assignments are made by determining the number of generations away from the grandparent. Thus, any gift to a grandparent will always result in no generational difference.

Answer (D) is also incorrect. Referring to the diagram above, it can be seen again that Hank is assigned to the third generation, and Hank's daughter is assigned to the fourth generation. Thus, Hank's daughter is only one generation removed from Hank, and she is not a skip person.

206. No, Answer (B) is still the correct answer. For purposes of assigning generations to lineal descendants, a relationship by legal adoption is treated the same as a relationship by blood. IRC § 2651(b)(3)(A).

207. **Answer (D) is the correct answer.** Unlike Question 205, above, the answer options also include individuals who are lineal descendants of Hank's parents but not Hank. For purposes of determining whether the transferee is a skip person, a transferee who is a lineal descendant of Hank's grandparent but not Hank is still related in a manner that requires use of the lineal descendant rules. Here, Hank's grandniece ("Gniece") is a lineal descendant of Hank's grandparents. Grandniece must be separated by two generations or more from Hank to qualify as a skip person.

Generation assignments are made by comparing (1) the number of generations between the grandparent and Hank, with (2) the number of generations between the grandparent and Hank's grandniece. Again, a diagram substitutes for many paragraphs of explanation:

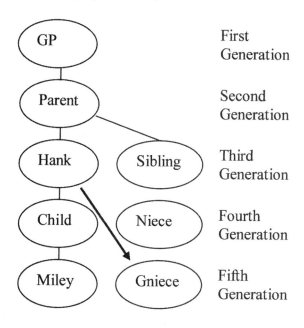

First Generation

Second Generation

Third Generation

Fourth Generation

Fifth Generation

The comparison between generations is determined by comparing (1) the number of generations between Gniece (e.g., fifth generation) and Hank's GP (e.g., first generation), which is three generations, with (2) the number of generations between the GP (e.g., first generation) and Hank (e.g., third generation), which is one generation of separation. Thus, comparing the three generations to one generation, it is seen that there are two generations of difference.

Because there are two generations between Hank and Gniece, Gniece is a skip person under the rules.

Answers (A) and (B) are incorrect. Hank, his brother, and his cousin are each in the third generation. Since they are all the same number of generations away from Hank's grandparents, there is no generational difference.

Answer (D) is also incorrect. Using the diagram above, it can be seen again that Hank is assigned to the third generation and that Hank's daughter, as his child, is assigned to the fourth generation. Hank's daughter is only one generation removed from Hank, and, therefore, his daughter is not a skip person.

208. Yes, a transfer from Hank to Harley's grandson is a transfer to a skip person. For purposes of determining generation assignments, a relationship by half-blood is treated the same as a relationship by whole blood. IRC § 2651(b)(3)(B).

209. **Answer (C) is the correct answer.** The answer options here include individuals that, while commonly perceived as family members and friends, are not lineal descendants of either Hank or his grandparents. Transferees who are not lineal descendants of the transferor's grandparents are assigned to a generation on the basis of age under the nonlineal descendant rules. IRC § 2651(d). A transferee who is born not more than 12 and a half years after the date of the transferor's birth is assigned to the same generation as the transferor. Id. A transferee born more than 12 and a half years but not more than 37 and a half years after the date of birth of the transferor is treated as being one generation younger than the transferor. Id. A transferee born more than 37 and a half years but not more than 62 and a half

years after the transferor is treated as being two generations younger that the transferor. Id. Hank's second cousin is a descendant of Hank's great grandparents, but the second cousin is not a descendant of Hank's grandparents. Therefore Hank's second cousin's generation is assigned under the nonlineal descendant rules. Hank is 57 years old, and his second cousin, who is 17 years old, is 40 years younger than him. Being 40 years younger, the second cousin is deemed to be two generations younger than Hank and is also deemed to be a skip person under the rules.

Answers (A), (B), and (D) are incorrect. Each of the individuals described in Answers (A), (B), and (D) are not descendants of Hank's grandparents. However, each of the individuals is less than 37 and a half years younger than Hank. Therefore, none of these individuals qualifies as a skip person.

210. The fact that Hank married his friend's daughter prevents the daughter from being a skip person. An individual who has been married at any time to the transferor is deemed to be assigned to the transferor's generation. IRC § 2651(c)(1). Regardless of the fact that Hank's spouse is 40 years younger than he is, she is not a skip person, and transfers to her avoid the GST tax. The same principles applied to the now infamous marriage between the late J. Howard Marshall and Anna Nicole Smith, also deceased. On June 27, 1994, 26-year-old Anna Nicole Smith married J. Howard Marshall, then 89 years old. After only 13 months of marriage, Marshall died. It is notable that even though Smith was approximately 63 years younger (three generations younger by age) than Marshall, Smith was not deemed to be a skip person, and no amounts that Smith may have received through Marshall's will would have been subject to the generation-skipping tax.

211. **Answer (A) is the correct answer.** A transfer to a trust may also be subject to the GST tax. A trust qualifies as a "skip person" if all interests in the trust are held by skip persons. Treas. Reg. § 26.2612-1(d)(2)(i). In general, an interest in a trust exists if a person has a present right to receive trust principal or income. Treas. Reg. § 26.2612-1(e). If a person merely has a future right to receive income or principal, then such person is treated under the rules as having no interest at all. IRC 2652(c)(1)(A). Hank's granddaughter has a present interest for 10 years in the trust income. Granddaughter is a skip person under the family generation assignment rules and, by having a present right to trust income, all interests in the trust are held by skip persons. Thus, the trust itself is treated as a skip person under the rules. Why is it that the remainder interest held by Hank's wife has no impact on the outcome? It is true that "all" interests in trust must be held by skip persons, and it is also true that Hank's wife, a non-skip person, owns a remainder interest. However, Hank's wife's interest is merely a future right to receive the remainder of the trust assets. As a future interest, Hank's wife is treated as having no interest at all for purposes of determining whether the trust is a skip person.

Answers (B), (C), and D are incorrect. In Answer (B), Hank's son has an interest in the trust income for life. Because Hank's son is assigned to the first generation below Hank, he is a non-skip person. Further, because as a non-skip person the son has a present interest in the trust, "all" of the interests in the trust are not held by skip persons, and a transfer to the trust is not a transfer to a skip person. Similarly, Hank's wife and his son, both non-skip persons, have a present interest in Answers (C) and (D), respectively. Note that the creation of the trust inter vivos or as a testamentary trust is not decisive.

Direct Skips

212. At this point, you are asked to calculate all gift and GST tax due on a direct skip. The amount of tax due upon the transfer is $551,250. The following calculations and citations attempt to support the amount of tax due and, although it is complex, students are encouraged over the next several problems to analyze why the Code imposes such a high tax on a generation-skipping transfer. The transfer from Hank to Miley is a transfer from grandfather to granddaughter. Miley is assigned to the second generation below Hank. IRC §§ 2612(c), 2613(a)(1), 2651(b)(1). The gift of the $500,000 constitutes a transfer to a skip person, and the transfer is also a direct skip for GST tax purposes. IRC § 2612(c)(1). The gift also results in a gift for gift tax purposes. Hank will incur gift tax of $225,000 (45 percent of $500,000). IRC §§ 2001(c), 2502(a)(1). GST tax will also be imposed on the taxable amount or *value of the property received by the transferee*, or $500,000 in this case. IRC §§ 2623, 2624. Applying the same tax rate, another $225,000 (45 percent of $500,000) of GST tax is due.

But the calculation is not done yet. IRC § 2515 provides that for gift tax purposes, any taxable gift must be increased by the amount of the GST tax on the transfer. Thus, another 45 percent of the amount of GST tax ($225,000) is treated as additional gift tax due on the transfer, resulting in $101,250 of additional gift tax. Aggregating all gift and GST taxes due results in a total tax liability of $551,250 ($225,000 + $225,000 + $101,250). Of the $551,250, there is $225,000 of GST and $326,250 ($225,000 + $101,250) of gift tax. Note that it costs $551,250 in transfer taxes to make a gift of $500,000 to Hank's granddaughter. By imposing $551,250 of taxes on a $500,000 transfer, the Code imposes an effective tax rate of approximately 110 percent ($551,250/500,000) on transfer. Do you find that to be a tax-expensive way to transfer assets to individuals who are two or more generations younger than the donor?

213. **Answer (A) is the correct answer.** With respect to gift taxes paid, the tax is imposed on the donor. IRC § 2502(c). In the case of a direct skip, the tax is paid by the transferor. IRC § 2603(a)(3). Under these rules, Hank is liable for $326,250 of gift taxes, and $225,000 of GST tax due.

Answers (B), (C), and (D) are incorrect. For reasons just explained, the remaining answer options are incorrect.

214. Because Hank is liable for all taxes due on the transfer, Miley will receive and retain the full $500,000, undiminished by any taxes due. This becomes important for estate planning purposes when analyzing the tax cost of making a gift to a skip person when compared to the tax cost and benefit to the recipient under taxable terminations and taxable distributions. Note for later that each type of transfer results in liability for the GST being placed upon a different person, which also may impact the amount of gift that ultimately ends up in the hand of the recipient.

215. This question addresses yet another aspect of analysis in comparing the tax consequences of making a gift during life versus transferring assets at death via a will or will substitute. In general, it is important to note that the system of taxation that is imposed by the Code upon gifts results in a tax that is "exclusive" of the gift that is made. In an exclusive tax system, the tax paid is not removed from the gift itself. Rather, the tax is imposed in addition to or exclusive of the amount of the gift that is made. By imposing the tax on the donor, the donor is liable for and pays the tax separate and apart from the amount of the gift. Like the gift tax system, the GST tax system imposes the liability for GST tax on the transferor exclusive of the amount of the gift that was transferred. Note again that it cost Hank $551,250 in transfer taxes to make a gift of $500,000 to Miley. Miley, on the other hand, receives the whole $500,000.

216. The purpose of this question is to address the possibility that taxpayers might try to avoid the GST tax by making sequential gifts. In Question 212, above, Hank makes a gift of $500,000 to his granddaughter Miley. The combined gift and GST tax was calculated in Question 212 to be $551,250. Another relevant number is the combined amount of $1,051,250, the amount Hank is out of pocket on both the gift and the taxes. In this problem, Hank gifts $725,000 to Mona. Applying the gift tax at 45 percent to this gift, Hank will owe $326,250 in gift tax ($725,000 × 45%). Note that, like the direct transfer of $500,000 to Miley, Frank is out a total of $1,051,250 ($725,000 gift + $326,250 tax) on a gift of $725,000 to Mona. Mona then gifts $500,000 to Miley and Mona is liable for $225,000 of gift tax ($500,000 × 45%). At the end of the day, the total amount of gift tax paid by both Hank and Mona is $551,250. Again, the effective tax rate on this transfer would be approximately 110 percent ($551,250/500,000).

217. Miley ends up with $500,000. If you don't already see where this has gone, you should note that Miley ends up with the same $500,000 as she did in a direct skip from Hank to Miley as seen in Question 212, above.

218. Neither method results in a smaller liability. The total amount that the U.S. government gets in Question 216 is $551,250, the same as the government got in Question 212. The combined tax due on a direct skip from Hank to Miley ends up being the same as the combined tax on sequential gifts from Hank to Mona and to Miley where Miley ends up with $500,000 in pocket. It is but one small additional step to conclude that in general the GST tax regime is largely designed to ensure that transfer tax is imposed at each generation. An attempt by taxpayers to make gifts that skip a generation will effectively be neutralized by the manner in which the GST tax system operates.

219. When a direct skip is made by means of a $500,000 devise at death from Hank to Miley, Miley continues to be assigned to the second generation below Hank, and

she continues to be treated as a skip person. A bequest to Miley as a skip person results in a direct skip and incurs GST tax on the taxable amount or *value of the property received by the transferee* or $500,000 in this case. IRC §§ 2623, 2624. Like a direct skip on a gift during life, the GST tax in a direct skip by devise at death is imposed on a tax-exclusive basis. The estate tax, however, applies to the full value of property held in a decedent's estate (less expenses allowed). IRC §§ 2001, 2031, 2033; see also Treas. Reg. § 20.0-2(b). The estate tax is an inclusive tax that is charged on all property held within the estate. IRC § 2001(b). Continuing with an assumed 45 percent rate, the estate tax on a $500,000 is $225,000 ($500,000 × 45%). This leaves $275,000 ($500,000 - $225,000) that is subject to the GST tax, also at 45 percent. However, because the GST tax is applied on a tax- exclusive basis, we must now determine what portion of the $275,000 is treated as the taxable amount or the "value of property received by the transferee." The calculation becomes circular in that the GST tax imposed may not be determined without first determining the taxable amount. However, the taxable amount may not be determined without knowing the GST tax due. The problem can be solved by applying the following algebraic formula:

$$\text{Taxable Amount} = \frac{[\text{Amount of Devise}]}{[1 + \text{Applicable tax rate}]}$$

Thus:

$$\text{Taxable Amount} = \frac{\$275,000}{1.45} = \$189,655$$

The amount subject to GST tax or $189,655 can then be multiplied by 45% to determine the tax due of $85,345. Note that the GST tax ($85,345) and the taxable amount ($189,655) together represent the $275,000 left in the estate after estate taxes. Finally, note that it cost Hank $500,000 to get $189,655 to Miley. Effectively, the rate of tax on a direct skip by devise is approximately 164 percent ($310,345/ $189,655). The reason for the higher effective rate on a devise at death as compared to a direct skip during life is due to the inclusive nature of the estate tax versus the exclusive nature of the gift tax.

220. **Answer (A) is the correct answer.** IRC § 2603(a)(3), the GST tax must be paid by the transferor. In this case, Hank has passed away and Hank's estate is liable to pay the taxes due. Thus, **Answers (B), (C), and (D) are incorrect.**

221. As alluded to previously, the GST tax is tax-exclusive with respect to a direct skip by devise. Thus, every direct skip is GST taxed on an exclusive basis. Again, per the lengthy discussions above, note the difference between the gift tax and the estate tax for effective rate differentials between inter vivos gifts and bequests at death. In general, a transfer during life under the gift tax is less costly than a transfer at death even though the nominal tax rates are the same.

Taxable Terminations

222. **Answer (A) is the correct answer.** A taxable termination occurs when an interest in a trust terminates and immediately after the termination only a skip person (or persons) has an interest in the trust. IRC § 2612(a)(1)(A); Treas. Reg. § 26.2612-1(b). Prior to Mona's death, Mona has an interest in the trust. Mona is a non-skip person because, as Hank's child, she is assigned to the generation immediately beneath Hank (e.g., one generation apart). During Mona's life, the trust is not a skip person, and a contribution to the trust is not a direct skip. Upon Mona's death, only Miley has an interest in the trust. Since Miley is assigned to the second generation below Hank, she is a skip person. After Mona's death all interests are held by skip persons, and a taxable termination occurs.

Answers (B), (C), and (D) are incorrect. With respect to Answers (B) and (C), Mona, a nonskip person, continues to hold an interest in the trust. Therefore, no taxable termination has occurred. Note that Answer C describes a taxable distribution that is discussed more fully below. Answer (D) is incorrect for reasons already explained.

223.   **Answer (D) is the correct answer.** Notwithstanding that when Mona dies (as is the case in Answer (A)) a termination of an interest in trust occurs, where the resulting transfer is subject to federal estate or gift tax, there will be no taxable termination for GST tax purposes. Treas. Reg § 26.2612-1(b). Because Mona had a general power of appointment over the assets, the value of the assets will be included in Mona's estate upon her death. *See* IRC § 2041. Upon including the assets in Mona's estate under the power of appointment rules, the value of the assets are taxed in Mona's estate. Thus, because the transfer from Mona to Miley was subject to estate tax, no taxable termination occurs and the transfer is not subject to GST tax.

Answers (A), (B), and (C) are incorrect. Again, because the transfer was subject to the estate tax, no GST tax can be imposed when Mona dies in Answer (A). In Answer (B), Mona continues to be a non-skip person and continues to hold an interest in the trust. Therefore, no taxable termination has occurred. Again, Answer (C) describes a taxable distribution, which is discussed more fully below.

224.   Since Mona was alive and had an interest in the trust up to creation of the trust, the trust was not a skip person and the original transfer to the trust was not a direct skip. Upon Miley's survival of Mona, a taxable termination occurs upon Mona's death because Mona's interest terminates and, thereafter, only Miley, a skip person, has an interest in the trust. Upon Mona's death, the amount transferred for GST tax purposes is the $1,000,000 of trust principal. GST tax on the termination of the trust at 45 percent is $450,000 ($1,000,000 × 45%), leaving $550,000 ($1,000,000 - $450,000) to Miley. Compare this outcome to a direct skip, in which the GST tax would be imposed only on the amount received by Miley and would not apply to the amount used to pay the tax.

225.   **Answer (A) is the correct answer.** In a taxable termination, the tax is paid by the trustee, and the trustee is liable for the tax. IRC § 2603(a)(2). Thus, Answers (B), (C), and (D) are incorrect.

Answers (B), (C), and (D) are incorrect for reasons already explained.

226. The GST tax on a taxable termination is calculated differently than it is on a direct skip. As previously discussed, the GST tax is imposed in an exclusive fashion on a direct skip. In a direct skip, the taxable amount is equal to the value of the property received by the transferee. IRC § 2623. On a taxable termination, the taxable amount is the value of all property with respect to which the termination has occurred less any deductions similar in nature to administrative deductions allowed under IRC § 2503. IRC § 2622(a). Since there are no expenses to deal with in the facts of the problem, the taxable amount is $1,000,000, the value of ALL property in the trust. Because the GST tax is imposed on all of the property, it is imposed on an "inclusive" basis. Note that here it costs Hank $1,000,000 to get $550,000 to Miley. The effective tax rate on this transaction is approximately 82 percent ($450,000/$550,000). Again, a tax that is imposed on an inclusive basis will result in a higher effective tax rate. Note, however, that this effective rate does not include any gift tax that may have been imposed upon creation of the trust.

Taxable Distributions

227. **Answer (C) is the correct answer.** The term "taxable distribution" means any distribution from a trust to a skip person (other than a taxable termination or a direct skip). Miley continues to be deemed a skip person because she is assigned to the second generation below Hank under the lineal descendant rules. When the trustee distributes one-half of the principal to Miley on her eighteenth birthday, the distribution is a taxable distribution to Miley. *See* Treas. Reg. § 26.2612-1(f)(example 10). Note also that the distribution does not qualify as either a direct skip or a taxable termination. Id. If the distribution qualified as either a direct skip or taxable termination, the distribution could not qualify as a taxable distribution. *See* IRC § 2612(b)(parenthetical).

Answer (A) is incorrect. Answer (A) describes a situation under which the original contribution would have been a direct skip. In Answer (A), Miley has a present interest in the trust while Mona, Hanks child, has merely a future interest. Because Miley has a current interest, a contribution to the trust will be a direct skip subject to GST on the date of contribution.

Answer (B) is also incorrect. The facts of Answer (B) describe a taxable termination. Again, even though there is a distribution to Miley at the end of Mona's life, meeting the requirements of a taxable termination prevents the distribution from qualifying as a taxable distribution under the rules. Id.

Answer (D) is also incorrect for reasons already explained above.

228. Again, Miley continues to be deemed a skip person because she is assigned to the second generation below Hank under the lineal descendant rules. When the trustee distributes $50,000 to Miley, the distribution is a taxable distribution for GST tax purposes. Note also that the distribution does not qualify as either a direct skip or a taxable termination. The taxable amount in the case of a taxable distribution is equal to the value of the property received by the transferee reduced by appropriate expenses. IRC § 2621(a). Applying the 45 percent assumed GST rate to the full amount of the property received by Miley results in a tax of $22,500. Thus, in a taxable distribution such as the one described in the problem, it will cost Hank $50,000 to get $27,500 to Miley. The effective tax rate on the transfer is approximately 82 percent, the same as a taxable termination. Again, this effective tax calculation disregards any gift tax that may have applied on the original formation of the trust.

229.   **Answer (B) is the correct answer.** Liability for tax imposed on a taxable distribution goes to the transferee. IRC § 2603(a)(1). In this case, because Miley is the transferee, Miley is liable for payment of the GST tax on the distribution. Note that in this fashion the liability for GST tax follows the distributed assets.

    Answers (A), (C), and (D) are incorrect. For reasons already explained, these answers are incorrect.

230.   The taxable amount in the case of a taxable distribution is equal to the value of the property received by the transferee reduced by appropriate expenses. IRC § 2621(a). Thus, because the taxable amount includes all property received by the transferee and because the transferee is liable for the tax, the GST tax on a taxable distribution is imposed on an "inclusive" basis.

Additional GST considerations

231.   For purposes of determining whether a transfer qualifies as a generation-skipping transfer, if a transferee's parent has predeceased the grandparent transferor, the transferee is deemed to be a non-skip person. IRC § 2651(e). Since Miley's mother Mona has predeceased Hank, Miley is not considered to be a skip person with respect to a transfer from Hank to Miley. Under these circumstances, no GST tax will be imposed upon Hank's gift to Miley.

232.   No, the GST tax is not applied twice. If there is a generation-skipping transfer to a great grandchild or even a great great grandchild, the transfer is not taxed any differently than transfer to an individual who is two generations below the transferor. The transfer from Frank to Miley will be subject once to GST tax at the applicable rate. Note that this is truly a planning opportunity for great grandparents to avoid multiple application of the GST tax and, indeed, will avoid substantial gift tax that would be involved in a gift to a child followed by a gift from the child to a grandchild and so on.

PRACTICE EXAMINATION ANSWERS

1. Federal estate tax is calculated under IRC § 2001. The formula for determining federal estate tax aggregates adjusted taxable gifts and the taxable estate to determine if decedent's taxable life time transfers exceed the $2 million applicable exclusion amount available to decedent's dying in 2008. Aggregation also ensures application of the appropriate tax rate. In 2008, the top estate tax rate applicable to estates in excess of $2 million was 45 percent.

   Adeline's taxable estate equals $1.7 million. Add to that amount adjusted taxable gifts of $1 million. Aggregate transfers made by Adeline equal $2.7 million as of her death in 2008. Note that Adeline's annual exclusion gifts are not taxable gifts, and, thus, are not included in adjusted taxable gifts. Then determine the tentative tax on aggregate transfers of $2.7 million. The tentative tax based on the tax rate set forth in IRC § 2001(c) is calculated as follows: $2,700,000 - $2,000,000 = $700,000; $700,000 × .45 = $315,000; $315,000 + 780,800 = $1,095,800. The tentative tax on the aggregate amount of the taxable estate and adjusted taxable gifts is $1,095,800.

   Next, subtract from the tentative tax of $1,095,800 the aggregate gift tax, which would have been payable on post-1976 gifts based on the estate tax rate effective as of Adeline's date of death. The tax that would have been payable on Adeline's $1 million dollar gift is zero, because the gift tax applicable exclusion equals $1 million. Thus, the tentative federal estate tax equals $1,095,800.

   In order to determine the amount of federal estate tax owed by Adeline's estate, available credits must be subtracted. The only credit available based on our facts is the unified credit under IRC § 2010. The credit amount in 2008 equals $780,800. The credit is subtracted from the tentative federal estate tax of $1,095,800.

   Federal estate tax, thus, totals $315,000 or [$1,095,800 - 780,800].

2. **Answer (C) is correct.** In order for IRC § 2033 to include the value of property held by decedent at death, decedent must own an interest in the property the moment before death, and be able to transfer the property at his or her death. Because the note canceled or terminated at death, Bill could not transfer the note at death. Under similar facts, the court in *Estate of Moss v. Commissioner*, 74 T.C. 1239 (1980), analogized the note to a life interest, and held that the self-canceling note was not includible in the decedent's gross estate.

   Answers (A) and (B) are incorrect. Answer (A) is incorrect because it is not enough to simply be entitled to an amount at death; the decedent must also be able to control its transfer on death. Courts do not always ignore a self-canceling feature, especially when it appears that decedent contracted at arm's length with an unrelated individual, and for that reason, Answer (B) is incorrect. Although the self-canceling installment note may escape inclusion in the gross estate, if the holder of the note does not charge a sufficient premium for the self-canceling feature, a gift may be deemed to occur. Also, where the holder and payor on the note are related, adverse income tax consequences arise. *Compare, Estate of Frane v. Commissioner*, 998 F.2d 567 (8th Cir. 1993), and *Costanza v. Commissioner*, 320 F.3d 595 (6th Cir. 2003). **Answer (D) is incorrect** as it is a red herring.

3.   The answer to the preceding question would change if the note did not have a self-canceling feature, and instead Bill forgave the note in his will. In that event, Bill would own the right to receive payments immediately prior to his death. He also possessed the right at his death to transfer the right to receive payments on the promissory note. The fact that he forgave the note in his will does not impact whether the value of the note is includible in his gross estate. *See Estate of Buckwalter v. Commissioner*, 46 T.C. 805 (1966).

4.   **Answer (A) is correct.** Property (1) transferred by the decedent (2) other than in a bona fide sale for less than adequate consideration in money or money's worth, (3) that directs trustee to pay the income to or for the benefit of decedent (4) for a period of time measured by decedent's life, for any period not ascertainable without reference to decedent's death, or (as here) for a period that does not in fact end before decedent's death is included in decedent's gross estate under IRC § 2036(a)(1). The facts indicate that Cassandra's transfer to trust satisfies each of these elements, including retention of an income interest. Treasury Regulation § 20.2036-1(b)(2) specifies inclusion whenever "the use, possession, right to the income, or other enjoyment is to be applied toward the discharge of a legal obligation of the decedent." Treas. Reg. § 20.2036-1(b)(2). For these same reasons **Answers (C) and (D) are incorrect.**

Answer (B) is incorrect because Treasury Regulation § 20.2036-1(a) indicates that "the value of the entire property, less only the value of any outstanding income interest which is not subject to the decedent's interest or right and which is actually being enjoyed by another person at the time of the decedent's death" is included in decedent's gross estate. In this fact pattern, no other person is enjoying the right to income other than Cassandra, as the income is being used to satisfy her support obligation to her child.

5.   If Cassandra instead dies at a time when her child is 22, no part of the trust will be included in Cassandra's gross estate under IRC § 2036. When Cassandra's child is 22 years old, generally, Cassandra would no longer owe her child a duty of support. Thus, at that point in time the income would no longer be applied to satisfy any duty of support owed by Cassandra. In addition, the changed facts do not trigger application of any of the requisite time periods of IRC § 2036. Cassandra no longer retains any interest in trust for a period that does not in fact end before her death.

6.   **Answer (D) is correct.** A standard that requires distributions of principal for support amounts is ascertainable and falls within the scope of determinable ascertainable standard. The court in *Jennings v. Smith*, 161 F.2d 74 (2d Cir. 1947), determined that such powers become "a duty enforceable in a court of equity. . . ." A duty enforceable by a court does not leave any room for an exercise of discretion

that could lead to application of IRC § 2038. **Answer (B) is incorrect**. Although a power held by a donor decedent to remove and replace the trustee with herself causes the trustee to be deemed to hold the powers of trustee, the powers of trustee in this fact pattern do not trigger application of IRC § 2038 in light of the ascertainable standard. **Answer (A) is incorrect** because Doug does not owe his niece any legal duty of support that could cause inclusion in the gross estate. **Answer (D) is incorrect** for the reasons indicated above.

7. **Answer (D) is correct.** Although Ellen should have been entitled to only 20 percent of the income of the family limited partnership attributable to her 20 percent limited partnership interest, Ellen in fact received 100 percent of the income. The terms of the limited partnership were not respected by the parties. The facts indicate an implied agreement that Ellen retain the income to the transferred property. Thus, IRC § 2036(a)(1) requires gross estate inclusion of the value of all assets transferred by Ellen to the limited partnership because Ellen impliedly retained an income interest in the property transferred for a period that did not end before her death. *See Schauerhamer v. Commissioner*, T.C. Memo. 1997-242. Answers **(A), (B), and (C) are incorrect** for the reasons stated above.

8. **Answer (A) is correct.** As of his death, Fred did not hold any interest in the trust, and, thus, did not retain an interest in trust for his life, for a period not ascertainable without reference to his death, or for a period that did not end prior to his death. Thus, IRC § 2036 does not apply to include any portion of the trust assets in Fred's estate. For this same reason, **Answers (B) and (C) are incorrect.**

Answer (D) is incorrect because IRC § 2035 applies to include trust property only if decedent transferred an interest or relinquished a power that had it been retained by decedent would have caused inclusion of the property in decedent's gross estate under IRC §§ 2036, 2037, 2038, or 2042. Fred neither transferred an interest in nor relinquished a power over the trust property within three years of his death. His annuity interest in the trust merely ceased at the end of the 10-year term.

9. **Answer (B) is correct.** IRC § 2040 applies to determine the rental property value included in Heidi's gross estate. Treasury Regulation § 20.2040-1(c)(2) indicates that Heidi's gross estate will include that portion of the rental property value corresponding to the portion of the purchase priced furnished by Heidi. Thus, 50 percent of the rental property value is included in Heidi's gross estate. Because Heidi and Ingrid do not die simultaneously, the holding of Revenue Ruling 76-303, 1976-2 C.B. 266, does not apply in this situation. When Ingrid dies, IRC § 2033 will include 100 percent of the rental property value in Ingrid's gross estate because at the time of her death she owned the property and was able to transfer it pursuant to her will. For these same reasons, the remaining **Answers (A), (C), and (D) are incorrect.**

10. **Answer (B) is correct.** IRC § 2013 allows a prior transfer credit for the purpose of avoiding double taxation when the transferor and the transferee die within 10 years of each other. The amount of the credit begins at 100 percent and decreases

by 20 percent every two years. Because Ingrid died within two years of Heidi, Ingrid's estate may take 100 percent of the amount of the credit. In order to determine the credit, the estate must calculate two limitations. The first limitation determines the amount of estate tax attributable to the transferred property in the transferor's estate, and the second limitation determines the amount of the estate tax attributable to the transferred property in the transferee's estate. The transferee's estate is allowed the lesser of the two limitations as a credit. Thus, Ingrid's estate may take a $30,000 tax on prior transfers credit. For these same reasons, the remaining **Answers (A), (C), and (D) are incorrect.**

11. **Answer (D) is correct.** During his life, Kyle can pay trust property only to himself for his support. A distribution standard limited to support falls within the list of ascertainable standards enumerated in Treasury Regulation 20.2041-1(c)(2). Because support is an ascertainable standard, Kyle's power to pay property to himself does not fall within the definition of general power of appointment. **Answer (A) is incorrect** because the concept of a legal obligation of support is not applicable to payments to oneself. It is applicable only to the extent a beneficiary must support someone else, such as a child. Thus, during his life, Kyle does not possess a general power of appointment. He also does not possess a general power of appointment at his death because he may not distribute property to his estate or to the creditors of his estate per the definition set forth in IRC § 2041(b)(1). A power to appoint only to one's descendants is a special power, and not a general power of appointment. *See* Treas. Reg. § 20.2041-1(c)(1)(a) and (b). For this same reason, **Answer (B) is incorrect. Answer (C) is incorrect** because the fact of exercise is irrelevant for federal estate tax purposes with respect to powers created after October 21, 1942.

12. **Answer (D) is correct.** IRC § 2035 includes in the gross estate those transfers made by decedent during the three-year period ending at death that otherwise would have been included in decedent's gross estate under IRC §§ 2036 through 2038 and 2042. Here Lannie transferred the insurance policy in 2008 and died the following year, well within the three-year time period. Had Lannie retained ownership of the insurance policy, she would have held incidents of ownership at her death that would have caused inclusion in her gross estate under IRC § 2042(2). Thus, the full value of the policy proceeds will be included in Lannie's gross estate. For these same reasons, **Answer (A) is incorrect.** The value included is not limited to the amount of the gift or of the taxable gift, and for that reason, **Answers (B) and (C) are incorrect.**

13. Lannie could have avoided application of IRC § 2035 by transferring cash in the amount necessary to purchase the life insurance policy and pay the first premium to her child. If the child had purchased the policy instead of Lannie, IRC § 2035 could not apply because Lannie would then never have held incidents of ownership over the policy that could have caused IRC § 2042 inclusion of the proceeds.

14. **Answer (D) is the only correct answer.** Property taxes are deductible as claims against decedent's estate if they accrue and become due and owing prior to

decedent's death so that they are an enforceable claim as of the date of death. Treas. Reg. § 20.2053-6(b). **Answer (A) is incorrect** because the expense for the reception was not one ordinarily incurred as part of a funeral that entails the burial and eulogizing of the decedent. In a case, *Davenport v. Commissioner*, T.C. Memo. 2006-215, the court disallowed reception expenses. Treasury Regulation § 20.2053-2 allows as funeral expense deductions only those (i) actually incurred and (ii) those allowable under local law. In addition, if paid out of property not subject to claims, the regulation requires the expense be paid within nine months after the date of death. **Answer (B) is incorrect** because the administration expense was not actually paid. To be deductible, Treasury Regulation § 20.2053-3(a) requires administration expenses to by (i) actually and (ii) necessarily incurred. The expense must also be allowable under local law. Treas. Reg. § 20.2053-1(b). The first element is not met. **Answer (C) is incorrect** because to be deductible a claim generally must be "contracted bona fide and for an adequate and full consideration in money or money's worth." Marvin failed to receive consideration "in money or money's worth" in exchange for the promissory note. Courts scrutinize transactions between family members, and would likely find the "loan" to be in fact a gift to child.

15. **Answer (A) is correct.** In order to obtain a marital deduction, the property subject to the deduction must be included in the decedent's gross estate. IRC § 2056(a); Treas. Reg. § 20.2056(a)-2(b)(1). The patent rights owned by Nancy would be included in her gross estate pursuant to IRC § 2033. The patent rights must pass from Nancy to Omar. If the patent rights pass to a qualified terminable interest property trust, the patent rights will be considered to have passed from Nancy to Omar under Treas. Reg. § 20.2056(c)-2(a)(2) and (b)(2). The interest passing must be a "deductible interest," or in other words, it cannot be a nondeductible terminable interest. Treasury Regulation § 20.2056(b)-1(b) specifically states that patent rights are not a terminable interest simply because they last for only the specified number of years allowed by federal law. Treasury regulations also indicate that property passing to a qualified terminable interest property trust qualifies as a deductible interest under an exception. Treas. Reg. § 20.2056(b)-1(d). Thus, the question becomes whether a qualified terminable interest property election can be made with respect to the trust created for the benefit of Omar. Here, Omar has a qualifying income interest for life because he is entitled to receive all trust income at least annually, and the facts indicate the patents pay substantial royalties. Thus, the executor can obtain a marital deduction for the patent rights passing to the trust by making an IRC § 2056(b)(7) QTIP election. **Answer (B) is incorrect** because Omar does not hold a general power of appointment over the trust assets. He holds only a limited or special power of appointment to direct trust property on his death to Nancy's children. **Answer (C) is incorrect** because IRC § 2056(b)(3) permits the spouse's interest in trust to be condition on up to six months survival. For the reasons stated above, Omar's interest in trust is a deductible interest and, thus, **Answer (D) is incorrect.**

16. **Answer (B) is correct.** In order to make a taxable gift, the donor must relinquish all "dominion and control." Treasury Regulation § 25.2511-2(b) indicates a gift is

complete when "the donor has so parted with dominion and control as to leave in him no power to change its disposition, whether for his own benefit or for the benefit of another. . . ." To the extent Peter retains the right to change who will receive trust income or principal, the gift remains incomplete. This is the case in Answers (A), (C), and (D). In Answer (A), Peter retains the right to name who will receive income and principal. In Answer (B), Peter retains the right to revoke the trust. In Answer (D), as policy owner, Peter retains the right to name a different beneficiary. Only in Answer (B) is Peter precluded from exercising discretion to change who ultimately receives the property. In Answer (B), Peter at most may affect the timing of when property is received. Thus, Peter makes a completed gift in Answer (B).

17.   Quincy will have made a completed gift because, although he retains the power to pay income and principal for his friend's support, support is a fixed and ascertainable standard. As such, Quincy upon making the gift has relinquished dominion and control pursuant to Treasury Regulation § 25.2511-2(c).

18.   **Answer (D) is correct.** IRC § 2503(b) allows a taxpayer to transfer up to $10,000 per person per year, as that amount is adjusted for inflation, so long as the transfer is one of a present interest. In 2008 the gift tax annual exclusion amount is $12,000. Penelope transfers only $10,000, so the entire amount will qualify for the annual exclusion provided it qualifies as a transfer of a present interest. The Ninth Circuit in *Crummey v. Commissioner*, 397 F.2d 82 (9th Cir. 1968), and the Tax Court in *Cristofani v. Commissioner*, 97 T.C. 74 (1991), acknowledged that a withdrawal right over property transferred to a trust is the transfer of a present interest. In this problem there is sufficient time for Rylan to exercise the withdrawal right, and it is assured that the trustee will notify Rylan of the withdrawal right. While the Service has made a substance-over-form argument, courts have consistently rejected this argument; thus, **Answer (B) is incorrect.**

Answers (A) and (C) are incorrect because both answers focus on the impact of a lapse of the withdrawal right held by Rylan. An analysis of whether the withdrawal right lapses is irrelevant to an analysis of the transfer made by Penelope.

19.   **Answer (B) is correct.** Rylan's right to withdraw property from the trust amounts to a general power of appointment over the trust property. An exercise or release of a power of appointment is deemed a transfer of property for purposes of the federal gift tax pursuant to IRC § 2514(b). A lapse is treated as a release pursuant to IRC § 2514(e), but only to the extent that "the property which could have been appointed by exercise of such lapsed powers exceeds in value the greater of the following amounts: (1) $5,000, or (2) 5 percent of the aggregate value of the assets out of which, or the proceeds of which, the exercise of the lapsed powers could be satisfied." Thus, when Rylan allowed his power to lapse, the lapse is treated as a release to the extent of $5,000, or, in other words, the amount by which $10,000 exceeds $5,000. For these same reasons, **Answers (A), (C), and (D) are incorrect.**

20.   **Answer (B) is the correct answer.** A skip person includes a natural person assigned to a generation that is at least two generations below the generation

assignment of the transferor. IRC § 2613(a)(1). Whether a transferee, who is a lineal descendant of Jerry's grandparent but not of Jerry, is still related in a manner that results in a skip requires reference to the lineal descendant rules. *See* IRC § 2651. Here, Jerry's grandnephew Jason is a lineal descendant of Jerry's grandparents. Jason must be separated by two generations or more from Jerry to qualify as a skip person. Generation assignments are made by comparing (1) the number of generations between the grandparent and Jerry, with (2) the number of generations between the grandparent and Jason. The number of generations between Jason (e.g., fifth generation) and Jerry's grandparents (e.g., first generation) is three generations. The number of generations between the grandparent (e.g., first generation) and Jerry (e.g., third generation) is one generation of separation. Thus, comparing the three generations to one generation, it is seen that there are two generations of difference. Because there are two generations between Jerry and Jason, Jason is a skip person under the rules. **Answers (A), (C), and (D) are incorrect** for reasons explained above.

21.   **Answer (C) is the correct answer.** A taxable termination occurs when an interest in a trust terminates and immediately after the termination only one or more skip persons has an interest in the trust. IRC § 2612(a)(1)(A); Treas. Reg. § 26.2612-1(b). Prior to Nancy's death, Nancy has an interest in the trust. Nancy is a non-skip person because, as Mary's child, she is assigned to the generation immediately beneath Mary (e.g., one generation apart). During Nancy's life, the trust is not a skip person, and a contribution to the trust is not a direct skip. Upon Nancy's death, only Judy has an interest in the trust. Since Judy is assigned to the second generation below Mary, she is a skip person. After Nancy's death, all interests are held by skip persons and a taxable termination occurs. **Answers (A), (B), and (D) are incorrect.** With respect to Answers (A) and (B), a non-skip person, continues to hold an interest in the trust. Therefore, no taxable termination has occurred. Note that Answer (B) describes a taxable distribution, which is discussed below. Answer (D) is incorrect for reasons already explained.

22.   **Answer (C) is the correct answer.** The term "taxable distribution" means any distribution from a trust to a skip person (other than a taxable termination or a direct skip). Einer continues to be deemed a skip person because he is assigned to the second generation below Frank under the lineal descendant rules. IRC § 2651(b). When the trustee distributes one-half of the principal to Einer on his eighteenth birthday, there is a taxable distribution to Einer. Note also that the distribution does not qualify as either a direct skip or a taxable termination. Id. If the distribution qualified as either a direct skip or taxable termination, it could not qualify as a taxable distribution. *See* IRC § 2612(b)(parenthetical). **Answer (A) is incorrect.** Answer (A) describes a situation under which there would have been a taxable termination. In Answer (A), when Martine dies, a taxable termination occurs as opposed to a taxable distribution. **Answer (B) is incorrect.** Answer (B) describes a situation under which the original contribution would have been a direct skip. In Answer (B), Einer has a present interest in the trust while Martine, Mary's child, has only a future interest. Because Einer has the only current interest, a contribution to the trust will be a direct skip subject to GST on the date

of contribution. **Answer (D) is also incorrect** for reasons already explained above.

INTERNAL REVENUE CODE (IRC) SECTION INDEX

TREASURY REGULATION INDEX

TREASURY REGULATION INDEX